Scottish Lifestyle
300 Years Ago

Compt=Book of Dame. Grisel Kar-
Countess of Marchmont Begun in Anno
1694 Pairtlie wryten by her own hand Pairtly
filled up from her Notes And ghe rest added.
since the 11th of October 1703 being munday in hen
the Lord took her at 4 of the Clock in the afternoon

The Index of the Book begins upon Page 201:
There are in this Book pages 232:

Frontispiece. Lady Grisell Baillie's frontispiece to her mother's Compt Book.

Scottish Lifestyle
300 Years Ago

New Light on Edinburgh and Border Families

HELEN and KEITH KELSALL

JOHN DONALD PUBLISHERS LTD
EDINBURGH

ISBN 0 85976 167 3

Exclusive distribution in the United States of America and Canada by Humanities Press Inc., Atlantic Highlands, NJ 07716, USA.

Phototypeset by Burns & Harris Limited, Dundee
Printed in Great Britain by Bell & Bain Ltd., Glasgow

Acknowledgements

Grateful acknowledgement is made of permission granted by the Keeper of the Records of Scotland to quote from the manuscripts identified in the references by their call numbers, and to the authorities of the National Library of Scotland and the Map Room in respect of the source material in their possession to which reference is made. The helpfulness of the staffs of these institutions and of the library of Sheffield University is acknowledged with gratitude. Miss S. D. Fletcher, Secretary to the Pictures Committee, Edinburgh University, kindly obtained permission for a portrait to be reproduced. Dr. Rosalind Marshall and the National Galleries of Scotland have also been of very great assistance. Help in finding a manuscript formerly held by Roxburgh District Council was given by the Director of Technical Services.

Of the many individuals who have given access to material or permission to reproduce portraits, thanks are particularly due to the Marquess of Linlithgow, M.C., T.D., M.A., the Earl of Hopetoun, Lady Brigid McEwen, Lord Polwarth, T.D., D.L., Mr. G. Riddell-Carre, Dr. Michael Robson, Sir John Swinton, K.C.V.O., O.B.E., Revd. Robert Thompson, Vicar of Norham, and Miss N. J. Tweedy Bratt.

List of Illustrations

Frontispiece. Lady Grisell Baillie's frontispiece to her mother's Compt Book

1. Map showing the relationship between seats mentioned in the text
2. Facsimile of a page of the Compt Book, showing Grisell's and her daughter's handwriting
3. The home of the Polwarths
4. Grisell Kar, aged about 18, by Scougall
5. Grisell Kar in middle life, attributed to Medina the Younger
6. Grisell Kar, Countess of Marchmont, by Kneller
7. Patrick Hume, 1st Earl of Marchmont, by Kneller
8. Patrick Hume, 1st Earl of Marchmont, by Aikman
9. Lady Grisell Baillie, by Medina
10. Anne Hume, artist unknown
11. Andrew Hume, artist unknown
12. Jean Hume, by Scougall
13. David Home, Lord Crossrig, attributed to Medina the Younger
14. Lady Margaret Hope of Hopetoun, by Medina
15. Sir Thomas Kar of Cavers, attributed to Scougall
16. John Carre of Cavers and West Nisbet, probably by Scougall

Contents

	page
Acknowledgements	v
List of Illustrations	vi
Prologue: What the Book is About	1
1. Principal Sources	5
2. Dark Days and Exile	15
3. George Home the Diarist	24
4. Close Friends of the Family	40
5. Children Growing Up	64
6. Lifestyle of the Merse Lairds	80
7. How People and News Got Around	107
8. New Beginnings	125
9. Housekeeping and the Compt Book	138
10. Crest of the Wave	171
Epilogue	192
Suggestions for Further Reading	201
References	203
Index	215

PROLOGUE
What the Book is About

Let's begin by explaining what this book is all about. How can it shed new light on life in seventeenth-century Scotland? It can do so in two ways. First, by relying very largely on *manuscript* sources, some of which have never before been used at all, and others hardly more than glanced at. And secondly, this can be done by concentrating attention on one particular family and its social network, that network being so extensive that the number of people whose lives we are going to talk about is not a mere handful, but runs into scores of men and women in all walks of life. The story will be told mainly in the words actually used by these people, so that as you turn the pages it is their voices you will be listening to. They will be telling us what they ate, what everything cost, how they got from place to place, what they wore, what illnesses they had and how they were dealt with, how marriages were arranged, what weddings and funerals were like, what they did in their spare time (if they had any), the songs they sang and the games they played, the books and newspapers they read, their gardening interests, the way politicians behaved, about the prevalence of quarrelling, stealing and superstition, indeed anything that was being talked about in the homes, the ale-houses and coffee-houses of Edinburgh and the Scottish Borders.

The family we have made the centre piece of the story is what they themselves called a middle-rank one. Not rich and powerful, with forebears who had controlled the destinies of Scotland for centuries, but not without some say at least in local affairs either. Sir Patrick Hume, the husband and father, was a Berwickshire laird, and had succeeded his father as baron of Polwarth. Apart from just being one of the landed gentry of his day, he held strong views on political and religious issues, and he is able to tell us from first-hand experience what it was like to have to flee the country to save your life, and then only a few years later to find yourself, against all the odds, Lord Chancellor of Scotland. Grisell, who shared all these adventures with him, was the daughter of a similarly-situated laird in Roxburghshire, and fortunately for us kept what she called her Compt Book, in which she noted down all the things she bought and what they cost, as well as many other matters of which she wanted to have a record. Not very unusual, you may think, but it so happens that only four such household account books kept by women in

1

the seventeenth century have survived in the whole of Britain, of which hers is one, and that kept by her daughter Grisell Baillie is another; and as the third was kept by a Roxburghshire lady, Magdalen Nicolson, we are given a unique insight into housekeeping in Edinburgh and the Scottish Borders in the last quarter of the century.

But we are extremely fortunate in one other respect also. For a certain George Home, Laird of Kimmerghame nearby, and a cousin and close friend of Patrick, was a compulsive diary-keeper, who has left four closely-written volumes recording his doings and those of his friends. Like all the best diarists, his interest in the love affairs, the marriage arrangements, and all aspects of the behaviour of his contemporaries was insatiable. And, luckily for us, Patrick and his family were the very centre of George's world. To have such a keen observer on the spot, in the very place and at the very time we need him, is something the importance of which, for the kind of enterprise on which we are engaged, can hardly be exaggerated. Indeed, this is a good point at which to start counting our blessings. Here we have, within the confines of the one family circle we have chosen, the following: two account-keepers (Grisell and her eldest daughter), a compulsive diarist (George Home), someone else who jotted down detailed recollections of his earlier adult life (David Home, afterwards Lord Crossrig), a whole bevy of prolific letter-writers, and hearth and poll-tax records for the two parishes most closely involved. And as if this were not enough, a high proportion of this tremendous output has actually survived the three turbulent centuries between when it was written and the present day. What more could anyone seeking to recreate the lives of this group of people possibly ask for?

These, then, are the three principal characters on the stage we have constructed for the performance — Patrick, Grisell and George. But, as we have said, it is not just their lives we are going to hear about, but also those of their children, of their wide circle of friends, of the many people who worked with them and for them. Some of the latter, because they were not sufficiently educated to keep diaries or account books of their own, cannot speak for themselves, but as far as is possible we will try to show what life must have been like for them, as well as for their more fortunate contemporaries. The three leading actors will, in what follows, be referred to simply by their Christian names, Patrick, Grisell and George, the rest of the cast by their full names on first mention, and afterwards in a shorter form.

Whilst on the subject of names, something more must be said. The spelling of names of people and of places will either be what contemporaries used or what we use today, depending on the context. But how people's names were spelt was so much a matter of the personal prefer- ence of the owner or the writer that one version is often no more 'correct' than another. Two examples may make this clear. David Home, after- wards Lord Crossrig, was one of the Blackadder branch of the Home family and always spelt his name in that way, as did all the others. But the editor of his life story arbitrarily altered it to Hume, and later writers have usually followed him in this. On the other hand our principal character, Patrick Hume, though from the same original stock, followed his father and grandfather in using that spelling in preference to Home. Or take the case of the name Grisell, where different possessors called themselves Grisel, Grizel, Grizell and so on through all the permutations of the single or double 's', 'z' and 'l'. Whatever spelling an unfortunate author adopts, someone is bound to tell him that he's got it wrong.

Some guidance should perhaps be given on the arrangement and con- tent of chapters. Those who prefer to have the full life story of Patrick and Grisell before looking at anything else should first read Chapters 2, 8, 10 and the Epilogue, and then go back to read the others. The life stories of the children are given individually in Chapter 5, and of the family's close friends in Chapter 4, also individually. George Home's story has a chapter of its own, number 3: thumbnail sketches of some of the prominent people who were at Patrick and Grisell's Edinburgh dinners will be found in Chapter 10. What life was like for lairds is shown in Chapter 6, and for everyone else in Chapter 9. The value of money and the cost of living are also treated in Chapter 9. Aside from this, the titles of most chapters are, it is hoped, self-explanatory.

The footnotes, or references, will all be found at the end of the book, those for each of the chapters being grouped together. In the case of *pub- lished* material, all quotations will have a footnote giving the source and the page number. For *manuscripts,* on the other hand, it has been thought sufficient to identify quotations by *date* in the text, and a footnote reference showing the place where the manuscript is kept, together with the reference number. Where the whole of a manuscript relates to a single date, some other point of reference will be given; for example, in lists of pollable persons, the parish will be identified. In the case of two of the manuscripts — Grisell's Compt Book and George Home's Diary — a slightly different procedure is followed. The date is given in the text but, as constant repetition would be tedious, there is only a single footnote mention, that in Chapter 1, Principal Sources.

It should be explained that where sums of money are quoted in pounds, shillings and pence they are always Scots, not sterling, unless otherwise stated; to translate into the sterling of that time, divide by twelve. Measures of length, capacity and weight are Scots, but guidance is given on their conversion into today's measures at appropriate points.

The illustrations reproduce portraits to show what some of our main characters looked like; in some cases it has not proved possible to find one. In addition, there is an unknown artist's impression of Polwarth House, a map showing the relationship to each other of some of the places mentioned, and a facsimile of a page of the Compt Book with the handwriting of both Grisell and her eldest daughter.

CHAPTER 1
Principal Sources

In writing the story of Patrick and Grisell Hume of Polwarth and the network of their relatives, friends, tenants and workpeople at the end of the seventeenth century, very many sources have had to be used, and it is desirable to describe at the outset the principal ones on which we have drawn. One of the central sources is a hitherto unpublished account book. Shortly after her mother's death, Grisell Baillie, her eldest daughter, set about doing several things to this account book. On the inside front cover she explained the situation: 'Compt-Book of Dame Grisel Kar Countess of Marchmont Begun in Anno 1694 Pairtlie wryten by her own hand Pairtly filled up from her notes and the rest added since the 11th of October 1703 being Munday when the Lord took her at 4 of the Clock in the afternoon'.[1] What Grisell Baillie in fact did was to copy into the book itself a variety of loose papers found pinned to certain pages, and also to provide an index of many of the people and some of the topics referred to by her mother. It is worth noting, and may in fact be a token of respect for the archive and its author, that she neither corrects slips and errors, nor does she supplement or complete anything that her mother had left unfinished.

Basically the book was used by her mother as a place in which to note down anything that was of a practical nature, and of which she wanted to keep a record. Where money was concerned, such items were of various kinds. First, if she had given some money to someone to spend on her behalf, an initial entry was made, and later the word 'cleared' would be added to indicate that the arrangement had been successfully concluded (though sometimes it was noted that corroborative evidence was lacking — 'without a tikat'). Secondly, there were straightforward records of money spent on purchasing goods or services. Sometimes, however, only the total amount spent on a number of miscellaneous items is given, making the entry of doubtful value either to the account-keeper or to later investigators. Thirdly, there were payments to workpeople or servants by way of wages, often with an indication (in the case of living-in staff) that these were only part-payments. Fourthly, there were sums of money given to members of the family, not always with an explanation of why this was being done. And a final type of money transaction consisted of rents and other receipts.

5

Many types of entry in the Compt Book had no sums of money attached to them. There were inventories of pewter and kitchen utensils when a new cook was taken on; lists of what she called furniture, consisting of curtains and bedding; catalogues of plate (i.e. silver); quantities of meal stored or changing hands; a count of 'lint and tou' including 'strekins and hardn', put up in pounds and half-pounds for sending to Polwarth and Greenlaw and also to her daughter Grisell Baillie; and a record of wine in the cellar, together with a note about cheesemaking. The period of time covered by the Compt Book is from 1694 to 1697, though some of the loose pages afterwards copied into the book are of a slightly earlier date. There is every reason to suppose that this is the only record of the type that was kept by Grisell, not merely because no other one has survived, but also because her daughter's explanatory note at the front would clearly have been differently worded had the book she was talking about been one of a series. Shortly after Grisell was married, she jotted down in a little notebook (the spare pages of which were long afterwards used by her husband Patrick for some jottings of his own) the sums of spending money she received from him, but this record was only kept intermittently for a very short time and contained no other information of any kind.[2] Moreover, not only did she herself not at any time keep any other record of the Compt Book type, but nothing else comparable kept by anyone else relating to the family at this period has survived. It is, therefore, a unique record.

As already pointed out, only two other account books of similar date for the Scottish Borders (containing much material on Edinburgh as well) have survived, and full use has also been made of the data contained in both of them. One is her daughter's household book, lengthy extracts from which, edited by Robert Scott-Moncrieff, were published by the Scottish History Society in 1911.[3] The second valuable supplement to the Compt Book has been the original manuscript of the account book of Dame Magdalen Nicolson of Roxburghshire, now in the Manuscript Room of the National Library of Scotland in Edinburgh.[4] A. O. Curle, to whom it belonged at that time, wrote an article on it which appeared in 1905 both in the *Proceedings of the Society of Antiquaries of Scotland* and in the *Hawick Archaeological Society Transactions*, but reliance on that alone would not have been sufficient for our present purpose. Reference to the other publications consulted containing comparable price, wage and inventory data from elsewhere in Scotland will be found in the notes to Chapter 9.

Of equal if not greater importance than the household account book as a source of material for social history is the diary, and we are, as has been said, extremely fortunate in that a certain George Home, Laird of Kimmerghame some five miles south of Polwarth House, kept a diary in the 1690s of which a great deal of the manuscript has survived.[5] As a later chapter is devoted to George Home, it will be sufficient at this point to confine ourselves to the scope, nature and usefulness of the diary itself. The first volume of manuscript begins on 7 May 1694, though there was originally an earlier volume which has disappeared. What has survived consists of four volumes of very closely-written, sometimes almost microscopic material, with an overall timespan of eleven years and four months, ending on 6 September 1705 just before his death. Within this overall timespan there are three important gaps. The first, of nearly eighteen months, is from 7 April 1696 to 20 September 1697; the second, of over four months, from 26 September 1700 to 3 February 1701; and the last, again of nearly eighteen months, from 3 June 1702 to 29 November 1703; these substantial gaps add up to three years and four months. There are several reasons for interruptions. One reason is that at particular times (whilst on a visit to London, or when he was keenly observing the proceedings of the Scottish parliament in Edinburgh) he recorded his rough diary notes temporarily in a little pocket book with a view to transferring them to the main book later, but failed to get round to doing so; these little books have disappeared, but a parchment pocket book of a different kind has survived and is referred to from time to time in subsequent chapters.[6] Another reason for a gap is not feeling well enough to write. A third reason, unfortunately, is deliberate destruction of parts of the manuscript by someone into whose hands the diary later came, and who clearly felt that certain portions of what it contained might, if not eliminated, operate to his own disadvantage in some way.

The diary entries themselves naturally vary greatly in length. On some days there was nothing to report, but at the other extreme as many as six pages might be needed for a single day. Some topics of very great importance to the diarist arouse less enthusiasm in someone reading through the material today. For example, he is often preoccupied with legal and financial worries, which are sometimes discussed at length in his diary. His account of these matters must have seemed lucid enough to him, and probably would have been also to any of his contemporaries in similar difficulties, but to the twentieth-century eavesdropper the effort of trying to understand them hardly seems worth while. Borrowing and lending of money takes place so often, with so many people, and in such a variety of forms that it is difficult to keep track of them. When Commissary Home, who has been his constant companion over the years, dies rather unexpectedly, George's main concern seems to be to discover as quickly as possible how, on balance, this is going to affect his own financial position, since his departed friend owed him more money than he was in debt to the Commissary.

Litigation, often with a view to securing financial benefit or avoiding loss, is a minefield for the social historian. For how, at this distance in time and without specialised knowledge of the often obsolete legal terminology, are we to make sense of the network of bonds of relief or of corroboration, declarations of trust, decreats of absolution, diligences, advocations, pursuits, assignations, escheats, precepts, intromissions, summonses and hornings to be found in the diary? Legal remedies seem to have been resorted to as a first, not a last resort, and no one was apparently unduly worried when legal proceedings were initiated against them even by their friends. One moment George Home is taking legal action against the Earl of Home for a wrong he thinks he has suffered at his hands, but the next moment he is rejoicing at being invited to the Hirsel for some social occasion.

Leaving aside those legal and financial memoranda too complicated to be worth trying to grapple with, there remains, fortunately, an enormous volume of diary entries which throw a flood of light on matters of the greatest possible interest to us today. What, then, are the virtues of George Home's diary as a source of social history? First, there is the immediacy of the entries, the feeling they give the reader that he is actually there when these things are happening. This is in sharp contrast to those writings where the author has had time to reflect on the events he is describing, where significant detail has been lost, and where what you are reading no longer has the freshness of material recorded that very night or at latest the following morning. This is well brought out by the case of the fire in the Edinburgh meal market on 3 February 1700. George's account of this is a marvellous piece of journalism: it would do credit to the star reporter of any of today's newspapers, and makes what was given in the news sheets of that time seem pedestrian and unexciting by comparison.

A second virtue of the diary is that it is not weighed down by one-sided presentation of religious or political issues. Unusually for a seventeenth-century Scottish diarist, he does not seek to convert us to his views; after saying what he wants to on these matters, he leaves it at that and gets on with other things. Again, though detailed accounts of his own and other people's illnesses, and of his grievances against particular fellow-men, are all there, they are never carried to such extremes that one wants to skip a page or two. Here was a man with a zest for living who was not going to allow adversity to hold up the action. He may sometimes, as has been said, be preoccupied with his own financial and legal worries, but never to the complete exclusion of everything else. Despite its length, the diary never becomes boring. To spend even the whole of one working day reading what in that time can only be a minute fraction of his diary is an emotional experience not easily forgotten.

George Home is, then, an indispensable guide to the way of life of a laird in lowland Scotland in the 1690s who spent a good deal of his time in Edinburgh, and who had ample leisure to move around and visit and talk to his extremely wide circle of friends. Though very interested in politics, he was able to stand on the sidelines because he was not an M.P. or a political activist, and could spare the time for diary-writing and reporting such things as the weather, the gossip, and casual conversations about nothing in particular. Yet in all this he provides the essential detail we need to make it all come to life — to whom he was talking, where they were, what else they were doing.

For the particular purpose of a study focussing on the Polwarths, his diary has the further merit that, as a first cousin of Patrick, he became involved in family discussions of many matters, including everything to do with the future marriage of each of the children. Being near at hand, and a widower with only one child, he attached himself to the family on every possible occasion, whether they were at home or in Edinburgh, and Patrick's position as Chancellor provided an added incentive for making frequent visits and having numerous discussions. His anxiety to keep in the closest possible touch with his most influential and important kinsman is evident on every page, and makes the diary almost as useful in studying the Polwarths and their children as if it had been written by Patrick or by Grisell. And, of course, a very high proportion of the people with whom George Home socialised were their friends as well. And through his diary we soon become able to understand the complex and puzzling intermarrying that was all the time taking place amongst the different branches of Border families with such wide ramifications as the Homes, the Johnstons, the Douglases, the Trotters, the Cockburns, the Pringles and many others.

In view of its importance, it seems quite extraordinary that the diary has hitherto been almost ignored for nearly three hundred years. Apart from a casual reference to its existence by the Historical Manuscripts Commission in 1894, only two writers seem to have made any use of this storehouse of historical material not to be found anywhere else.[7] A. C. Swinton, in *The Swintons of that Ilk and their Cadets*, published in Edinburgh in 1883 and of which only 150 copies were produced, printed a few very brief extracts from it because of their relevance to the family he was studying.[8] And Margaret Warrender, in *Marchmont and the Humes of Polwarth*, which came out eleven years later, reprinted the same extracts (and Swinton's comments on them) together with one or two others, though she remarked that 'copious use has been made [of it] in compiling this sketch of the Marchmont family'.[9] And that is all.

It seems very doubtful whether anyone still living, save the present writers, has ever read the diary in its entirety, or even a substantial part of it. In addition to Swinton and Warrender, several of the diarist's descendants no doubt did so, including the person who, to our tremendous loss if to his temporary personal advantage, maliciously cut out with a sharp knife and then destroyed many pages of it. Perhaps someone will eventually publish what has survived in full. In the meantime, we must be thankful that so much of this unique manuscript record of what life was like in southern Scotland three centuries ago is now at last in the safe keeping of the Scottish Record Office, where it can sustain no further damage.

A contemporary of the diarist, Dr Pitcairne (who is also discussed in a later chapter) once in conversation with George ran through those of the name of Home who had been the first to distinguish themselves up till then in different fields. Sir Patrick Home, he said, was the first Lord of Session. Commissary Home was the first Writer to the Signet, Dr Home (son of Patrick Home the Minister of Hutton) the first physician. To these one must, in 1986, add quite a number of others — professors of many different subjects, particularly in the medical field, in the eighteenth and nineteenth centuries and, of course, a twentieth-century Prime Minister. It would be a fitting tribute if, as a result of the outstanding nature of his contribution to our knowledge of the social history of Scotland being made clear in the present book, the name of George Home the Diarist could now, however belatedly, be added to this distinguished list.

Though a contemporary diary, such as George Home's, is clearly of crucial importance, an autobiography written by a relevant person living at the time is also of great value, and for our particular study we have one primary source of this type. An uncle of George's, David Home, afterwards Lord Crossrig, who was also a close friend of Grisell and Patrick, left a highly unusual autobiography which he began to write on 28 April 1697, and the manuscript of which was eventually published in 1843. He has become so well known for another writing of quite a different character, his 'Diary of the Proceedings in the Parliament and Privy Council of Scotland, May 21 to March 7 1707', presented by one of its members as a contribution to the Bannatyne Club in 1828, that his autobiographical sketch has virtually been forgotten. He himself called it 'An Accompt of my Estate and Fortune (so far as I can remember) ever since I had any'. When, well over a century later, it was published in Edinburgh, the title chosen was *Domestic Details*, a very fair description of his own story of his life from 1657 to 1707.[10] It is full of information of great value to the social historian, and one reason why almost no use has subsequently been made of it is that only seventy copies were produced on small paper, twenty-four on large, and one on vellum. The editor provided an introduction of eight pages, as well as notes extending to a further nineteen pages. He chose to remain semi-anonymous, simply giving the initials W.B.D.D.T.; but as the publishers were Thomas and Stevenson, one would guess that he was probably the Thomas in that Edinburgh partnership. The text of the Accompt itself covers eighty-three pages (roughly 12,500 words), and it is particularly useful to us, both because of Crossrig's ties of kinship and friendship with our principal characters, and because, like them, he lived and worked in Edinburgh and the Scottish Borders. The full story of who he was and of the part he played will be given in a later chapter.

A primary source of a rather unusual nature, which at first sight might not seem to be of much interest, consists of two manuscript lists of the names of people invited to special dinners at the Abbey, Holyrood House, organised by Patrick and Grisell.[11] The first of these relates to a series of thirty-five such events, from 14 May to 31 December 1696 and is headed 'Memorandum. Who have dined with my Lord upon invitation'. The second covers the period 7 January 1697 to 3 February 1698, during which nineteen more were held, and is a list of 'Persons at the Lord Chancellor's public dinners'. A bare list of names, all in such shortened form, so hastily written, and with such idiosyncratic spelling that it is often almost impossible to identify the person concerned, is not much to go on. But once you know who these people were, and how often each of them came to this series of dinners, it becomes possible to see just how they fitted in to the pattern of the social and political life of the host and hostess. There are over a hundred guests to choose from, all of them quite important figures in the Scotland of that day, men and women about whom we know enough to provide thumbnail sketches of what each of them was like, and to make reasonable guesses as to why they were invited, often or seldom, to join Patrick and Grisell round the dinner table. From the unpromising beginnings of these two rather dull manuscripts, something is constructed making a significant contribution to our understanding of politics in late seventeenth-century Scotland.

In any historical reconstruction, letters form an indispensable primary source. In the present case, letters to or from Patrick, mainly concerned with politics, are very numerous indeed, and a certain number of these have been drawn on. By contrast, letters from his wife, or from George Home, are very few, and almost all of them have been found to be of value for our present purposes. All this correspondence has been unearthed from so many different manuscript bundles and printed volumes of letters that it would be tedious to list them all here; appropriate acknowledgement will, however, be found in the notes to individual chapters.

Up to this point, the sources discussed in the present chapter have all been private ones — Grisell's Compt Book, George Home's Diary, Crossrig's story of the domestic details of his life, the lists of dinner guests, and correspondence. In a moment some account will be given of the main public records used in our study, but in between the private and the public category comes another principal source, the newsletter, which is in a sense neither the one nor the other. It so happened that, because it contained an item connected with the family, a single copy of the one-sheet *Edinburgh Gazette* for March 20-23, 1699 was found loose between two pages of Grisell's Compt Book and this, supplemented by material from other Edinburgh newsletters available for consultation in the National Library of Scotland, has been used in putting together an account of the dissemination of news in late seventeenth-century Scotland.

That brings us to the last category of primary sources, the public records. In our particular case the most useful of these have proved to be the hearth and poll tax rolls. If in the twentieth century one wanted factual information about the living conditions of different families in any given area, there would be two obvious public sources to consult. The rateable value of the houses concerned would give some idea of their relative size and economic standing, while the electoral roll would show the names and the number of adults living in each house. Rather the same kind of information was collected in Scotland in the 1690s, and a little of it has survived for certain parishes. Instead of rateable value we have records of hearth money collected, whereby a tax of fourteen shillings Scots was levied on every hearth except for hospitals and paupers receiving parish relief. And when poll taxes were collected, the minimum except for exemptions was six shillings Scots per head, but with a scale of payment varying with the rank and means of the individual. Because of this last provision, a record had to be kept of the name and status of each adult (and sometimes children also) living in each house, with the appropriate tax payable in every case, and a broadly similar statement to today's electoral roll emerges (fuller in some respects, less full in others, and of course with an entirely different purpose). We are fortunate in that a few hearth and poll tax records have survived, and that some of these relate to parishes of particular importance for the present study. They have proved of enormous value, and extensive use has been made of them in what follows. A fuller description of the nature of these records, and the information relevant to our purposes that can be derived from them, will be found at appropriate points in the chapters that follow.

A second type of public record of which substantial use has been made relates solely to the capital city of Scotland and not to the country, or to the towns of the Borders. Extracts from the Records of the Burgh of Edinburgh have been published for much of its history, and between 1954 and 1967 three volumes appeared, covering the years 1681 to 1718.[12] These throw light on many of the matters with which we are concerned, and have proved a very useful source; reference to them will be made at the relevant stages in our narrative.

So far all the sources mentioned have been primary ones — contemporary material either in manuscript or printed form. We can now move to secondary sources; first of all the rather special case of people who were not quite contemporary, being children at the time, but who heard parents or other adult relatives talking and, being gifted with good memories, were able with their recollections to provide a sort of worm's eye view of what was going on. Our first source of this kind is an account, headed 'Facts relating to my Mother's life and character. Mellerstain, December 12th 1749'. It was written by Grisell, one of Lady Grisell Baillie's two daughters, who made an unfortunate marriage with Sir Alexander Murray of Stanhope, whose fits of violent jealousy made a separation necessary. Her manuscript first appeared in print in 1809 in the unlikely form of an Appendix (headed 'Lady Murray's Narrative') in George Rose's *Observations on the Historical Work of the late Right Honourable Charles James Fox*.[13] Thirteen years later it was republished on its own by Thomas Thomson. Its usefulness to us is enhanced by the light it sheds on her grandmother's, as well as her mother's, life and character.

A second source of the same type consists of the recollections of someone born in 1698 who died in 1784, Lady Anne Purves, daughter of Patrick's son Andrew, 2nd Earl of Marchmont. In the last year of her life she recounted many of her memories of people and events, and these were 'wrote in this connected state by Sir Alexander Purves's particular desire, who often heard them Narrated by his Mother', and eventually in

1894 printed (with a few — too few — factual amendments) by Margaret Warrender in her book described below, as the second part of that book under the heading 'Anecdotes of the Family of Marchmont'.[14]

Though secondary sources of this type often provide very colourful material, the dangers inherent in using them without extreme care can be illustrated by just one example. Lady Anne Purves gives a detailed story of an occasion when (presumably in 1689 or 1690) Patrick was asking his daughter Grisell which of her suitors she had heard from. 'Have you heard from Cavers?' receiving a negative response, he tries 'Have you heard from Jerviswood?' and the reply confirms his suspicion that this is the favoured one. The Purves account is very specific: 'Mr Carre of Cavers and West Nisbet (a widower) had paid his addresses to her, and was much encouraged by his Uncle and Aunt'.[15] But we know that the only person to whom this could refer, Mr John Carre of Cavers and West Nisbet, was not a widower at that time and did not become one except for a short spell after 1702. Moreover, Patrick and Grisell were not his uncle and aunt, for the young man of whom that would have been true died, and John who then became laird was a cousin. There are other errors even in this one short piece of text, but enough has perhaps been said to show with what caution this and similar secondary sources have to be approached.

Finally, the only secondary source not written within earshot, as it were, of the events described, but to which such frequent reference has been made that it constitutes for us a principal source, is Margaret Warrender's *Marchmont and the Humes of Polwarth*, published 'by one of their descendants' in 1894 but with a dedication on one of its first pages making it clear by which one of them it was written.[16] The particular value of this book in our case stems from two of its features. First, she has sifted and reassembled her raw material with such meticulous care as to make it unnecessary for much of that work to be done again. Secondly, she had access to a number of family sources of information that have since disappeared. Indeed, but for her efforts in the 1890s, a significant number of important threads in the tapestry of the Marchmont saga would have been missing today and for all time to come.

CHAPTER 2

Dark Days and Exile

Grisell Kar was born on 1 August 1642. Her father was Sir Thomas Kar of Cavers Carre, situated in Bowden parish, north-west Roxburghshire, three miles south of Melrose. Sir Thomas had been twice a widower before he married Grisell's mother, Grisell Halkett. By his first wife, Agnes Riddell, who died in 1635 aged 34, he had a son Andrew who succeeded him. His second wife is unrecorded, and gave him no children. Grisell Halkett, second daughter of Sir Robert Halkett of Pitfirrane Park, near Dunfermline in Fife, gave him four daughters. She lived to the age of 85 and died in 1682. The daughters of the marriage were: Margaret who married Deas of Coldenknows (Cowdenknows), Christian who married Scott of Mangerton, Grisell who married Patrick Hume of Polwarth, and Isobel who married Hugh Scott of Galashiels.

On 29 January 1660, when Grisell was 18 years of age, she married Sir Patrick Hume, the eighth baron of Polwarth. Although we have no information about Grisell's early years, we do know a little about Patrick's childhood. The original home of the barons of Polwarth had been Polwarth Castle, which was replaced by Mains House, and it in its turn by Redbraes/Polwarth House. Of these three early houses there is nothing now to be seen, although the sites are known. His father and grandfather, both Patricks, had each in their turn been favourites at court. The 'young Laird O' Polwarth', one of the twenty-five gentlemen appointed to attend King James VI when out riding, was Sir Patrick the sixth baron; and subsequent honours were bestowed on him when he was made Master of the Household, a Gentleman of the Bedchamber and a Warden of the Marches against England.[1] His son, the seventh baron, was also a member of court circles. This Patrick married Christian, daughter of Sir Alexander Hamilton of Innerwick. Of the marriage were five children: Julian who married Richard Newton of that Ilk, Patrick, his heir, born on 13 January 1641, Christian who died unmarried, Alexander who went to Russia and served in the Tsar's army, and Anne who married Alexander, one of the Manderston Homes (known to us later in this book as Commissary Home). Of the four children Julian, the eldest, was born at the Mains House, the second home of the Polwarths. The three younger children were all born at Redbraes, which replaced the Mains. The seventh baron died in 1648, a comparatively young man, when the Patrick with whom we are concerned and who became the eighth baron was only seven.

His mother, who was his guardian, brought up her children very strictly on episcopalian lines, but at an early age young Patrick broke loose in religious matters and adopted presbyterianism. Throughout his entire life his religion was of prime importance to him. He remained a staunch presbyterian, never altering his views, though in his middle years it would have paid him handsomely to do so. We are told that the young Patrick was a bit of a rascal, playing tricks on his mother, especially where he could score a point or two against her rigid episcopalianism. She was in the habit of inviting the Scottish bishops in turn to Redbraes, and of asking them to participate in family prayers. This bored the boy who, to the annoyance of his mother, would fall asleep, thus opting out of the psalm singing. So, on a subsequent occasion when a bishop was conducting the little service and reading aloud, Patrick sang continuously throughout the proceedings.

Lady Polwarth married a second time, Robert, 3rd Lord Jedburgh, but this proved to be a much less fortunate alliance. He had been imprisoned for very heavy debts. These were paid by his new wife with monies from the Polwarth estate, leaving things in a very poor state for her children. Jedburgh showed little gratitude for her generosity. He had as little stomach for her religious practices as had young Patrick. Sometimes she would coax him into absenting himself from the services and retiring into her closet. But all her husband did there was to pass the time by eating up her sweetmeats. It is also said that he treated his wife very badly. She died in 1688.

Patrick was 19 years of age when he married Grisell on 29 January 1660, a partnership that was to last for 43 years until her death on 11 October 1703. It was a very happy marriage in spite of trials and tribulations which at times must have seemed beyond human endurance. Children came thick and fast, though they had to wait fours years before they had an infant who survived. In all, Grisell was pregnant 18 times, and was child-bearing over a period of almost 28 years, from March 1661 to September 1688. Her final miscarriage occurred at The Hague when she was 46 years old. To modern wives this would be a totally unacceptable pattern of married life, but at that time it was relatively common. The sequence of pregnancies reads as follows:

1661 March, daughter, died unbaptised.
1662, son, died unbaptised.
1663 30 June, Christian, died.

1664 11 November, Patrick.
1665 25 December, Grisell.
1667 29 April, Thomas, died.
1668 7 May, Christian, died in Holland 1688.
1669 10 July, Robert, died unmarried 1692.
1670 9 November, Julianne, died.
1672 15 June, Thomas, died.
1673 16 August, Julian.
1675 1 January, Alexander.
1675 August, miscarriage of a daughter.
1676 19 July, Andrew.
1677 4 November, Anne.
1678 September, miscarriage of a son.
1683 22 March, Jean.
1688 September, miscarriage of a child at The Hague.

The life of a country laird did not satisfy Patrick. He soon involved himself in politics and at the age of 24 he went to the Scottish parliament as representative for Berwickshire. In spite of his youth he was determined to stand up for his principles to a degree which soon antagonised the parliamentary leaders of the day, in particular the very powerful Duke of Lauderdale whose control over the country seemed to Patrick to be little short of tyrannical. As a result of his anti-government stance he was brought before the privy council in 1675 and declared to be 'a factious person, having done what may usher in confusion, and therefore incapable of all public trust'.[2] There followed spells of imprisonment in the Tolbooth in Edinburgh, the Bass, Dumbarton Castle and Stirling, his release coming ultimately through the good offices of his influential relations in England, notably his cousin, the Countess of Northumberland. It was during this period that his daughter Grisell first had the chance to show her worth. Anxious to exchange messages with his very close friend Robert Baillie of Jerviswood, he asked his eldest daughter, then only 12, to dress in country clothes and go to Edinburgh with the common carrier. It was while executing this mission that the young girl first met George Baillie, Robert's son, who was later to become her husband.

After his experiences Patrick and a number of his friends who held similar political views came to the conclusion that they would be better able to lead a peaceable existence if they emigrated to North America. So, in 1682 a move was set going to found a settlement in Carolina. The prime promoters of the scheme, apart from Patrick, were the Earls of Haddington and Callendar, Lord Yester, and a number of Scottish advocates. They got so far as to gain King Charles's consent to the establishment of such a settlement, but the scheme had to be quickly abandoned in consequence of the political disturbances associated with the Rye House Plot. Some of those who had subscribed to the Carolina venture were accused, justly or unjustly, of being implicated in the plot against the King and his brother.

Patrick claimed throughout his life that he was innocent, and that he had never engaged in any activities which would harm the King or his brother the Duke of York. But everyone who at any time had been known to be critical of the government was in danger, for soldiers were scouring the countryside for possible scapegoats. In such a situation the only thing he could do was to disappear before he could be apprehended. The story is well known of how he hid in the vault of Polwarth church on the estate. The little church, which still stands today, and has ecclesiastical records going back to the sixteenth century, had by that time fallen into disrepair, but was later restored by Patrick and Grisell in the early years of the eighteenth century. It was in the confined space of the vault beneath this building that he hid, and the church itself measured only 55 ft. by 24 ft. on the outside. There was no light at all, except what penetrated through a very small grating at ground level. He could not have candles nor any form of heating, for no one except his wife, their eldest daughter Grisell and one trusted servant, Jamie Winter, a carpenter at the house, knew where he had concealed himself. With Winter's help, a folding bed, bedding and night clothes were smuggled to the vault to avoid Patrick having to rest on the bare earth.

There are differing accounts of the amount of time Patrick spent confined in this way; they vary from one to twelve months, the former being much the more probable. It is said that his only way of passing the time was to walk up and down the aisle, and to repeat to himself Buchanan's version of the Psalms. His daughter, Grisell, who was now 18 or 19, visited him every night, taking him food and regaling him with news of what was happening at home. The church was about a mile from Polwarth House, and she had to make her way through the churchyard guided only by the light of a small lantern. This was an ordeal in itself, for there could have been soldiers lurking about, and she also had to make the return journey before dawn broke. On one occasion she was very frightened by the barking of the dogs at the minister's house nearby. But her mother saw to it that this at least would not trouble her again. She informed the minister that a mad dog was running loose, and suggested that it would be safer if his dogs were destroyed, and this he did. Food had to be procured surreptitiously without the servants noticing, so at mealtimes, young Grisell would quite often transfer her own portion to her lap so that she had enough for her father. Once, so the story goes, Alexander drew attention to the rate at which Grisell ate, complaining of her greed: 'Mother, will ye look at Grisell; while we have been eating our broth she has eaten up the whole sheep's head!'[3] This amused Patrick when it was recounted to him, and he gave instructions that Sandy was to have his proper share next time. The little lantern carried by Grisell Hume on these perilous and dismal trips was subsequently given to the then Antiquarian Museum in Edinburgh.

After a spell of incarceration in the vault it was decided that Patrick could be concealed in Polwarth House itself, as the search for him had somewhat subsided. But a bolt hole had to be prepared in case the need arose. In a room on the ground floor, Lady Grisell, her daughter Grisell and Jamie Winter lifted the floorboards under a bed, and each night with great secrecy they dug a hole with their bare hands. Young Grisell's nails were quite worn away with scraping the earth, which had then to be put into a sheet and eventually carried out into the garden. When they were able to insert a box big enough to hold Patrick, it was fitted with bedclothes, then planks with air holes bored in them were placed on top. But after a week or two Grisell went one morning, as was her custom, to inspect the box, and when she lifted the planks the bedding floated up to her, the box being full of water. Thus they were faced with having no possible dependable refuge in an emergency, so they realised that safety for Patrick could only be assured by his fleeing the country. Although many of his friends had already taken such a step, not all of them were in even as favourable a position as himself. His near neighbour and very close friend, Robert Baillie of Jerviswood, had again been seized, and confined in the Tolbooth. Little time was wasted and in September 1684 he left the country. He, himself, gives the exact date of finally leaving — 'I had gone off the kingdom 11th September, 1684' — and Crossrig says 'he fled in the harvest'.[4]

The exact circumstances of his escape and eventual arrival in Utrecht are the subject of confusing accounts which vary in several respects, including the route taken. Most confusing of all are two particularly colourful stories regarding his indebtedness to a miller known as Slap, whom Patrick afterwards recompensed by a grant of a tenement and yard to him and his descendants. The first version of the story is that given by Abraham Home, writing the section on the parish of Greenlaw in the 1834 Statistical Account of Scotland. Here Patrick is said in his flight to have encountered Robert Broomfield, of Greenlaw Mill, engaged in repairing a slap in the mill cauld and, using what he was occupied with to improvise a name for him, said, 'Slap, have you any money?' whereupon the miller supplied him with what he needed and earned his undying gratitude. One misleading element in this version is that Slap was the name of the place where Broomfield lived, and he was usually addressed in that fashion in any case. A second version of the story makes the incident take place on an earlier occasion, in 1683 or 1684, when the Broomfield family were building or repairing dikes, and they are said to have erected a makeshift cairn of stones around him until those who were in hot pursuit of him had gone by, earning his gratitude in that way. This second version was handed down to James Richardson of Greenlaw, who died in 1885 aged 95, by his mother who was herself a Broomfield born in 1749, which makes it a family tradition rather than merely a local one and therefore, in the view of Robert Gibson (*An Old Berwickshire Town*, 1905), lends it greater credibility.[5]

Once Patrick eventually reached Holland he made contact with William of Orange, found himself a house in Utrecht and sent for his wife and children. Forfeiture of the Polwarth estates was declared on 22 May 1685, and from then on the only resources available to the exiled family were from his wife's jointure, and these were hardly adequate to sustain so large a family. Nevertheless, Grisell set forth from Scotland with her tribe of children, showing great courage and determination. Her youngest child, Jean, was still a babe in arms when they reached Holland. Julian had to be left in Scotland as she was ill when they left, so young Grisell returned after a month or so to help her sister make the journey, and to collect some money which was owing to her father.

Their return journey to Holland must have been a nightmare. They had paid for a cabin bed, but an unscrupulous captain first sold it to other passengers and finished by occupying it himself. He also ate the small amount of provisions they had with them for the journey. So they had to make do with sleeping on the bare boards, using books which their father had asked for as pillows. A violent storm developed, which terrified them, and it was fortunate that help was given to the two girls by a kindly gentleman who was, like themselves, seeking refuge in Holland. They landed at Brill, where there was no transport, and had to make their way to Rotterdam on foot. Julian was still far from well, she slipped about on the muddy pathways and soon lost her shoes. Grisell then took her sister piggy-back into Rotterdam, and the kindly gentleman gave further assistance by carrying their luggage. They were met by their brother Patrick and his young friend George Baillie of Jerviswood who escorted them on the final lap of their journey to Utrecht where the family was at last reunited.[6]

It was four years after Patrick's departure before the family was all safely back in Polwarth House, during which time they were more poverty-stricken than at any other stage in their lives. They must have been living at what for them was near subsistence level. There was no money for servants, they had only one little girl to wash the dishes. The girls in the family did the housework, but the bulk of this was borne by young Grisell. She cleaned, cooked, went to market, to the mill to have the corn ground, and mended the children's clothes. She was devoted to her brother Patrick, and took great pride in seeing that his little point cravats and cuffs were properly laundered. Their mother was the needle-woman, giving instruction to her daughters, and their father attended to the education of all his children. He was a scholar, and could teach them Latin, French, and the Dutch language, as well as dealing with more general studies. During the time spent in Holland, Patrick lived incognito, keeping indoors as much as possible, and using the pseudonym of Dr Wallace; but many people knew his identity. This was certainly true of the other exiles who were close enough to use his house as a favourite meeting-place, often resulting in there being many guests to be entertained and fed. Christian helped with the entertainment. She was the musical member of the family, and would play and sing for the company on many evenings. It was natural that, as the eldest daughter, Grisell took over the duties of housekeeper from her mother who had her hands full caring for the younger children. And the straits in which they frequently found themselves gave her ample scope for developing further the traits of leadership for which she was well known throughout her later life.

The small remittances from Scotland on which they had to rely were often late on account of ships being delayed. Without ready money, they had to part with the few treasures they had managed to take with them. The little plate they had often went into the Lumber (or pound) until the arrival of the ships. Fortunately, most of it was retrieved before they returned to Scotland. As an indication of their poor circumstances, Grisell Baillie used to tell of how on one occasion when a door-to-door collection was being made on behalf of the poor, they had only one coin, the smallest in Dutch currency at that time. Everyone was too ashamed to offer it, but at last their father took it, saying, 'Well, then, I'll go with it; we can do no more than give all we have'. He had some sketchy medical knowledge and, as 'Dr Wallace', he occasionally used this to augment their income when things got very difficult.

In spite of their privations, the years spent in Holland were pleasant in many ways. Later in life, Grisell Baillie would talk tirelessly of their experiences, claiming that it was one of the happiest and most delightful times in her life. The family was a happy, close-knit one, and they were all together. Their friends, all exiles themselves, found the Polwarth home a haven where troubles could temporarily be forgotten. George Baillie of Jerviswood, whose father, Robert, had been so summarily executed in Edinburgh, was a close friend. He and young Patrick were members of the Prince of Orange's Guards, and usually tried to organise their sentry duties together. Some degree of friendship had already been established between George Baillie and Patrick's sister Grisell, and in such a propitious situation, where he was almost accepted as a member of the family, it was not surprising that this eventually developed into a stronger and more permanent relationship.[7]

Undoubtedly the most anxious time for the family during the years spent in Holland was in 1685 when Patrick joined the Earl of Argyll's disastrous expedition to the West of Scotland, designed to support the Duke of Monmouth. He himself left a lengthy account of the mishaps and wanderings this entailed, which almost cost him his life. A detailed story about the affair is also given in 'Anecdotes of the Family of Marchmont' by Lady Anne Purves.[8] The Earl of Argyll and other exiles in the Netherlands, including Patrick, landed in the West of Scotland hoping to create a diversion which would support Monmouth and split the King's troops. They were set on by soldiers and engaged in a bitter fight from which Patrick was lucky to escape alive. After much hardship and making a slow journey by stealth he eventually made his way to the coast and from there to Bordeaux. He had a lengthy journey through France into Switzerland, landing up in Geneva where he spent some months before he was finally able to return to Holland in the summer of 1686.

Two years were to pass before the 1688/89 Revolution which so drastically improved the fortunes of the Polwarth family. Patrick writes that he returned to England with the Prince of Orange on 5 November 1688, his son Patrick and George Baillie accompanying them. Their first sailing had to be abandoned on account of a gale which scattered the fleet. The storm was so severe that Baillie maintained a rigorous fast on one day a week for the rest of his life as a gesture of thanks for his deliverance. When the political situation was felt to be more settled the younger children were sent to Scotland, presumably to the care of relatives. Their mother and the eldest daughter, Grisell, accompanied the Princess Mary, who tried to persuade young Grisell to accept a post at court as Maid of Honour. This offer she did not accept, being too fond of her family to want to leave them and (one suspects) by this time being too fond of George Baillie to consider a move which would put so many miles between them.

After William and Mary had accepted the Scottish Crown they did not forget to reward those who stood by them while the claims to the throne had been in the balance. In due course Patrick's family was favoured, partly because of real gratitude on William's side, and partly (as we shall see in a later chapter) because it proved to be a politically advantageous arrangement. On 22 July 1690 the forfeiture of the Polwarth estates was rescinded by parliament, and on 26 December of the same year Patrick was created Lord Polwarth by King William and Queen Mary. Exceptional royal gratitude was shown by the patent assigning to him, in addition to his armorial bearings, 'an orange proper ensigned with an imperial crown, to be placed in a surtout in his coat of arms in all time coming, as a lasting mark of his Majesty's royal favour to the family of Polwarth, and in commemoration of his Lordship's great affection to his said Majesty'.[9] (See Plate 7.) In due course, after the estates had been returned to the family, on everything possible at Polwarth House (and long afterwards at Marchmont House) the crowned orange was emblazoned, down to the spines of the books in the library. Further recognition of royal approval was shown by the King sending Patrick a large single diamond set in a ring.

CHAPTER 3

George Home the Diarist

Who was George Home? He was Laird of Kimmerghame, only a few miles from Polwarth House, and a first cousin of Patrick. Even the briefest catalogue of the key points in his life up to the age of 34, when the surviving parts of his manuscript diary begin, will show how crowded with traumatic events it had been, despite the fact that he was not directly involved in the Scottish troubles of those years. Born on 28 June 1660, he was pressganged by his father and a group of his relatives into marrying a young heiress when she was only 12 and he was 17 (we discuss this in a later chapter as an example of how marriages were sometimes arranged at this time), and he was then imprisoned for a few months as a result. Losing his father immediately afterwards and succeeding him as laird, and losing his wife six years later, he then went to France with the young Laird of Blackadder, Sir John Home, returning to Scotland in 1687. Four years after his return, on 26 May 1691, he married for a second time, but on this occasion the choice was his own, his father no longer being there to influence things. He chose as his bride Margaret, daughter of Sir James Primrose of Barnbogle (seven miles west of Edinburgh). She went to stay with her mother when her first child was on the way, and Robie was born on 2 March 1692. She herself died there a few weeks later, however, and was taken to Berwickshire for burial on 2 April. Sir John Foulis of Ravelston, a close relative of the Primroses, travelled south from Edinburgh for the funeral and stayed that night at Polwarth House, where his accounts tell us that he left £5–16s. in drink money.[1] So, when the surviving part of George Home's diary begins just twenty-five months afterwards, the diarist is a Border laird of 34, already twice widowed, with a two-year-old boy to look after.

In all the circumstances it was inevitable that little Robie should be of central importance in his father's life. Hardly a day goes by without reference to him in the diary. He took the baby with him on his jaunts when he was only two: 'I went to Blackader and took Robie before me on the black mare, and his woman behind John Murdo [his manservant]'. As soon as he was old enough he clearly had to have a pony of his own. In today's terms, this was equivalent to giving him a bicycle, rather than the luxury item a pony has now become. He records with pride on one particular Sunday: 'I went to church and Robie rode alone on his pouney better than I expected'. The boy was then six and a half. Six months later: 'I went to Blackader and took Robie with me: we walked and rode time about having the pouny'. Naturally enough he took the boy with him as often as he could, whether he was going hunting or just to visit friends. At nine he had his first taste of Edinburgh: 'Mr John Dickson got me a chamber in James Belchasses, a very nasty holl, but I must be content, the town is so throng that lodging is hardly to be had for money. Robie lay with me'. When he was younger, relatives in Edinburgh and elsewhere sent toys to Robie by carrier to Kimmerghame — a little play-thing like a tortoise, a bow and two arrows (though the feathers could sustain damage in transit), a drum, ninepins of ivory, and sometimes 'another plaything that was lost in the carrying'. When the boy was nine, John Dickson sent '10 elles of a crape, in fashion for clothes, to Robie, with lining, mohair buttons and mohair for the knots', with the in-junction 'send back the crape if it please you not'.

George Home took a keen interest in the boy's education. On 13 November 1702 'I was trying Robie in his Latine and find he is quite neglected'. So a fortnight later he was forced to put away Mr Walter Patersone who had been teaching his son since February: 'Beside that he neglected his business, he was so nasty I could not bear it'. For a while father took over the teaching, and on 17 December 'Robie and I are bussie at Terence. Instead of causing him repeat I cause him write the English off the Latine and then ask the Latine from the English which succeeds, blest be God, very well'. He took great trouble to avoid having anyone incompetent to teach his boy. When Doctor Trotter brought along a prospective Latin teacher, Mr Robert Wood, George tried him on a section of the Second Book of Horace 'but he could not make sense of it, though it be one of the easiest, so I told Dr Trotter he could not be for me'. In desperation at one point he wrote to John Dickson in Edinburgh asking him 'to get me one to waite on Robie who has taught before, though it should coast me double what it has or more'. He was, indeed, not easy to please where teachers were concerned, even when Robie himself was not involved. When David Robisone brought along a Mr James Watsone, applicant for the post of local schoolmaster, the diary entry reads 'I hear he is a little notional'.

Robie's health had never been of the best, though at the age of eleven he was so keen on football as to be prepared to miss his dinner rather than miss the opportunity of playing football on Blackadder Green. On a memorable day in June 1699 his father had been so worried about his seven-year-old son's state of health that both Dr Abernethy *and* Dr Trotter were summoned, and a message was rushed through to his sister in Edinburgh to seek advice on suitable treatment for the boy from Dr Stevenson as well. In addition 'I sent to Edrom Church to desire Robie might be remembered in the prayers of the congregation'. Although the boy recovered on this and other worrying occasions in George's lifetime, in the event he only survived his father by some five years, dying at the age of 18. George's deep affection for his son is never in any doubt, and the diary entry on his ninth birthday sums it all up: 'Lord bless him to make a right use of the years thou allows him, and lengthen them to glorify thee in his generation'.

Apart from his one son, George had only three other close relatives living at the time he wrote the diary — his younger brother David, and his two sisters Julian and Isobel. Relations with his brother tended, particularly in his younger days, to be clouded by resentment over money matters. There are various papers with dates ranging from 1680 to 1693 setting out what David has received both from George himself and from Patrick and others — 'for clothes boarding at Kelso' £120 is quoted — and there is a memorandum: 'he stayed with me for the most part of 1687 to 1689 and from 1690-93 and had a horse which will more than double exhaust this summe [unstated] besides I am sure I have not all the particulars of all the summe he has got'.[2] Later, when David had rooms in Duns, George occasionally got in touch with him to find out in winter time how traffic was getting through on the easterly route to Edinburgh. On 7 July 1699 his brother, then a cadet in Row's regiment, turned up at Kimmerghame: 'He tells me he is designing to go to America with the ships that are now going'. Relations are obviously strained, as the diary entry for that day records advice to George from Sir John Home that he should forget and forgive his brother's usage of him. Finally, on 2 February 1700 he gets news of David having died of a fever on the preceding 25 October when taking part in the ill-fated Darien expedition. The diary entry is suitably laconic: 'he has been a poor unfortunate lad'. George was not one to indulge in mournful reflections about the past, and this was not only in connection with his brother. For it is noteworthy that there does not appear to be a single reference in the entire diary to either of his departed wives.

With his sister Isobel, money matters also caused strained relations. If we are to believe the diary, most of her letters to him asked for money to which she thought she was entitled, but about which he often took a different view. Nevertheless, when she moved to a house in Edinburgh he made constant use of her to buy things he needed and send them by carrier to Kimmerghame, and these requests she seems always to have acceded to very promptly. She also made innumerable shirts for Robie.

It is not clear whether he ever stayed with her on his frequent visits to Edinburgh, for he often details where he found lodgings and what they cost. Isobel apparently remained unmarried, though in one moment of exasperation she quotes her 'husband' as having instructed her to complain to George about something, perhaps as a piece of sarcasm. Relations with Julian, his other sister, seem to have been rather better. He was probably quite pleased when, in October 1698, she married Dr Trotter, and he busied himself, as always, with the important matter of the marriage settlement. When Dr Trotter spoke to him of a match with Julian 'and desired my Countenance, I told him my sister's part was to please herselfe in a choice: mine to see provisions etc'. Once all that was arranged there were presumably fewer money problems to be disagreed about; and when the couple settled in Duns there was a good deal of friendly interchange, helped by the usefulness of Dr Trotter as an additional family doctor, and by George's natural interest in the forth-coming appearance of nephews or nieces upon the scene.

Turning to George's domestic arrangements, Kimmerghame was a very much more modest establishment than those of his friends, having only seven hearths as compared with, for instance, seventeen for Polwarth House, sixteen for Blackadder, fifteen for West Nisbet and Jerviswood's thirteen even before the new Mellerstain was built.[3] His domestic staff was correspondingly small — in the 1695 poll tax roll it is given as one manservant and two women (one a nurse for Robie) together with a gardener — almost spartan for a laird.[4] There may also have been Margaret Home, who died early in December 1702. She was clearly an old and trusted retainer, and had been 'under a decay' for some time; her death calls forth the comment, 'a great pity of an honest servant'. With no wife to help him in such matters, he has difficulty even over the size of the rooms to be furnished. Although David Robisone told him in a letter to Edinburgh that the main room was nineteen ells, 'I had better trust my aunt who writes that the hall is twenty ells and two ells hight'. Also in his little parchment notebook, under the heading 'To be bought for my house', there are some rather confusing memoranda about the suits of hangings (with poles) required — one green of 38 ells for the hall, the other purple of 32 ells. As to what cloth will be suitable, he is to seek advice from Lady Hilton and others. He also plans to buy a dozen chairs; if timber, they must have cushions or be covered with the colour of the hangings, and until all this can be arranged, chairs must be borrowed from friends. He is also going to have two wainscot tables for the hall, two chamber boxes and two iron chimneys. If any pewter vessels need to be changed, new ones are to be bought at Berwick. Drinking glasses, and two looking glasses, must also be obtained.[5]

In his diary, under the dateline 16 May 1694, he gives a list of his personal linen. First, the linen he uses at present:

6 Nightshirts
4 Holland half shirts
5 pairs of sleeves
7 caps for nightcaps
5 snuff napkins
4 long muslin cravats
4 muslin cravats with stocks
4 long holland cravats
3 linen night cravats
4 pairs of linen thread stockings.

'I gave Margaret Turner my linnens for present use to be washed. I gave her likewise a haggabag tablecloth which is not in her account and some days ago 2 pair of linnen sheets and half one which are likewise not in her account.' He had 'besides, lying in a trunk in the little study in my chamber:

5 laced cravats
1 point cravat
2 pair of laced ruffles and ane old one
2 holland shirts'.

The problem of what to put up with from servants presented itself quite frequently. If he had still had a wife, particularly one like Grisell Baillie who, on her own evidence, stood no nonsense and summarily dismissed the unsatisfactory ones, things might have been easier for George. As it was, he had to cope as best he could, and occasionally lost his temper. Saturday 3 March 1700 was one of those days. His man, Jammy Scot, having stayed out all morning until nearly eleven, and reproofs on previous occasions having been useless, received 'on the cheek, a cuff, at which he gave so indiscreet language that he provoked me to beat him again. He still repeated he would not be beat, so I bid him get him gone'. This time things were patched up afterwards, but sometimes dismissal seemed the only solution. A case in point arose when Jammy Orange, who had come back from performing errands for George in Edinburgh on the Saturday or Sunday, failed to turn up at Kimmerghame until Tuesday night. He had evidently been drinking at Duns and came no further than Jammy Robison's where, hearing he was there, George sent a message demanding the letters he had brought. These letters were his undoing, for their dates proved when he had left

Edinburgh, so he was got rid of as being no use. It was not only the men servants who proved unsatisfactory. George's sister Julian, who had married Dr Trotter and was living at Duns, told him in July 1700 'several base things of the hussy' who was currently serving him. It seems that when Mr James Redpath went to Edinburgh in March, 'she made treat for him of hens and pock-puddings and pancakes at 10 o'clock at night'. Worse still, 'Some were there who ought not to have been there'. The last straw was that she applied to her own use the money George had given her to serve the poor, to whom she only served milk. No doubt she was got rid of as well. To try and ensure that all difficulties of this kind did not arise, George's aim was to hire only those whom someone had recommended. In one case he took on a servant who had previously worked for Lady Hilton and had given satisfaction. In another, finding that a prospective servant came from Stirling, he sought out someone else's servant who also came from there and obtained a verbal character reference. Then, of course, it was important to be very specific as to what you were going to do for them, and what they must do for you, before taking them on: 'I am to give him a livery coat and breeches, and a pair of shoes in the half year, and six pounds Scots. The livery is mine, and he is to wear his own clothes at work: and is to run and ride as I shall order him: thrash: ditch: and go to the coals'.

'Going to the coals' was a much more complicated business than one would suppose. For the position was that to heat even a modest-sized country mansion such as Kimmerghame meant fetching substantial quantities of coal a long way, fifteen miles or so, from one of the small Northumberland collieries on the English side of the Tweed, which meant crossing the river by boat at Norham. Because many of the roads on such a journey were unfit for any kind of wheeled vehicle, the task was a packhorse one. And as each horseload could not be more, in today's terminology, than two or three hundredweight at most, the few horses George himself possessed were insufficient on their own. The terms on which his tenants held their land, however, included an obligation to provide so many 'carriages', and a 'carriage' meant the services of a horse, and someone to lead it, for a day. So it was George's servant's duty periodically to organise a convoy of his own and his tenants' horses to go to the coal hill and back again to replenish the coal stocks at the house. There was no question of George himself wasting a day doing this — it was not laird's work — so his servant had to see to it. In June 1694, for instance, the diary records that George Archer 'has brought home 8 loads of coals upon my horses and cobled twice'.

What were George Home's main interests, apart from Robie?

Undoubtedly the dominant one was socialising, which meant visiting his friends and receiving visits from them. There was an astonishingly wide circle of people with whom he was on terms of this kind, and apart from each others' houses there were many settings in which to meet them. In the country there were, of course, taverns and ale houses and in Edinburgh also an assortment of coffee houses, chocolate houses, and places to eat. An example of how he and his cronies played pranks on each other in Edinburgh is provided by the hitherto unexplained case of the Earl of Home's Club. Careful readers of that storehouse of published information, Foulis of Ravelston's account book, will have been puzzled by two related entries, on 2 February and 1 March 1699. The first records a payment of £2 'to mr rentoune all my bygane absents from E of Homes 12 hours Society'; the later one mentions £2–18s. 'to E of Homes club for payment of our dinner at Mitchells'.[6] An item dated 25 February 1699 in George Home's diary at last solves the mystery: 'I have never set down anything about Our Club ordinarily called the E of Homes Club where we goe allwise betwixt 12 and half an hour after: those of the Company decoy as many as they can, if there be but one he pays the reckoning, which at first was but small, the company increasing . . .' So now we know.

Then he was also a regular churchgoer. To him, it is true, the most important element there consisted of the sermons, since on certain Sundays his reason for not going was that there was not to be one — 'there being no sermon . . . I went not abroad'. And often there were *two* sermons, with or without a break between them. Oddly enough, he rarely tells us anything of their content, except when it had to do with some topical issue, such as the ill-fated Darien expedition. Thus he describes one sermon in Edinburgh on Thursday 7 March 1700 in which the minister 'asked God to deliver our friends there from the *cruelty* of the Spaniards, the *malice* of the English, and the *treachery* of ill men among ourselves'. But churchgoing was also, of course, a social activity, and he tells us which of his friends he went with, or encountered there, on each occasion, and his Sunday diary entries nearly always include news he has picked up, usually relating to illness or death. Funerals — and he rarely missed one — were also important socially, to see and be seen, and as he apparently had only one set of clothes suitable for such occasions, this was constantly being sent from Kimmerghame or Edinburgh, depending on where a forthcoming funeral was to take place.

Much of the conversation on these numerous social occasions was, of course, concerned with news and gossip about relatives and friends. But though he was actively interested in all such matters, he was also a keen and knowledgeable student of home and foreign affairs. That he himself was skilled in debate and argument can be inferred from many of his diary entries, but also from an unusual passage in his little parchment pocket book, beginning: 'I hear a great contest about the Virgin Marie's being known by Joseph, but the matter is not so hard as men imagine'. He then proceeds to set out the arguments that have been advanced, and ends up with a lucid statement of his own conclusions having considered all the points raised.[7]

This brings us to a second dominant interest in his life, books and reading. Since he was a highly educated and intelligent man, with plenty of time on his hands, this was a natural outlet. Though he occasionally worried about the cost of adding to his already extensive library, as when in June 1694 'I counted what I have given out for books these two years; I find it is £171–19–0 which is too much for me', he went on being a regular customer of three of the Edinburgh booksellers. The one he visited most frequently was George Mosman in the Luckenbooths. He was a man of substance, with two apprentices, a manservant and a maidservant.[8] His was a three-hearth establishment, and he was also a bookbinder, who did in fact bind up the sheets that formed the volumes of George Home's manuscript diary. Two of the other Edinburgh booksellers he patronised were John Vallance (or Vallange) and James Wardlaw. Besides this, he always asked friends who happened to be going to suitable places such as London or Paris to buy particular books for him. Apart from adding to his considerable library, he and his book-loving friends were constantly borrowing books from each other. They were quite undaunted by Latin, French or Italian; if they bought or borrowed dictionaries or grammars, these were probably for the children as much as for themselves. When he started to make a list of the books in his library on one occasion, no fewer than 67 were in Latin. The books in English would hardly suit today's taste, but then the selection available was much more restricted. Dr Gregory's Astronomy, the Works of the Learned in five volumes, the second editions of Kirkwood's Disputer, and of William Dampier's New Voyage round the World, the History of the Popes, and the History of the Wars of England, Scotland and Ireland are all mentioned, together with an anonymous book about the Christian Education of Children — a natural choice because of Robie. Some pamphlets are referred to — Dr Sybbald on the Independence of Scotland in Church and State, and The Short Way with Dissenters: ''tis said some of themselves writ it.'

When you lend books there is always the problem of getting them back, and on at least one occasion, in 1694, George was able to retrieve a book which he must have given up hope of recovering. On a visit to one of his friends (who was away), and while his lady was out of the room for a moment, George 'found upon the table Bacon's History of Henry 7th which I had lent him 10 years ago. I brought it home with me, but he has spoilt the binding of it miserably and beside inked it in several places that it is not or very hardly legible'. Forgetfulness, even if accompanied by ill-treatment, was one thing, outright stealing quite another. In February 1703 we find him writing to his sister Isobel in Edinburgh to try and retrieve for him the two-volume Cervantes' *The Delightful History of Don Quixot* (in English) 'which Mr James Trotter I suspect stole, being informed it is his custom, and I mist them one day when he was here'. Isobel went into action on the matter fairly smartly, for less than a fortnight later he heard that 'she chanced to be in Elshy Trotter's when Mr James's books came in from the country and found the 2 volumes of Don Quixot which I suspected him for and has brought them away'.

Did his reading of books in English include poetry? The only clue to this is that in his little parchment notebook he has, under the heading 'Pastoral of Rochester', transcribed one beginning 'As Strephon gasping on his death-bed lay'. This piece of verse is not *by* John Wilmot, Earl of Rochester, but *about* him, and is a poem by Thomas Flatman (1635-88) 'On the death of the Earl of Rochester'; the correct version of the opening lines is

> As on his death-bed gasping Strephon lay,
> Strephon the wonder of the plains,
> The noblest of th' Arcadian swains . . . .

It first appeared in Flatman's *Poems and Songs* (1674) in the 1682 edition, and has since been reprinted in George Saintsbury's *Minor Poets of the Caroline Period* (1921) and more recently in *The Penguin Book of Pastoral Verse* (1974).[9] Whether its appearance in his notebook means that George Home particularly liked Flatman's poetry, or that this particular pastoral's *moral* appealed to him (that caring too much for pleasure led to repentance when it was too late), we have no means of knowing. In view of George's own fondness for the Latin tongue, however, it may be significant that Flatman also provides a Latin version of this Pastoral.

Were we to rely solely on his diary, we might well conclude that George Home had no interest in music either. For apart from one isolated item, when Patrick's son Lord Polwarth, in March 1703 sent a flute he had promised to lend him, there is not a single reference to anything connected with music in the entire text. In the same little parchment notebook, however, much of which seems to relate to the very early 1680s, there are twenty-six entries under the heading 'Airs'.[10] Some of these defy identification, such as number 3, 'The air Rowistone plays', the Laird of Rowistone merely being one of his friends; or numbers 12 and 13, 'A trumpet air' and another trumpet air he learned from a friend. In others, too many of the words are illegible to attempt a reconstruction. There remain fifteen items, however, where the writing is at least partially clear, and these are as follows:

4. Under her apron
5. The Duke of Albany
7. When Phyllis full of . . .
8. Macbeth
9. Show me the lass that's true country bred
14. Saw ye no ma piggy [or peggy]
15. The braw lass [or lads] of Gallowa'
18. Sandy's never be my love
19. As I gaed down . . . . . side
20. Bonny lass an thou wert mine
22. O no tis in vain
23. New corn rigs
24. The black ewe
25. There was a K. . . . . . . wine
26. When Phyllis steps. . . . .

None of these airs seems to be referred to in Thomas Crawford's *Society and the Lyric: a study of the Song Culture of Eighteenth Century Scotland*, (Edinburgh, 1979), the most recent authoritative work available. It looks, then, as though we have here over a dozen hitherto unrecorded songs being sung in Scotland in the seventeenth century. We may only have their first lines, and some of these not in complete form, and no melody to go with any of them, but this nevertheless represents a very exciting discovery in a field where such discoveries are increasingly rarely made.

So many of George's contemporaries had their portraits painted that it is surprising, and also disappointing, that he himself appears not to have had this done at any time. Whether when he was younger and had a wife he did not want to incur such an expense, and later when he became a widower, having no one to press or encourage him to do the fashionable thing, he consequently still failed to do it, we do not know. For he certainly notes in his diary visits of this kind by his friends, as when in

January 1696 he records Cavers having been sitting for Scougall, and the Blackadders having been painted by the Frenchman Eude (Nicholas Heude); he also tells us that in September 1699 'I got from My Lady Marchmont 2 prints of my Lo: Chancellour's pictures and one of hers'.

However, the diary provides a good deal of evidence to show that he held strong views on another art, the design of country houses. He comments unfavourably on Mellerstain as it was in September 1700: 'They have ane old tower with but one room off a floor, about 5 stories high, but it looks very ruinous. There has been much building about it, but the stone is much wasted, being bad'. In the same year he visited Archibald Primrose's place at Rosebery. Primrose, who had just been made a peer as Viscount Dalmeny, was George's father-in-law's half-brother. George was impressed by the garden, a very fine plot of ground just behind the house, and also by the large park with planting in it, and was told of a plan for a deer park. The house was large, the second storey very noble, the drawing room taking up the second and third storeys up to the roof, and being finely painted above. Heude, the French painter, was doing other rooms as well. The main fault, in George's eyes, was the lack of a fine staircase: 'I find Dalmeny has thrown down one that was in the middle of the house, and designs to built it up again, but it will be an eyesore . . .' In March 1705 he criticises a rough plan of a house Patrick's son, Lord Polwarth, would like to build, 'the product of some idle hours, a world of rooms and but 3 tollerable bed chambers . . .'

Like a good many of the other Merse lairds, George began as he grew older to take increasing pride in his garden, and there are frequent diary entries about sending for seeds. In March 1700 in Edinburgh he 'bought some garden seeds in one Fraser's, and a pruning knife'. In February 1704 John Dickson sent him from Edinburgh a hundred apple stocks and six apricot trees, but 'the apples are small and not for grafting as I expected'. August 1702 proved to be a red-letter month for apricots — they were the first he had ever had, as many as fifty or sixty on one tree on the west side of the gate. So proud was he of this achievement that he took three of the apricots with him to Polwarth House, where the Chancellor commended them, and George gave one each to him, Sir John Home and Frank Pringle. Earlier that month he had been very depressed because 'the apricocks at Polwarth Hous are allmost all done and not one of the few I have here ripe as yet'. Sometimes his gardener got the blame when things went wrong, as when on 29 March 1704 'yesterday I caused uncover the Asparagus which by the gardener's negligence was not uncovered though it was shooting under the dung'. Advice on gardening problems was sometimes sought in his letters, as when in April 1698 he entreated Sir John Home, who was then on a visit to London, to get some cure 'for Moles and the "shear mice" as we call them, or water rats as the English'.

Apart from the *interests* of this gregarious, scholarly, compulsive diary-keeper, what were his outstanding characteristics as a person? Though he never actually says so, the evidence in the diary all points to a belief that lairds and men of similar rank should not soil their hands with manual work of any kind. To him gardening meant arranging to have seeds or young trees sent, and engaging in the planning of operations, not actually carrying them out. Even the home brewing of ale was a task to be undertaken by others, not by him. His favourite way of putting it is that he 'caused' this or that to be done, never that he himself did it. A mixture of male chauvinism and status consciousness gave a very restricted meaning to the term 'work' in its application to him personally; in this, however, as in so many other respects, he was merely a man of his time.

Even the most casual glance at his diary makes another characteristic clear — an inability to make ends meet, to live within his means. It may well have been a common complaint then as now, but he seems to have been a chronic sufferer from cash-flow problems. Time and again we find him asking his friends as a matter of urgency to pay what they owe him, or lend him some money; or imploring John Dickson to raise something for him in Edinburgh as quickly as possible 'in my present pinch'. And equally frequently he has to fend off similar requests from those to whom *he* owes money. His extensive library does not seem to have included Gervase Markham's *A Way to get Wealth*, which had already reached its 12th edition in 1668; but perhaps its 738 pages did not contain any usable advice for people in his particular situation. Yet with all his money problems, we know that he still managed to give to the poor. And gentlemen in distress were not forgotten either. In August 1698 'I got a letter from the Lady Hiltone desiring me to send her what I had a mind to give George Carmichael (who is in a Low Condition and asking a contribution from his friends). She being to go to Edinburgh tomorrow I wrote to her and sent her £12 Scots'. There is no obvious evidence of extravagance on his own part, and there are plenty of examples of 'making do' rather than going to unnecessary expense. He paid George Wilson the tailor 'for making Robie a suit of cloath of ane old coat and a silk waistcoat of mine'. And once when he was in Edinburgh, finding that his feet would get wet on going out, 'I was forced to get ane old hat and make soles of it to put in my shoes'.

Another dominant characteristic is his preoccupation — whether excessive or not must be a matter of opinion — with the weather and with his health. These two seem often, but not always, to have a close relationship in his mind. One Tuesday in October he records having a letter from the Chancellor asking him to go to Polwarth House next day. But on the Wednesday he tells us 'it rained so I could not goe'. At other times the weather cannot be blamed for his failure to go out: 'I went no wher. It was fair with some wind all day'. Much the more usual situation, however, was exercising caution and, when not feeling too well, not risking going out. Even before the diary as we know it had begun, we find him writing a letter of apology to Patrick for not being well enough to attend a meeting 'but these 2 days I have been troubled with a sore throat'. A fortnight later 'I am hindered from waiting on Your Lordship by the badness of my health, for though I find myself better I dare not as yet venture abroad'.[11] Four years later, being again troubled with a sore throat in October, 'I think the weight of the new periwig was the cause of it'. The terms he uses to describe his other ailments include 'ane aguish or feverish distemper', 'the gripes', 'a violent fitt of the gravell' and, most frequently of all, 'shortness of breath'. One morning there was 'a violent pain in my stomach and I broke out into lumps all over my body with such ane itch I was like to tear myself. I sent for Dr Trotter but, blessed be God, found ease before he came, one mouthful of brandy eased me'. On most occasions his first reaction was to reach for 'a vomit' (a purgative or emetic), though if one of the doctors or Mr Auchinleck was there to treat Robie, they took blood from him *before* he took the vomit; and if the frost was keen, the procedure was postponed until the weather became soft. Robie's vomit was seven drams of *vinum ameticum* or, alternatively, syrup of pale roses. Blood-letting (which was Mr Auchinleck's speciality) was the normal treatment, though when Robie had a cough and six leeches were put on his neck it proved rather much for him. For himself, George was critical of Mr Auchinleck for making 'the orifice too small and ther came so little away at a time that he got but about 3 ounces, for I fainted. Whereas had the orifice been big enough, 6 ounces — the quantity I designed — might have been got'. As treatment for the gravel, the doctors 'ordered nothing but the common things of clysters, fomentations and laudanum, which had no effect'. Some of the treatments recommended by doctors meant a spell in some other place. Several times we are told of 'Jerviswood sweating at the salt pans [Prestonpans] for his deafness', though he also resorted to a silver ear trumpet, the efficacy of which, we are told, was 'to cause the air beat his ear more strongly', but 'I did not see him make use of it'. When in England, several friends were put on ass's milk or goat's milk, but the most usual recommendation was a spell at Scarborough Wells. When George had kidney trouble in 1704, Dr Abernethy is quoted as wishing 'I could get Scarburgh water to drink'; its popularity is mentioned again in Chapter 6.

If he became ill when he was in Edinburgh, it was Dr Stevenson who was called in, and particularly great reliance seems to have been placed on getting his help. His advice was sought when Robie was ill in the country, even though he could not examine the patient. And when the Earl of Home, who was in Edinburgh, got news from the Hirsel in March 1700 that his sister Lady Anne was dangerously ill, and two of his children sick, he went to the country that day and took Dr Stevenson with him in the coach. In their Berwickshire homes the normal practice was, however, to call in Dr Abernethy. His house was in Kelso, so this meant sending your man on horseback to deliver a letter to him. He might, of course, be out seeing a patient somewhere, in which case the letter merely awaited his return. All told, it might be several days before he could visit you; but if the day was already far advanced when he arrived, he would in any case have to stay the night, and proceed to his next visit or back to Kelso at first light. In the early 1690s he seems to have been the only medical practitioner in the area, so everyone patronised him — everyone, that is, except the bulk of the population who could not afford to pay for his services. Later in the decade Dr Trotter appeared on the scene, married George's sister Julian and settled in Duns, so an element of choice came in; and Mr Auchinleck, whose speciality as already noted was bleeding, could also be sent for if you were in a financial position to do so.

To George, Dr Abernethy was much more than just the family doctor: he was a personal friend. They lent each other books and discussed them together at length. They probably talked of many other matters not specifically referred to in the diary. Because of this personal relationship, Dr Abernethy sometimes refused to take any fee for his visits; when he was persuaded to accept one, it was, in 1695, five rix dollars. One other non-medical aspect of the doctor's life was his determination to visit Newcastle Fair, whenever it came round; but what the particular attraction was to him we have no means of knowing. There were, in fact, at least three other doctors in Kelso besides Abernethy — Somervell, Richardson and Thomas Inglis. If George Home does not mention visits to himself or his friends by any of these, it may be because their patients were to the west of Kelso or even in the town itself. There was also an apothecary there, James Robisone. And a bonesetter by the name of William Clavern lived somewhere within reach, for (February

1704) 'I knew him when he set Sir John Home's arm here when he disjointed it one day at hunting in 1681 or 82'.

George may have been unduly preoccupied with his own (and Robie's) health, but at least he cannot be criticised for indulging in nostalgia, or wallowing in self-pity. Once some close relative or friend has died, they receive no further mention in the diary, and though this may sometimes seem heartless, it is perhaps better than the maudlin sentimentality indulged in by some diarists. Not to look back was almost a matter of principle with him, but occasionally it presents problems when reading what he has written today. For our knowledge of his pre-diary life has to be built up from other sources, and inevitably there are aspects of his previous history of which we know little or nothing. So it comes as a shock when, uncharacteristically, he suddenly reveals something of his past of which we think we have been quite unaware. What at first appears to be a startling example of this is when, coming face to face with Carstares in Edinburgh in March 1698, and not being recognised by him, he reminds himself in the diary that the two of them had been fellow prisoners in Edinburgh Castle twenty years before. And then it all falls into place — George was there on that occasion for a very different reason from that of his companion in misfortune, merely because of non-payment of his fine for breaking the rules in marrying clandestinely and irregularly, and this we already knew about from other non-diary evidence.

He was, like many of us, a once-a-year maker of good resolutions. In his case this took place on his birthday, when he always resolved to live a worthier life in future and follow the wishes of his Maker, but these resolutions were probably quickly forgotten in the hurly-burly of actual living. One character fault of which it would be difficult to accuse him is vanity. There is virtually nothing in his diary to suggest this, and had he been vain there would surely have been some indication of it somewhere in this immensely long story of a substantial slice of his life. The only hint of such a possibility lies in a slight fussiness about the colour of his wig — he sent back the one his sister had got for him in Edinburgh as being too dark; and in ordering another later on he sent a sample 'of this I have for the colour'. Hardly enough to justify a charge of vanity. One other matter connected with wigs we may be shocked or surprised at today. In his little parchment notebook is a reminder 'to try among my tenants wives daughters servants or others whether any of them have a good head of hair and will part with it'.

He certainly thought of himself as a tolerant man, and this comes out in his comments on what the less broad-minded would have categorised as the follies of youth. There was, for instance, the time when, in February 1699, Mr Meldrum gave two young ladies of quality in the Tron Church in Edinburgh a public rebuke for laughing and making a noise during the service. 'Some say', and George obviously agrees with them, 'he should have given them a *private* rebuke, especially they being young and youth having some thing excusable in its wantonnesse.' He also thought that one should be more tolerant of country folk and not write them off as hayseeds: 'I find it is a gentleman's interest who is conversant in country affairs to hear country people, especially the most intelligent, talk of business, they think of nothing else and so are ready to make more solide remarks than gentlemen who are more taken up with other things'. Occasionally, however, he himself slipped into what might be construed as a form of intolerance, however harmless, as when he and Cavers 'thought it odd to see Mrs Jane, his Lady's Aunt, eat fish to her supper at the age of 75'. And Cavers mentions with equal astonishment that 'Sir Thomas, her Father, would have done the same at 85, and did till he died at 88'. George certainly showed remarkable toleration regarding the behaviour of one of his pets. Reporting on 5 April 1703 that he had his windows mended, he explains 'the tame Corby I have breaks them yet I'm loath to put him away. Though he is very mischievous, he is a pleasant kind of pet, speaks some words and imitates the dogs barking exactly. He stole the Glasier's diamond yesterday, which we had work enough to find again'. Some of the things of which he shows intolerance are matters about which most of us would feel the same way. On one occasion he was wakened at four in the morning and unable to get to sleep again because the tailor turned up at that hour to start work on the family's clothing and made a great noise. And then there was the time when he and Patrick's son Andrew made an unfortunate choice of a bed: not only was there the noise of the kitchen where the children lay and cried all night, but the activities of the fleas also prevented them from sleeping.

Leaving aside the unchallengeable value of his diary as history, how then does its author come across as a man? Not, perhaps, with any particular distinction, though not as an insignificant figure either. Yet there is one final question each of us might usefully ponder. If *we* had, from some inner compulsion, produced a daily record of our thoughts and doings as full and frank as his, for posterity to scrutinise, would we pass this character test with as much credit as George does?

CHAPTER 4

Close Friends of the Family

The Humes of Polwarth and the **Homes of Blackadder** had been friends for some time. The family seats were only eight miles apart, and of roughly the same size, and their status in the community was similar. Patrick's contemporary Sir John Home, the Laird of Blackadder, died early in 1675; his wife Mary, whom he married about the same time that Patrick married Grisell, had died two years earlier. So it was not until after Patrick's flight to, and return from, Holland that friendship could be re-established with the new generation of Blackadders. The new Sir John followed in his father's footsteps as an M.P. for Berwickshire from 1690 until his death in 1706. His political leanings were very much the same as Patrick's, and he soon became known as one of his staunchest allies. Indeed, the unflattering terms used about him by the Duke of Argyll, writing to Carstares in September 1698, clearly had more to do with this than with his merits or abilities: 'If any mention be made of Sir John Home beware of him, for he'll make mischief amongst us. And though he went as to the cess alongst, yet, in the polls he opposed us. He is light in the forehead, full of notion, always talking and most uneasy to be in business with . . .'[1] Disgruntlement at the lack of reward for his earlier political services led him to join with the opposition from 1700 onwards.

The new laird was of an age with George Home the diarist. In 1684, when they were in their twenties, the two of them had been to France together. Whilst abroad (probably in 1686), Crossrig tells us, 'a wofull accident befell Sir John Home at Angiers, having in a scufle receaved a wound in his head from a Frenchman that had well nigh cost him his life, and cost him great expenses in his cure', but it does not appear to have had any long-term effects (unless we take Argyll's strictures literally).[2] He and George remained firm friends, and it was at the Blackadder seat that the tossing of dogs in a blanket took place (see Chapter 6). From the diary we get a good deal of incidental information about Sir John and his family. As they were a lot better off than he was, it was usually George who borrowed things from Sir John. In bad travelling weather for a trip to Edinburgh, we learn that he 'sent to Blackader for a loan of his black sword and his cloakbag, saddle and maille pillion'. A 'Maill Pullion and Girths', we may note, cost Cunningham of Craigends sixteen shillings in 1680.[3] On another occasion George again sends his man to Blackadder, this time for half a dozen bottles of table ale, 'mine being done'. We learn something about the arrangements for the education of the boys when, in May 1700, 'the Lady Blackader came this way before noon with her two sons going to Stichell, where they are to be to learn to write, Stichell's son's governour teaching extremely well'. We also hear of their having had portraits done by Nicholas Heude, the member of the French Academy who was expelled from France as a Protestant and came to Scotland around 1688. On 20 February 1696 in Edinburgh 'I went to a French painters, one Eude, who had been at Blackader taking the Lady's picture, and Jamie's, and Robie's and was finishing them there'. George was, naturally, present on all important family occasions. He went to the baptism of baby David on 15 September 1695, and to his funeral in November 1702. And when Sir John came back from a London visit with a calesh and two black mares to draw it, George was the first to be taken in it and, as mentioned in Chapter 7, was highly critical of it as a means of locomotion.

Sir John and his wife, Catherine, daughter of Sir John Pringle, first baron of Stichell, had three sons, John, Robert and David, and a daughter Helen. The family seat had sixteen hearths, and in the mid-1690s there was a living-in staff of nine, comprising four manservants (including a groom and two cooks), a gentlewoman and four maidservants.[4] It was here that, some twenty years before, Crossrig (who was Sir John's uncle as well as George's), had brought his first wife and settled down for a while to look after the orphans and cope with the management of the estate.

David Home was also a Blackadder, but one of the older generation, a contemporary of Patrick and Grisell. He was born on 3 May 1643, the second son of the Laird of Blackadder. Tremendously helpful in putting together the following account of his life has been what amounts to his autobiography; he left a manuscript 'An Account of my Estate and Fortune (so far as I can remember) ever since I had any', which was, as we have seen, published long afterwards with the shorter title *Domestic Details*.[5] His elder brother John, who succeeded to the estate, married his cousin Mary Dundas, daughter of Sir James Dundas of Arniston. There were four sisters, and when they married we have another example of the extent to which intermarriage was customary among the landed gentry, with the usual bargaining between the families concerned. Like many of the Homes, the Blackadders were cadets of the Homes of Wedderburn, their origin being traced to the '4th Spear' of that family, all well known for their valour on the battlefield.

David was only 14 when his father died on 31 October 1657, and as he himself notes in his *Domestic Details*, it was Hallowe'en. By this time his sister Margaret was already married to Robert Home of Ninewells; Katherine married Robert Home of Kimmerghame in September 1659; Jean died of a fever in May 1668; and Isabell married Patrick Cokeburn of Borthwick in June 1674. In the case of Isabell he does not forget to mention that she was married at his mother's house, at *his* expense. Like many of his contemporaries among the Merse lairds he was obsessed by financial matters. A substantial proportion of his reminiscences consists of calculations of monies owing to him, and of details as to how things might or might not be straightened out.

With his father's death his mother was left to care for the remaining three girls and the younger son, David; she had, of course, her jointure of the Blackadder estate to support them. As a younger son, however, David had to fend for himself if any sort of livelihood was to be secured. He was not, fortunately, one to idle his time away; later in his life he tells us that he judged it 'an indecent and evil thing to be altogether idle'.[6] A month after his father's death he made the first move: 'In November 1657 I entered *bajin* in the College of Edinburgh'.[7] First-year students normally began their studies at the start of October, the course lasting eleven months, with one month of vacation. They went by the rather peculiar name of bajans (or bajins); no one seems very clear what the origin of the word may be. One suggestion is that yet again we have evidence of the French connection, and that it may be traced to *bas gens*. The third year was known as the bachelor class, and between these two, the second year students were the *semies*. The fourth and final year students were the *magistrands*. Examinations were very strict, and students were required to speak and write fluently in Latin.

David's bajan year seems to have passed uneventfully, but in the semie year he got into trouble. The semies had a tradition of attending a football match on the Borrow Moor (now Boroughmuir) on 11 March, something that was prohibited by the College rules. He had, in a moment of folly and under oath, promised to take part in this enterprise. His tutor tried to talk him out of the escapade, but with no success. The punishment for breaking the College rule was to be whipped in class, but to this David refused to submit, and as a result he was forced to leave the College for the rest of the session. His uncle, Dundas of Arniston, put in a good word for him, in consequence of which he was readmitted to the semie year in November 1659, and finally laureated (graduated) in 1662. By this time his mother had moved to live in Edinburgh, though David did not lodge with her. She left Blackadder when her son John married in April 1660, as things were not as happy for her as they might have been after the marriage.

No more formal study took place for a couple of years after graduation, and according to his autobiography David spent a good deal of this time studying old family accounts, trying to assess what his brother was owing him, and making endless calculations of his own disbursements. Although his father had made appropriate 'bonds of provision' to ensure that all members of the family would have no financial difficulties, there were all kinds of new agreements being made between John, the young laird, and his mother, many of which were not altogether agreeable to David. And when his sister Jean died, there was further acrimonious argument among the family as to how her portion of her father's provision should be shared out. On 30 September 1664 he decided to go to France, where he again carried on his law studies, at Poitiers, until April 1666, his return being hastened by war having been proclaimed with England. Even after this further course of study he still felt insufficiently prepared to consider entering as an advocate, and decided that a temporary change of plan might be beneficial. So, for the next few years, he embarked on some trading ventures.

In 1672 and 1673 he involved himself in wine trading and invested money in a brewery. These investments failed to produce profit and were speedily sold. He then joined with one or two of his friends and 'had a one-sixteenth interest in a ship'.[8] To finance this he had to borrow money, but here again he had no success and says sadly, 'this was the beginning of my debt'. It was during this time that his sister-in-law, the Lady Blackadder, died of a fever in childbirth in December 1672. The laird, desolated by the loss of his wife, decided to go to France in the following autumn. He was away for a year, from September 1673 to August 1674, leaving Mr John Craw of Greenlaw in charge of his estates, and some responsibility for his family with his brother, though the two girls, Jennet and Mary, stayed at his mother's house. On his return, John stayed in Edinburgh, and in January 1675 he developed a fever from which he died. Inevitably more responsibility for the young family then fell on David's shoulders, and things must have been made more complicated by the fact that by this time he had married (28 April 1674) and had his own establishment. The marriage was a happy one; his bride was Barbara Laurie, relict of William Laurie of Reidcastle, brother to the laird of Maxwelton.

The next year or two were full of upheaval and change for the couple. First, David's uncle Kimmerghame (the diarist's father) died in May 1677. He had not been on the best of terms with his uncle, again over money transactions which he felt were unfavourable to himself. But he went to the burial 'and found in his cloathes, as I remember, a list of debts owing to him and owing by him, the latter very far short of what I found it to be afterwards'.[9] We are not told if he made any effort to help in clearing up these problems. In May of the following year his mother died, and apart from feeling her loss keenly, this involved him in further difficulties. With his brother, his uncle and his mother all gone, there was no one to look after the affairs of the little family of four children (two boys and two girls) at Blackadder, particularly the young laird who had not yet reached his majority. His other uncle, Lord Arniston, had been for some time pressing David to go and live at Blackadder, to keep an eye on things. Until the death of his mother he had felt he could not do this, as he did not want to leave her alone in Edinburgh, and she could not be moved. Now, with this obstacle gone, he and his family of three children moved from Edinburgh to Berwickshire soon after Whitsuntide 1678. Not surprisingly, he complained about the 'great expense in flitting', and when in November of the same year his wife died, he bemoaned the cost of her sickness and death, all of which 'straitened me exceedingly'. At the same time he praised his wife as having been 'the most wise, religious, virtuous, pleasant-spirited woman and kind wife, that ever man had'.[10] His nephew was attending the College in Edinburgh from 1680-83, and used to spend the vacations at Blackadder for three or four weeks each year, accompanied by his brother, a governor and a servant. The expense of all this was felt keenly. And although young Blackadder finished at the College in the spring of 1683, he lived with his uncle for another year, till May 1684 when he went to France with his cousin, George Home, the diarist.

David Home married a second time, on 8 January 1680 when he was living in Edinburgh for a short spell. He seems to have favoured widows, for his choice again fell on one, Mrs Smithe, relict of James Smithe, an Edinburgh merchant, and eventually in June they moved back to Blackadder with the children. In the year following his marriage David sustained an accident at Berwick. His leg was hurt in some way; he does not give us any details of the injury, but it did not heal, and after a couple of months amputation was carried out. Thus he was left to hobble around with a wooden leg for the rest of his life. Probably what upset him most was that all this 'occasioned him a vast expense'. Further family duties were now thrust upon him, for Borthwick and his lady, David's sister, both died in October 1682. On her deathbed Isabell had charged him with caring for her two children, John and Ann Cokeburn. So these two joined the family at Blackadder and were the responsibility of their uncle for some five years. Soon after Ann Cokeburn arrived, he sent her to Mrs Shiens, mistress of manners, for (he says) about two years, though she later reminded him that it was three years. The cost was £5 sterling in the quarter, besides presents. And when young Blackadder went to France with his cousin the diarist in 1684, Uncle David looked after Kimmerghame's estate as well. In his reminiscences he says 'I was curator [guardian appointed by a court or an individual] to this Nynwell's father . . . I was curator to this George Home of Kimmerghame . . . I was tutor and curator to Sir John Home of Blackadder . . . I was curator to George Seuttie, my son-in-law . . .'[11] All of these duties he carried out, eventually receiving legal discharges acknowledging that his responsibilities had been satisfactorily completed. If we forget about his obsession with financial matters (which pervades every page of his autobiography), we must admit that from the point of view of shouldering other people's burdens he was the kind of uncle every family would be glad to have. Of course he had worries of his own as well. At this time the authorities were taking proceedings against many people who could not really be thought of as anti-government, and David was apprehensive. On a trip to Berwick, rumours reached him that a party of soldiers had been sent to apprehend him. So he lay low in Berwick for some days till the danger had passed, though in the event he learned that it had been a false alarm. He did, however, along with other Merse lairds, respond to the call for support when Argyll made his ill-fated expedition to Scotland, was taken by the militia, and made a 'free prisoner' for some twenty days.

By 1687 he felt the urge to go back to legal work, but thought perhaps he was too 'rusted' in his studies to pass the examination required for acceptance as an advocate. After consultation with the authorities, he established himself as a special case in view of all the family affairs he had had to deal with, and, having paid the fee to the Faculty of Advocates, was duly admitted. For a time he commuted between Blackadder and Edinburgh while carrying out his legal work, but he finally moved north to the capital. He tells us that the house he ultimately occupied cost 430 marks for the first year and 400 marks annually after that (a mark was 13/4 Scots). He also had a cellar in another house at a cost of £11 yearly.[12]

We can in fact say a little more about his Edinburgh house, for we know that what he called his 'lodging' there paid tax in 1690 on its eight hearths (quite a large house for a town dwelling). We also know that when a poll tax was taken in 1694 the members of his own family living in that house were himself, his wife and their five boys and four girls. In addition there were three lodgers — George and James, sons of the late

James Seuttie, merchant, together with his niece, Agnes Cokeburn of Borthwick. The servants consisted of two men (one paid £60 and the other £15 a year) and two women (£16 and £14).[13]

In June 1689 he received a pleasant surprise. Earl Crawford, president of the parliament, informed him that he had been nominated as a lord of session. He was unsure who had put his name forward, but guessed that it was the lord secretary, Lord Melville, whom he had to thank. This was followed by an appointment as lord of justiciary, and by his being knighted. The salary attached to the post of lord of session was a substantial one, and for lord of justiciary there was also a small annual payment. But as in the case of all official posts the recipients were fortunate if salaries were paid when they were due; it was more frequently the case that they were in arrears. In 1689 he took his seat on the bench, styling himself Lord Crossrig. The choice of name was an obvious one. For a number of years he had been engaged in legal wranglings with Robert Home of Crossrig and the Earl of Home over property to which he felt he had an entitlement. Finally, some agreement was reached: 'After many jars, wos and froes in my business with Crossrig and the Earl of Home [it] came to a settlement'.[14] One feels that, temporarily at least, some of his financial worries must have been forgotten.

Lord Crossrig's greatest misfortune was the disastrous fire in Edinburgh which broke out in the Meal Market on 3 February 1700, reducing a substantial part of central Edinburgh to a shambles. We have a vivid description of the damage caused in the letter written by Duncan Forbes of Culloden to his brother: 'Ther are burnt, by the easiest computation, betwixt 3 and 400 familys: all the pryde of Eden[r] is sunk; from the Cowgate to the High Street all is burnt, & hardly one stone left upon another. The Commissioner, President of the Parl[t], Pres[t] of the Session, the Bank, most of the Lords, Lawyers, and Clerks, were all burnt, & many good & great familys'. This all refers to property, for later in his narrative Culloden says 'Few people are lost, if any att all'. Everything was in confusion and disorder, 'twenty thousand hands flitting ther trash they know not wher . . . . These babells, of ten and fourteen story high, are down to the ground, and ther fall's very terrible. Many rueful spectacles, such as Corserig naked, with a child under his oxter, happing for his lyffe'.[15] In the fire, Lord Crossrig lost all his papers, legal and personal, and the latter part of *Domestic Details* is taken up with his attempts to reconstitute from memory all the documents that had been burned.

Sir David Home, Lord Crossrig, died on 13 April 1707 aged 64. He had three children by his first marriage and several more by his second; a grandson, Francis Home, became the first Professor of Materia Medica in Edinburgh University. The 1843 editor of his autobiography, looking at the official portrait of his Lordship by young Medina, sees him as 'a quiet, comfortable, cosy-looking person, with the expression rather of a country squire than of one learned in the laws'.[16] He suggests that he was perhaps more a man from whom one could expect honesty, friendliness and good common sense than evidence of superiority of intellect.

Alexander Home was not merely a close friend but was also Patrick's brother-in-law. He was a younger brother of the Laird of Manderston, and, as all younger brothers of lairds had to do at that time, he had to make a career for himself. He chose the law and was successful enough in that field to become the first of the whole of the Home clan to be a Writer to the Signet. He was made Commissary of Lauder in 1690, and continued in that office until his death in May 1702. The court in which a commissary presided was concerned with wills, successions, marriage, divorce and related matters. There were commissaries at Edinburgh and also at Lauder; matters arising in Berwickshire were dealt with at Lauder.

He married Patrick's sister Anne, which gave him strong links with the family, and accounts for his always being welcome to stay at Polwarth House. She had a reputation for being particularly knowledgeable in cases of sickness. We learn from George Home's diary on 11 January 1699 that 'Lady Anne Hall [who was her niece] went yesterday to Com. Home's lodgings, his Lady being very dextrous about sick folk'. Alexander and Anne had a son and several daughters; the son, Sandy, evidently studied at St Andrews, for the diary records in May 1698 that 'Com. Home was not in toune, being gone to Fife. I think it is to St Andrews to see his sone'.

Although his official duties were in Lauder, Commissary Home chose to live in Edinburgh, presumably to carry on his practice as a Writer to the Signet. He was very much part of the Edinburgh scene, and met John Foulis of Ravelston and his cronies there on a number of occasions. At the end of March 1698, for instance, we learn that he got together with them twice on one day, the 30th, and then again on the following day. Maggie Black's was where they foregathered for some of these meetings, and the others present included James Hay, another Writer to the Signet, James Nicholson, also in law, Commissary Elphinstone, Crawford of Crawfurdstoune, and a cousin of Sir John Foulis's, Colonel Adam Rae.[17]

His death in 1702 was sudden. George Home tells us 'He went out of

Ed^r on Mund with his sickness on him to Lauder . . . came in on Wed at night and was ill but concealed it. His Lady sent for Mr Auchanleck who would fain have taken blood of him'. Apparently this was not possible, and he died on the Friday afternoon. As we have already noted, George's main concern at the death of his great friend was the monetary loss it was likely to entail for him personally.

John Carre of Cavers and West Nisbet was not only a neighbour and close friend of the Polwarths, he was also related to Grisell as a cousin. Sir Thomas Kar had one son, Andrew, who was Grisell's half-brother, and his cousin John owned the estate of West Nisbet some five or six miles from Polwarth House. Sir Andrew (Grisell's half-brother) had only one son, a strong, healthy young man, whereas the heir at West Nisbet was a very sickly lad. With the idea of uniting the two properties of Cavers Carre and West Nisbet, the fathers of these two boys together made a legal arrangement to ensure that this would happen. Whichever of their sons survived the other was to inherit both estates. Very soon afterwards Sir Andrew's son died, and John of West Nisbet therefore fell heir to the two properties. By his marriage in 1679 to Agnes, Sir Andrew's elder daughter, a further link between the two branches of the family was forged.

It may seem odd that the spelling of the name should now be Carre, when we know that Grisell's father always signed himself Thomas Kar or Ker, and she, even after her marriage, used the name Grisell Kar. The explanation is that when John's father married Jean, daughter of the Carres of Crailing, he decided to adopt this spelling of his name. John and Agnes (often called Nance) set up house in West Nisbet. With sixteen hearths it was roughly equivalent in size to Polwarth House. The anonymous author of a contemporary account of Berwickshire describes it in enthusiastic terms: 'The Palace of West Nisbet . . . an estate with large Planting and fruitful Orchards'.[18] When details of those living there were recorded in the mid-1690s for poll-tax purposes, four sons are mentioned, Robert, John, James and Thomas, and three daughters, Jean, Margaret and Anne (the last of whom died within a few years of the poll tax being taken).[19] Two other relatives were also living there. The first was simply given as Mrs Christian Ker, and could either have been Cavers's sister (as the person who made out the list described every member of the family as a 'Ker') or else his wife's aunt, both of whom were called 'Christian'. George Home records seeing both of them on separate occasions at West Nisbet, so his evidence does not help to resolve the issue. There is no doubt, however, about the second relative living there. She was Jane, 'sister of the deceased Sir Andrew Ker' and therefore an aunt of Cavers's wife. She was in her early 70s at the time, and in Chapter 3 we have already noted the astonishment of both Cavers and the diarist that she should still be eating fish at that age. They had a slightly larger domestic staff than the Polwarths, consisting of eleven men and eight women. And they also employed a resident schoolmaster, Mr William Knox, decribed as 'pettegougie'.

Cavers and his wife were often at Polwarth House, as George Home mentions in his diary. He also frequently encountered them at the houses of other lairds in the neighbourhood. We learn how keen he was on fox-hunting from George, who tells us that on Saturday 6 April 1695 'Went to West Nisbet and Cavers was gone to the hunting, he going now every Tuesday and Saturday'. And in October of the same year he mentions 'Cavers and his Lady having been at Hutton Hall all night, he was going to the fox-hunting in Langton parks among the broom'. The younger Cavers boys were fond of Robie, George's son; and he notes the visits they made to Kimmerghame from time to time. Other interesting incidents relating to the Cavers family emerge from George's diary. On Saturday 11 January 1696 'I met with Cavers and Mr Wedderburn who were going to Scougall's the Painters . . . Cavers sat to his picture for the first time'. And later, in November 1697 when George Home was in Edinburgh, he met Cavers and his Lady and two of their sons: 'the boys are come to the humanity [Latin] classe'.

Agnes died on 18 February 1702, and Cavers was a widower for a short period; during this time there seem to have been a number of upsets in the family over the children's marriages. George Home was asked by Cavers on 5 May 1704 for his opinion about his daughter's two suitors (one of whom was approved by him, the other not). George gave a very diplomatic reply. But eventually he reported that 'Mrs Jane, Cavers being from home, went out in the night time and went away with young Blair Drummond who was waiting for her near the house'.

Robert, the eldest son, also married without parental consent. John, his younger brother, ultimately succeeded to the estates. He should have been relatively wealthy, for as a young boy he had been left substantial legacies both by Lord Jedburgh and by his aunt Christian Carre. But his father, who in any case seems to have been a great spender, apparently charged much of the cost of his son's education and maintenance to these legacies, thus leaving young John with little in the way of resources. When Cavers remarried it was to Margaret Wauchope; he himself died on 28 June 1737 in his 70s.

Marie Douglass became Lady Hilton on marrying the laird, Joseph Johnston, son of Archibald 'with the beard'. They had four boys and three girls and then he died, quite unexpectedly and unnecessarily, as a result of an unprovoked attack by a close friend following a game of cards at the Hirsel on 26 December 1683. The story of this tragic affair will be given in Chapter 6. Marie found herself a widow with six children to bring up (one of the boys having died very young). And she naturally turned to her close friend and relative Sir Patrick Hume for advice and guidance on the many problems arising. A number of letters she wrote to him in the difficult months following her husband's murder have survived in manuscript.[20] In one of the earliest of these, dated 13 February 1684, she asks for his comments on the advice she has been given by Coldenknows (Home of Cowdenknows) in connection with the conveyance of property to the elder of her young sons. Then on 3 March 1684 she writes again, asking how she should invest forty rix dollars (£168 Scots); and the letter proceeds: 'I must intreat you'l be pleased to doe me the favour as to speak to Mr Scougill Limner to draw a little pocket picture by that pichlers of My Dears which was gott from Mrs Anne Dundas and be pleased to desire hime gett it as soone as possible and let it be in a wike and take another by it of the bigness it is for Mis Anne which she desirs for it the little one I hope may be soone gott ready; the other as soone as he can . . . Your Affectionate and humble servant Marie Douglass'. Marie was obviously feeling the need to strengthen her family ties by commissioning further portraits, or copies, of her children. Later in the letter she mentions that she expects Patrick to visit her soon, and hopes he will bring the small portrait with him.

Another business letter follows a month later on 13 March, and yet another on 17 March. On 4 April she writes again: 'I expected you here long before this . . . my service to your Ladie and my cussins; my mother is very Ill and I think very weak since she keeps her bed constantly and has taken noe meat this great while . . .' Further letters follow on 16 May, 27 May and 28 June, in which she asks Patrick to look at some papers relative to her father's affairs, and discusses family troubles which concern her sister Sophia. Sophia Douglass had married the Laird of Kettleston, in the parish of Linlithgow, and Marie is very worried as her brother-in-law is obviously seriously mentally ill; she hopes that 'they may get him conveyed away being weary of this burden'. Knowing that the Kettleston family is in financial difficulties, she says she has 'writ to Gorg Cessford to give a years annual rent of 4,000 mks [over £5,000 Scots] to Kettlestone which you see he writs he has not yet received. I earnestly desire you [i.e. Patrick] may speak to Georg to see if it can be got to him, for I know he has very great need of it'.

We do not know just what happened immediately after this, but we hear again of the troubles at Kettleston when Marie's friend, Grisell, writes to Lord Melville, the secretary, on 24 June 1689 on Sophia's behalf. Kettleston had committed suicide in London at that time, and Grisell asks that some financial help be given to his widow for, if he is declared bankrupt, 'his lady and children will be perfitly beggers if they are not helpt that way'. She encloses a letter from Lady Hilton with her own, sending the package to Hampton Court; but Grisell is anxious in case the letter missed his Lordship, so on that same day she writes another letter to him, explaining that she had already written, detailing the circumstances again and finishing: 'That Lady has had nothing this long time but what she has had from her sister, and it will be charity to do for her'.[21] We have no further information about the Kettleston family, nor do we know how Lord Melville reacted.

Returning to 26 July 1684, Marie writes to Patrick that when her servant called with a letter about her son's inheritance he got no answer. One wonders whether he was lying low at this time? Finally, after a number of years, we have the letter of 30 November 1689 in which, as will be explained in Chapter 8, she makes an extremely generous gift to Patrick and Grisell to help them out of their current financial difficulties, and then one or two other interesting comments follow. She says her uncle George is made close prisoner in Edinburgh Castle, and that 'one Wilsone who was prisoner there and Dunbar that was in the Tolbooth are sent to the Bass'. In spite of her worries over matters of this sort, she does not forget to think of another kindness to one of her friends. She asks Grisell 'to buy a quilted petticoat for Sir John Sinclair's ladie off an Indian striped stuffe if you can have it and Indian quilting'.

Marie Douglass might be thought already to have had her share of family problems by the mid-1690s, but there were more to come. Joseph, the oldest surviving boy, went to the College in Edinburgh as a student where, in January 1695, George Home reported that he had died. John Carre of Cavers took an interest in Robert, the new heir, and helped him to acquire some of the skills thought to be appropriate to a laird, and took him foxhunting, to such effect that Lady Anne Purves in her 'Anecdotes' describes the young man as 'a great Nimrod'.[22] Meanwhile the eldest daughter, Katie, had married the Laird of Mangerton (Manderston), and in due course the diarist records that Lady Hilton visited her daughter, 'the Lady Mangerton being to ly in'. Unfortunately, shortly after a boy was born the laird took ill, and went to England where he was fed on ass's milk. But he failed to recover and died. In a relatively short time the little boy died as well. She had not long been a widow when she and Patrick's son Andrew fell in love with each other. There were, however, too many adverse factors to make their marriage possible, as we shall see in Chapter 5.

Marie Douglass was a very sociable woman, and was happy to spend a lot of her time travelling around visiting her many friends and relatives in the area; she was frequently at Polwarth House, sometimes staying there several nights. On these visits, which were always on horseback, as she did not have a coach, she was usually accompanied by one or two of her children. Like the others in her social circle, she found visits to Edinburgh attractive, for in the capital plenty of entertaining was always taking place. Foulis of Ravelston, for instance, reports that on 24 February 1694 he bought '1 mutchkin new hard seck to dinner, L. and Lady Raith, Mr francis montgomerie, Lady Hiltoune and her doughters dyned w^t us'.[23] In her case there was an added reason for Edinburgh visits, for her brother-in-law Patrick Johnston had since 1677 established himself as a major figure in the capital, as merchant, Lord Provost and M.P. for the Burgh. Though he was not popular with the masses (because of his support for the Union), he played an important part in social as well as other activities.

Back in Berwickshire, Hutton Hall was a house with around fifteen chimneys, making it of comparable size to the seats of Cavers, Blackadder or Polwarth.[24] Lady Hilton must have found herself comfortably off financially when, as a widow, she was able to give generous help to her friends when they were in trouble, as we have already seen. When the poll tax was taken in 1695, apart from Lady Hilton herself, living in the house were her son Robert, her daughter Susannah, John, another son, Elizabeth Douglass 'designed Lady Kettlestone', Mrs Sophia Johnston, 'aunt to Hiltone' and 'Hiltone's governour', whose annual wage was £60. The domestic staff consisted of five women, one being cook, and two men.[25] One of the men was James Oringe who was subsequently employed for a time by George Home. This was a relatively small staff for the size of the establishment and the number of adults and children in residence.

Lady Hilton took ill of a fever in March 1700. The Marchmonts were most concerned, and paid visits to Hutton Hall in their coach. She died in her 40s on 4 April and the funeral took place five days later. Everybody was there, and George Home sent his man to Edinburgh to fetch his black clothes. Lady Anne Purves recollects an occasion a little while afterwards when Grisell, with her family all around her, burst out crying: 'My Lord immediately said, 'Fill a Glass of Wine to my wife, she is a Cup too low'".[26] She said that she had been thinking of her good friend Ladykins (as she was affectionately known in the family).

Sir John Swinton of that Ilk was another great friend of the Polwarths and their circle; his life story was a highly unusual one. His father John's estate in Berwickshire had been declared forfeit in 1651, and this was unhappily confirmed in 1661 when the Stuarts returned. He died in 1679, his eldest son Alexander surviving his father by only a few years. John, Alexander's younger brother, was next in line. He had by that time built up a successful business as a merchant both in London and in Holland, where he then was. In 1674 he had married Sarah Welsh whose father, William, was either another London merchant or a minister. They had quite a large family only one of whom, Frances, survived childhood; she ultimately married the minister of Swinton, Henry Veitch, and died there in 1741, aged 51. John, returning to Scotland in 1690, was faced with two main problems. The first of these was to have his father's forfeitures rescinded. Sir John Lauder of Hatton (brother of the more famous Lauderdale) argued and won the case for him. The second and more difficult problem was to try and rehabilitate the estates themselves, which had suffered devastating damage over such a long period of time. He still continued, however, to be highly successful in his business undertakings, and in 1695 he was one of the people named in the Act establishing the Bank of Scotland as well as in the Act setting up the Company of Scotland trading to Africa and the Indies. His friends made full use of his coach on journeys between Edinburgh and Berwickshire. Sir John was a sociable fellow, and when in Edinburgh he would often entertain his friends and business acquaintances. There is a record of a small dinner party he held at Mrs Kendall's tavern in September 1697:

Sir John Swinton To Mrs Kendall

For broth,	£00–03–00
For rost mutton and cutlets,	01–16–00
For on dish of hens,	03–00–00
For harenes,	00–05–00
For allmonds and rasens,	01–06–00
For 3 lb. of confectiones,	07–16–00
For bread and ale,	01–00–00
For 3 pynts of clarite,	06–00–00
For sack,	02–16–00
For oysters fryed and raw,	03–16–00
For brandie and sugare,	00–06–00
For servants,	02–02–00
	£30–06–06 [27]

When the list of pollable persons was drawn up in the mid-1690s he was recorded as living at the eleven-chimney family seat of Ellbank House, Swinton, with his wife and their sole surviving daughter, Frances; the domestic staff comprised only a solitary maidservant.[28] When his wife died very soon afterwards he decided to marry again, and the story of his pursuit of the daughter of Sir James Stewart, the Lord Advocate, is fully reported in George Home's diary, beginning on 29 September 1697: 'Jo: Swintone has now gaind his Mistres the Advocats daughter and ther is a minute of a Contract signed by them'. Two weeks later he understands that 'Sr Jo: Swintones marriage is like to blow up. They say the Advocats daughter has told him that though she will obey her father in what he commands her, yet if the thing be left to her own choice, and death were laid in one balance and he in the other she would choose death; and that her affection is otherwise engaged. I know not what truth is in this but I see him very pensive all Tuesday and he went to the Country on Wednesday'. There proved to be plenty of truth in it, and it emerged that the other suitor was 'Mr James Scot, the Advocat's Last Lady's nephew'. Sir John, well versed in business negotiations when neither party will accept defeat until the very last minute, continued his pursuit in spite of all rebuffs. He no doubt hoped that the young pair would be discouraged by 'the Advocat having threatened to ruin James Scot and his family if he married his daughter'. He went on pressing his suit until the 10th November, but to no avail, as Scot won the day. By February 1698 he had found someone else, and married Anne, daughter of Sir Robert Sinclair of Longformacus, by whom in due course he had four sons and four daughters.

In 1702, with his wife's consent, he sold some of his Berwickshire lands, probably, as his nineteenth-century descendant remarks, 'to retrieve in some measure the shattered fortunes of his family'.[29] Despite his business interests, he found time to attend parliament from the second session of 1690 onwards, though he did not play a very active role there, and almost always simply supported the court. He died in 1724 and was succeeded by his eldest son John, an advocate. One of Sir John's daughters was Sir Walter Scott's grandmother; and another of them was the Aunt Margaret from whom Sir Walter heard many of the tales of which he made use in his novels.

Lady Margaret Hope of Hopetoun was very much involved in Edinburgh life in the 1690s, and was also a friend of the Polwarths. Her background is interesting and unusual, and it is therefore relevant to say a little about it before developing her own story. John Hope of Hopetoun, Lady Margaret's husband, was born in 1650, and was the fifth son of James Hope, Laird of Hopetoun, and Anna Foulis. John's mother was heiress to the important Leadhills mines in Lanarkshire, and on her marriage she made over all her inheritance to her husband. Realising the potential of the Lanarkshire property, her husband, James, devoted himself to its development, and also applied himself diligently to the study of metallurgy. He not only produced the ore, but started up an export in it to Zeeland, by way of Leith, and by the time of his death in 1661 he had made Leadhills a very profitable enterprise. John succeeded his father as laird, also inheriting Leadhills. He was just as successful as his father had been, and thus was able to make considerable additions to the Hopetoun fortune and estates. On 21 December 1668 he married Lady Margaret Hamilton, eldest daughter of the 4th Earl of Haddington; there were two children of the marriage, a daughter and a son, Charles, born in 1681. In 1678 John Hope purchased lands in Abercorn and Winchburgh, as well as Niddry Castle, where the family made their home. But, besides being a man of business, John was a frequent attender at court, where he was often in the company of Charles II and his brother the Duke of York. Returning from an expedition with the Duke on the frigate *Gloucester*, John Hope was drowned when the vessel foundered.

Lady Margaret Hope was left with a daughter and an infant son to rear, as well as a prosperous business to look after. In discharging both of these responsibilities she showed herself to be highly competent. J. P. Wood, writing in 1794, in his account of the inhabitants of the parish of Cramond, described her as 'a lady eminent in all the virtues of her sex'.[30] Flattering as the tribute may be, she was made of much sterner metal than this would suggest, and her ability in many activities would indicate that in character she must have had much in common with Lady Grisell Baillie. As the young Laird of Hopetoun, Charles became M.P. for Linlithgowshire in 1702 at the age of 21. The following year the Queen made him a privy councillor and raised him to the peerage with the title of Earl of Hopetoun. He was a zealous supporter of the Union with England, and in later years played an active part in Scottish affairs. In the 1690s Lady Margaret and her son commissioned Sir William Bruce (the noted Scottish architect, responsible for major Holyrood extensions and other important buildings) to design their new home, the present Hopetoun House. The original house was completed in 1703, and later enlarged by William Adam and his sons. When Patrick held his Edinburgh dinner parties in 1696 he was thoughtful, as we shall see in Chapter 10, in arranging that, on at least one occasion, Lady Hopetoun and her son were invited along with Sir William Bruce.

During the years of Charles' minority, when his mother was handling his affairs, the lead enterprises continued to flourish. So the Hopetouns not only had income from rents of their estates, but also from the mines; and when Charles came of age he found himself one of the richest men in Scotland. We have another pointer to the high regard in which Lady Margaret's abilities were held by her contemporaries. Scott-Moncrieff, writing in 1916, tells us of how, when Andro Hog died in 1691, the tutors or guardians who had been appointed to look after his children were seeking advice as to what would be the best way to deal with things. Help was sought from three people, an advocate, a writer to the signet, and Lady Margaret Hope of Hopetoun. Scott-Moncrieff, clearly puzzled, comments: 'One can understand the advocate and the writer, but why Lady Margaret Hope?'[31] In the light of what we now know about her, this is not so difficult to explain. Sometime in the late seventeenth century a windmill, used for crushing the ore, had been built at Leith, and a factor and servants installed there to manage it. In 1692 Lady Hopetoun ran into trouble over shore dues levied by the Edinburgh Burgh Council on merchants whose boats made use of the foreshore and harbour. The tacksman wanted to deal with her as a stranger (i.e. non-resident in the Burgh) and to exact double dues from her. She refused to pay, and successfully petitioned the Council on behalf of her son and herself. The Council declared in her favour, noting the advantages her business brought to the town of Leith; the petitioners were 'only lyable for single dues as any burges being ane residenter within the liberties of the City'.[32] An interesting sequel to the progress of the Hopetoun trading may be noted when much later, in 1719-20, a Dutchman, Henry Kalmeter, travelled round Scotland. He has been described as 'the first and possibly most interesting of the industrial spies who came to Scotland in the course of the 18th century'.[33] Kalmeter gives a detailed account of the techniques of lead-mining at Leadhills, and tells us that the Dutch merchants shipped the ore themselves at their own expense, using it to make all grades of porcelain; because of its use in this way it was known as Potter's Ore.

Lady Hopetoun no doubt took part in much of the social life of Edinburgh, and of this we have some evidence. Foulis of Ravelston mentions in his diary that on 5 September 1699 he 'dyned at my Lady Hoptouns', and in February 1697 when the Polwarths were at Lady Hopetoun's they contributed £8–16s. towards the fiddlers.[34] She was clearly a remarkable woman, ahead of her times in her outlook, and able to take full advantage of the opportunities available to her. She died and was buried at Tynninghame on 31 January 1711, in her 60s.

Duncan Forbes, Laird of Culloden, was a friend on whom Patrick relied more than on anyone else in his political dealings. If, because of the many miles between Inverness and the Merse, they were unable to plan procedures which would suit their aims, there is evidence that an extensive correspondence was conducted between the two. More than that, if Patrick wrote most of the letters to other people setting out his wishes, he could rely on his trustworthy friend to append a note of agreement and his signature, and this frequently happened.

The exact date of Duncan Forbes's birth is not certain, but it has been put as probably 1644. His father, John Forbes of Culloden, was a member of parliament for Inverness-shire and had been provost of the county town. His mother was Anna, daughter of the Laird of Grange. John Forbes was known to be a very frugal man. He had refused to take the Test, accordingly he did not prosper under the government of Charles II. This had some rather unexpected consequences. Careful by nature, he economised in every possible way, and to an extent which resulted in his accumulating sufficient fortune to extend his property by purchasing the barony of Ferintosh and the estate of Bunchrew. In spite of his economies in private living, however, he saw to it that his eldest son Duncan received a very good education at Bourges and in other places on the continent as well. John Forbes died about 1688 and his son Duncan succeeded to the family estates. In 1668 Duncan married Mary, a daughter of the Laird of Innes in Morayshire, and of the marriage there were two sons — John, who in his turn fell heir to the family estates, and Duncan, as well as several daughters. The subsequent eminence of this latter Duncan, who became one of the foremost legal figures of his day and ultimately president of the court of session, has to a large extent eclipsed the contribution to political life made by his father in the latter years of the seventeenth century.

The two young boys, John and Duncan, were brought up very strictly. Although their mother was said to be a kind and affectionate woman, the rigidity of her presbyterian principles must have had a somewhat dampening effect on the home life of her children. When the two sons were in their 20s and already making their way in the world, she wrote to Duncan that she had been deeply wounded because when they left home they had started their journey on the Sabbath. Duncan, their father, was among the most active Scottish supporters of the revolution against the Stuarts. Perhaps, therefore, it was not surprising that in the year following the revolution his estates were laid waste by Jacobite supporters, the damage being assessed at a figure of around £50,000 Scots. He petitioned parliament, and they recommended his case to the consideration of the King. We know from an extract from a journal kept by Duncan Forbes that his services were valued by King William: 'At that time I continued the sending him [his brother John] to the Prince of Orange with our address, which took effect. I was in London in 1690, and wrote down scrolls of such letters as I would have his colonel write to Portland anent his officers; and by that means, and other management, got him made major of that regiment, the Secretary Melville being jealous for Carlipp, and Mackay for his cousin Roubigill. The King upon knowing that John was my brother immediately caused write him down major, because he meant to gratify me, to whom he then looked upon himself to be beholden, nor would he be brought to alter it in favour of either Mackay or Melville'.[35]

The result of the petition was not in the form of a monetary recompense for the devastation, but the laird of Culloden was granted perpetual liberty to distill the grain grown on the Ferintosh estate and to pay only a small amount in lieu of excise. The acreage of the Ferintosh estate was considerable and yielded a sizeable amount of barley. In turn this produced a large quantity of whisky, or usquebaugh, and in this way the family were for the best part of a century more than compensated for their hardships and damage to their property. In 1784 the government had to pay the very large sum of £21,500 sterling to recompense the family for the withdrawal of this privilege — even that amount was not thought to be adequate to replace the lucrative revenue they had lived on for so many years.

It is hardly surprising that the Forbes family themselves enjoyed the produce of the estate, particularly the sons, John and Duncan; the two boys attended the grammar school in Inverness, and even at this early age they were known as 'the greatest boozers in the north'. John, who succeeded his father as laird in 1704, was famous for his hospitality, which was referred to as almost without bounds. Familiarly known as 'Bumper John', he kept a hogshead of claret on tap in his hall, to be emptied in pailfuls free to all comers, and you could have as much as you could hold of any other wine you chose. According to an English visitor to the house, 'Few go away sober at any time; and for the greater part of his guests, in the conclusion, they cannot go at all'.[36] Duncan, later lord president of the court of session, officiated at his mother's funeral in 1716. The assembled mourners followed the custom of the house and drank their fill. When it came to what was called the 'lifting', the company proceeded to the burial place, some on horseback, some on foot. At the churchyard it was realised that the most important part of the ceremony could not proceed. They had left the corpse, Lady

Culloden, behind. A small group was hurriedly despatched to 'bring on' the corpse, and eventually the funeral was concluded with as much decorum as circumstances would permit.

But it is not with these two convivial gentlemen that we are concerned here, but with their father, the earlier Duncan Forbes. One cannot imagine that he would have approved of some of the excesses for which his hard-drinking descendants were so well-known. He would, however, have been very proud of the eminence achieved by his younger son, had he lived to see it. But Duncan Forbes died on 24 June 1704, and his son did not begin his law studies until after that date. We have noted his close involvement in politics, and the trust and intimacy between himself and Patrick. Forbes, like his father, was member of parliament for Inverness-shire from 1689 to 1702, and then for Nairnshire until his death. Apart from political activities, one of his great interests was genealogy, this in particular relationship to his wife's family, and in 1698 he compiled the scholarly work *Ane Account of the Familie of Innes*, important enough in its particular field to earn him a place in the *Dictionary of National Biography*. From Burke's *History of the Commoners* we learn that a personal acquaintance of Duncan Forbes described him as a deeply religious and really good man. There is no doubt that some of the ability which manifested itself in his son was transmitted from his father.

The best way of illustrating the close ties between Duncan Forbes and Patrick, as well as throwing light on the behaviour of politicians, is to reproduce in full one of the letters that Patrick sent to him. This transcript has been taken direct from the manuscript in the National Library of Scotland, and differs slightly from the version printed in the *Culloden Papers*:

'Marchmont to Culloden.

London
28 April 1698

Sir,

In the beginning of this month I wrott to Sir Alexander Monro upon the publick occurences and changes in our affairs and becaus I had not then time to write to you, I laid it upon him to acquaint you what I had written and did not intend to have written myself till I could [have] given you some fuller account of matters then I yet can. Now findeing that matters go slowly at court in the fashion which you and I are well eneugh acquainted with I would not delay longer.

I do believe you nor other honest men with whom I have sometimes assisted to bear a weight and get through difficulties of bussiness shall not have matters which I have lately past in a true light till we meet together. You will be the more easyly persuaded of this when you understand that till I had been some-time here I was in the dark and did not descern naither the motives the means nor the designes which now are pritty clear to me. The argument which I would press upon you, and by you upon other worthy men, who knows us well, and whom we know, with whom you may have occasion to converse, is, that it is no wayes fitt to draw conclusions far less to form resolutions, upon premises and suppositions not well discovered, examined and found to be true in fact, and sound in their subject matter. I shall, God willing, when we meet, treat honest men honestly and truely, and pretend to prevail no more upon them in reasoning, then they find the strength of reason to oblige them. You know I am no young man, nor a novice at this court and I hope many more know; that I will never debase myself to manage a trick; tho I were dealing with persons of weack understanding. but of all they upon whom I can pretend to have any influence are persons of understanding and worth, and truth. So I hope to approve myself of the like part towards them: and becaus storys by telling and retelling takes strange shaps in a long course I shall be glad that honest men be armed against them. I have been only thrice in the King's closet with him, the time I had was wholly upon publick business as to which his Maj^{ty} proposed nothing but what was very moderate, and what he gave good reasons for of which I doubt not to be able to satisfie all dyscreet men, well affected to the King, and the establisht government. His way towards me has been very gracious and obligeing, but he is so much taken up at present with the forrain ambassadors and ministers and with the busyness of the Parliment here, now drawing near to a close, that it occasions some delay in ordering the Matters of Scotland yet I hope to be in Edinbrough in the beginning of June, and for aught I yet know the Parliament may meet in the beginning of July, but what happens you shall know either from me or from Alexander Monro. My wife and I kindly salute you your lady and family and I remain your very humble servant and faithfull friend.

Marchmont.'[37]

Sir John Maxwell of Pollok and Patrick had many common interests and experiences in the course of their lives, which not unnaturally forged a strong bond between the two men. John was born in January 1648. His mother was Anabella Stewart and his father Sir George Maxwell who, like many others, had been imprisoned in 1665 in consequence of his religious principles, and thereby removed from the charge of the Pollok estate. Arrangements were made which would allow John, the eldest son — or failing him the second son, George — to have possession of the Pollok inheritance, but at this time John was still a minor. In his teens he went to Edinburgh to study law, and proved himself able and hardworking in his studies. In 1671 he married Marion, daughter of Sir

James Stewart of Kirkfield, and between his marriage and his father's death in 1677 he was known as the Laird of Pollok, younger. Some years after his father died John applied to King Charles II for the restoration of the dignities and titles of the Pollok estates, and the King duly regranted these on 12 April 1682, conferring on him and his heirs male the title of knight-baronet.

Having successfully established these claims, other trials beset Sir John Maxwell. Like his father he was a strict presbyterian, and when the occasion demanded he consistently sided with those who supported civil and religious freedom of thought and action. Up till this time he had escaped the fate of many of his contemporaries who held views similar to his own, but in September 1682 he found himself in conflict with the authorities. On the grounds of having attended house and field conventicles (i.e. separate from the parish church), of having listened to fugitive and vagrant teachers, and of having been involved in an irregular child baptism, all of which contravened an Act of Parliament, a fine of £93,600 Scots was imposed on him, an exorbitant sum which he refused to pay.[38] No action was taken against him immediately, but in the following year he was charged with harbouring and assisting rebels, and on these grounds being guilty of high treason. He could have absolved himself by taking the so-called Test, but this he refused to do. The Test was an oath, ordained by Act of Parliament, and was considered to assess an individual's loyalty to the crown. Large numbers of landowners and commoners were asked to submit to the Test; those who did so were exonerated, those who did not were liable to imprisonment. With many others, Maxwell found himself cast into prison, spending lengthy spells in the notoriously bad Tolbooth in Edinburgh. Further charges of having harboured and supported rebels were trumped up against him and his fellow prisoners, all being fined substantial sums, Sir John Maxwell's being £8,000 sterling. To all these charges against him he pleaded innocent, and the vicious fines were, of course, well beyond his means. He had intermittent spells of freedom, some because the prisons were so overcrowded, some on bonds of surety for his return, but he was not finally freed until March 1687. He then set off to London to petition King James II to give some consideration to the justness of his fines.

Things did not work out quite as he expected; King James did apparently at least lend a sympathetic ear, but the Revolution in 1688 relieved Sir John of the enormous burden, which had been imposed on him by the previous government — fines which were entirely disproportionate both to his so-called faults and to his means. Like Patrick, his star was now in the ascendant. In 1689 he was made a privy councillor by

King William, and for a number of years he represented his own county of Renfrew in parliament. His integrity and diligence were outstanding, and were noted even in London. To show his appreciation of so loyal a servant, early in 1696 the King appointed him one of the lords of treasury and exchequer in Scotland. Portland was at some pains to point out that these favours were granted by the King's own choice, and were an indication of the esteem in which he held Sir John for his zeal in his work, his honesty and his moderation. One privilege which accrued to a Scottish privy councillor was that of granting passes to England. So Sir John Maxwell was able to grant passes to his wife, his sister-in-law and their servants to go to 'Scarburgh Wells' in England and return at their convenience. For a number of reasons the authorities did not permit unrestricted crossing of the Border, though in practice most of those who had influence managed to make visits when their needs were pressing enough.

This indeed was a changed situation. Sir John Maxwell was recognised as someone with great influence at Court, and Carstares, King William's trusted adviser, wrote to Sir John suggesting that he would like to hear from him more frequently, as his thoughts would always be given careful consideration. His close friendship with Patrick is shown in a letter from the Chancellor, dated 16 April 1697: 'I have, according to my promise, forborn to invite you in to toune as long as possibly I can. Now since we were disappointed of meetings of Treasury & Exchequer for want of a quorum upon Wensday and Fryday last, the Lord Raith's condition of health having hindered him not ansuer my call, I must intreat you earnestly to come in upon Munday nixt that we may bestoue the week upon publick business, and that I may get the moneth of May of vaccation to refresh me in the countrey, if emergent occasiones will alloue it. I hope you will, not only with regaird to the publick affaires which press, but also with complyance to my ease and accomodation, be at the paines to make this journey'.[39]

In April 1698 Sir John was made an ordinary lord of session; he took his seat the following year as Lord Pollok. Almost immediately, in 1699, he was appointed lord justice-clerk. When the treaty of Union between Scotland and England was being debated he was nominated one of the commissioners. Queen Anne was less appreciative of Sir John Maxwell's qualities than her brother-in-law had been, and during her reign (as with Patrick) some of the favours which had been bestowed on him earlier were withdrawn. Apart from his political work Lork Pollok undertook many honorary duties, interesting himself particularly in education. He was a commissioner for visiting Glasgow University, and held the office of Lord Rector of the University for some twenty-seven years. Much of his time was spent visiting schools in the south of Scotland in which Latin was taught, a subject in which he had a particular interest. He died on 4 July 1732, a man who was respected and trusted by his friends and, more surprisingly, well spoken of even by some who were his enemies.

CHAPTER 5

Children Growing Up

Of Grisell and Patrick's eighteen children, nine reached adult life. As in all large families, there are plenty of contrasts amongst this disparate collection of individuals. We also come across a certain number of quarrels, though on the evidence we have these can fairly be said to be infrequent, and the family truthfully described as a relatively happy and close-knit one. Let's take them one at a time in the order in which they were born.

The Polwarth's had disappointments in their efforts to start a family. Three small girls had died, then on 11 November 1664 a son, **Patrick**, arrived safely. We have no information about his boyhood. When he was 21 he was living in London at the time when his father was with Argyll's unsuccessful expedition to Scotland, and young Patrick was put in prison there for a while as a hostage for his father. He does not seem to have suffered any great hardship in his confinement, for in a letter dated 4 July 1685 he writes, 'I am in verry good health and verry good company . . .'[1] He was able to go to Holland in May 1686, and in a letter written in December of that year says 'I have verry good ground to expect to be an ensign in the Prince of Orange's guards'.[2] This was, indeed, the start of his army career. When the Prince and Princess came to England, Patrick Hume was with the troops who accompanied them. He was a dearly loved and respected member of his family. This was particularly true of his sister Grisell; according to Lady Murray he was 'her most dearly beloved'.[3] There was only one year of difference in their ages, and they were reared together. We have already noted the pride she took in seeing that her older brother was always turned out as smartly as any other member of William's guards, even though the cost must sometimes have put extra pressure on their slender finances. In his subsequent career as a soldier, much of his time was spent abroad in the fighting William was engaged in overseas.

In 1696 he came home on leave; he was now Sir Patrick, as his father had been Lord Polwarth for six years. While at home he met two young Irish girl cousins who had been invited by his parents to spend some time in Scotland and to join the family in the festivities in the Scottish capital. In view of Lord Polwarth's important position as Chancellor there were now plenty of opportunities for gaiety presented by living at Holyroodhouse and by the demands made by protocol. The climax of the entertainments came at the end of the year, when the Chancellor's New Year's Eve Ball on 31 December took the form of a Masquerade. Sir Patrick fell in love with one of the girls, Elizabeth Hume of Castle Hume in Ireland; she returned his affections, but their marriage had to be postponed, as his regiment was ordered to Flanders. Elizabeth, or Bettie as she was known to the family, was, we are told, a sweet-natured and attractive-looking woman. It was a quiet wedding. George Home's Diary entry for Thursday, 2 December 1697 is as follows: 'I stayed in my Chamber till afternoon, I went to the Chancellour's lodging. My Lo. Polwarth was maried to Mrs Betty Home. I stayed ther till near 12. They were married by Mr George Meldrum. It was quiet, nobody being ther but my Lo.'s own children, Madam Irvine, Sir Pa: Home [the advocate], Com: Home and I'. And for Friday 3 December: 'I went to the Chancellour's and dined, The Bridegroom and Bride had been in the Tron Church in the Morning, so the Ceremony is over'.

Their happiness was short-lived, lasting only four years. According to Lady Anne Purves, Lady Polwarth and some friends were on a visit to Dunglass when, sitting with their backs to the sea, they did not notice the incoming tide, and she was badly soaked by the water.[4] She developed a chill from which she never completely recovered, and eventually consumption set in. During the year 1701 she was very ill, and in his Diary George Home tells us that on 9 June 1701 Dr Stevenson and Dr Abernethy were both at Polwarth House, that Lady Polwarth was still in some danger, and that she wanted to go to England. The doctors were not sure that either baths or wells would do her any good, but they thought a little travelling might be beneficial, presumably to give her some change of surroundings. We do not know if any journeys were embarked on, but her health did not improve, and she died in December 1701. Lord Polwarth had been passionately devoted to his wife and had nursed her during her illness. It is highly probable that it was from her that he contracted the same disease which was to cause his own death eight years later. He never really recovered from the loss, he was heartbroken and his health deteriorated. The whole family grieved, for Lady Polwarth had been a great favourite. Months after her death, her father-in-law Patrick wrote to her brother, 'The death of my kind, and, upon all accounts, beloved daughter Bettie, your sister, is a weight upon me still . . .'[5]

Concerned about the unhappy and distracted state of Lord Polwarth, his sister Lady Grisell and Lord Marchmont urged him to remarry, but he had no heart to do so. Finally, however, he agreed, they selected his bride, and he dutifully married her to please his family. Their choice fell on Lady Jean Home, daughter of Charles, 6th Earl of Home. She was young, and so attractive-looking that she was known locally as 'Bonnie Jean o' the Hirsel'. As Margaret Warrender remarks, 'It was a curious marriage for her to make; and one wonders now what was its secret history, and what inducement there could be to persuade a woman of high rank and great personal attractions to marry a man much older than herself, in broken health and spirits, who evidently did not care in the least for her'.[6] She then goes on to speculate whether the few surviving verses of an old and forgotten ballad could provide some clue:

> Bonnie Jean o' the Hirsel,
> Bonnie Jean o' the Hirsel,
> She has slighted baith lairds and lords,
> And ta'en up wi the Laird o' Stichill.
>
> Stichill never will get ye, Jean
> Stichill never will get ye;
> For a' his gear and his bonnie black horse,
> He may come but he'll gang without ye!
>
> Bonnie Jean o' the Hirsel,
> Bonnie Jean o' the Hirsel,
> She's forsaken baith lairds and lords,
> An' she's off wi' the Laird o' Stichill.[7]

This second marriage, despite the bridegroom's lack of enthusiasm, contrasted strangely with the first which, as we have seen, had been a very quiet affair indeed. This time the uniting of the less important house of Marchmont with the premier family of Berwickshire was, from the Marchmont side, an occasion for great rejoicing. George Home's own relationship with the Hirsel had, as we know, always been a love/hate one, and on Wednesday 21 April 1703 we find him giving as his two excuses for not being at the wedding next day, first 'want of cloaths' and second 'fear of being incommoded by ill lodging'. However, even such lame excuses do not seem to have gone down too badly, for on the Saturday a message reaches him that it would be taken kindly if he were at the Hirsel that afternoon to be a witness to the contract of marriage, and saying that he would be able to get home by nightfall. The following Wednesday, having had a formal invitation from Marchmont to come to dinner and bring Robie (now 11) with him, 'I went ther, ther was a great deal of company, fidles and dancing, Jerviswood and his Lady were ther and Sir James Hall who had strained his ankle dancing at the Hershill'. So a good time was evidently had by all.

In 1707 Lord Polwarth was promoted to colonel of his regiment, the 7th Queen's Dragoons, but because of deteriorating health he had to relinquish the post during the summer of 1709. In writing to his friends, Patrick expressed anxiety about his son, who was by this time living with the family. A lot of new building and repair work was being undertaken at Redbraes in the autumn of that year, so it was felt advisable that Lord and Lady Polwarth should spend the winter elsewhere to avoid the cold and damp conditions created by this work. The couple went to accommodation in Kelso where they hoped to spend the winter months, but Lord Polwarth slipped still further downhill and died on 25 November 1709. His father was heartbroken. Writing to George Baillie in March 1710, he says that 'he was a good man, having the fear of God in his heart; . . . he was a person of great probity and honesty; . . . he was a most dutiful child to his parents and a good husband to his wife; . . . he was a faithful and steady friend, where he professed it; and . . . as a soldier he was both diligent and daring, composed and courageous, brave and benign'.[8] Margaret Warrender describes his portrait, painted by John Scougall in 1698, as showing 'the bluff honest features of their soldier son'.[9]

With the exiles safely back in Scotland it was only a matter of time before the forfeitures of their estates were rescinded and their possessions restored to them. George Baillie had inherited Jerviswood in Lanarkshire and Mellerstain in Berwickshire; both were bought by his grandfather, another George. The former property had been acquired in 1636 and the latter in 1643. Unfortunately the titles to these estates along with his 'best clothes, his silver and goldsmyth work, were all totallie burnt', in August 1645. They were kept in 'ane trunk and ane kist' in 'the tyme of the Lamentable fyre that was then in Edinburgh'.[10] However, apparently there was no difficulty in establishing the Baillie claim to the lands. After settling down in Scotland, George was appointed commissioner of supply for Lanarkshire and for Berwickshire, as well as receiver-general of Scotland. This last appointment gave him a salary of £300 sterling a year, which was a lot of money in the 1690s. Feeling himself in a position which allowed him to make such a move, he now asked Patrick for the hand of his daughter, **Grisell Hume**. He was not the only suitor, however, for according to Lady Murray's *Memoirs* there were 'two gentlemen in their neighbourhood at home, of fortune and character, who had done nothing to forfeit either, and with whom they thought it would have been happy to settle their daughter at any time; she earnestly rejected both, but without giving any reason for it, though her parents suspected it, and it was the only thing she ever displeased or disobeyed them in'.[11] Grisell's parents were very fond of George Baillie, and he was fond of them, so her father consented when he knew where her heart lay. The marriage took place at Polwarth on 17 September 1691, and proved to be an extremely happy one. They were deeply attached to each other during the whole of their married life, and George Baillie, a very careful and canny Scot, was content to leave all his financial affairs to his wife.

He was right in doing so, for she was a most competent business-woman. Whether her acumen as an accountant was natural or whether she had taken some lessons we do not know. Soon after her marriage she did have some instruction in cooking and in dancing. We know that her brother-in-law, James Baillie, had some lessons in 'lairning book-keeping in pairt' at a cost of £2 sterling, so it was apparently not difficult to get such instruction. But Grisell Hume was probably at least partly, if not wholly, self-taught. For during the years in Utrecht she had had to sit up late two nights each week 'to do the business that was necessary for the household', and some of this effort is likely to have involved wrestling with the accounts in her efforts to make ends meet. After proving her worth so effectively when, at a very early age, she success-fully carried out her father's difficult mission of taking messages to Robert Baillie imprisoned in Edinburgh, she was looked on as the main-stay of the family. Even after her marriage she still helped to manage her father's financial affairs. She went regularly to Polwarth House to super-intend his estate business and general accounts, and she would, if necessary, stay with the family until things were as orderly as she wanted them to be. In later life she undertook the entire management of her brother Alexander's affairs while he was abroad, caring for the education of his children as well. She was a meticulous bookkeeper; one feels she must have derived great satisfaction from this work which she carried out so conscientiously.

The accounts for her own household were started in autumn 1692, the year after her marriage, and when one reads them it is clear that little — even the smallest detail — escaped her attention. Her *Household Book* was published in 1911 with an introduction by Robert Scott-Moncrieff, and has been widely studied and referred to ever since. But though she was careful, she was not mean, and from time to time she enjoyed spending on luxuries much more than did her husband. All that he was concerned with was that he would never be in debt; he trusted his wife completely, and was justly rewarded for his faith in her.

After their marriage the young couple set up house in Edinburgh, in Warriston Close, off the High Street, nearly opposite St Giles; the rent of this house was £200. George's mother died in 1697, which freed her jointure on the estate, thus making the young Baillies better off. They moved again to a more expensive establishment in which they stayed only a short time, but it is interesting to note that the flitting cost them £11. Finally, they took another house which was probably situated in Fowlis Close; the rental was £400, and here they stayed until they left Edinburgh in 1707. We know that when the poll tax was collected in 1694 they employed six servants in Edinburgh.[12] Three of these were men, one being paid £24 a year, another £18 and a third unpaid; one of the women received £36, the others £14 and £12 respectively. On leaving Edinburgh, they made Mellerstain their main residence in 1707. Mellerstain was only 8½ miles from Polwarth House, so the move was one that would undoubtedly delight Grisell. The house, which at an earlier time was known as Whitesyde, was described in 1659 in the *Diary of Andrew Hay* as 'ane old melancholick hous that had had great buildings about it'.[13] George Home, on his first visit to Mellerstain in September 1700, says, as already noted, 'They have ane old tower with but one room off a floor, about 5 stories high, but it looks very ruinous'. We know from Grisell's own accounts that she was constantly having repairs done to the buildings, and we also know from the hearth tax collected in 1690 that Mellerstain was assessed at thirteen hearths.[14]

Of all the Polwarth children, undoubtedly the one best known to posterity is Lady Grisell Baillie. It would be wrong to leave the impression that she was interested only in household management and book-keeping. She was a woman with considerable talent in many directions, talent which when she was younger she was unable to develop to its potential, being too busy attending to the day-to-day needs of the family. As we saw, while they were in Utrecht she undertook pretty well all the household drudgery. According to Lady Murray her mother would very much have enjoyed contributing to the entertainment of the family and friends, and would have been competent to do so, but she was prevented by the pressures of her domestic responsibilities. Apparently she and Christian used to joke about the very differing roles they had to fulfil at that time. But in her description of their lives in Holland Lady Murray says, 'I have now a book of songs of her writing when there; many of them interrupted, half writ, some broke off in the middle of a sentence'.[15] As far as we know this book no longer exists, but two examples of Lady Grisell's songs can be found in Margaret Warrender's study of the Marchmonts.[16] As a family the Baillies all loved music and enjoyed it together. They all studied it, the children being taught to play a wide range of instruments, the virginals, the viol, the flute and the harp.

The Baillies had three children, Grisell born in October 1692, Robert in February 1694 (who died two years later) and Rachel born in February 1696. The two girls both grew up and married, though there had been some anxious moments as when, in August 1700, they both contracted smallpox in Edinburgh, as we learn from George Home. The elder daughter, Grisell, made an unfortunate marriage with the son and heir of Sir David Murray of Stanhope; her younger sister, Rachel, married Charles, Lord Binning, eldest son of the Earl of Haddington, and was extremely happy. Their parents seem to have enjoyed reasonably good health, the only troubles we hear of being that both of them suffered from deafness, in the hope of alleviating which George used often to sweat in the saltpans.

Lady Grisell Baillie was beautiful, as can be seen from portraits of her by Gainsborough, Maria Varelst, Kneller, Scougall and Medina. Her daughter describes her as 'middle-sized, well made, clever in her person, very handsome, with a life and sweetness in her eyes very uncommon, and a great delicacy in all her features; her hair was chestnut, and to her last had the finest complexion, with the clearest red in her cheeks and lips, that could be seen in one of fifteen, which added to her natural constitution, might be owing to the great moderation she had in her diet throughout her whole life'.[17] George Home in March 1698 talks of 'she who I look on as one of the best friends in the world'. She lived to be 81, and died in London on 6 December 1746, being brought back to Mellerstain for burial, as she had wished. After her death Lord Cornbury wrote of her benevolence, good humour, good sense and cheerful dignity.[18] On all counts, a woman to be remembered.

Christian, second daughter of Patrick and Grisell, born 7 May 1668, was just over two years younger than Grisell. We do not know about her early life, really only hearing of her during the time when the family was exiled in Holland. Her niece, Lady Murray, tells us that she was a lively, vivacious girl.[19] She was an accomplished musician and could both play and sing well. Unlike her older sister, though, she had no head whatsoever for business. While they were in Utrecht they managed to buy a harpsichord cheaply, and on this Christian played while the company sang. The family and their friends were all fond of music, and in this way they passed many pleasant evenings. Sadly, Christian did not accompany the younger members of the family when they set out on their return to Scotland. She was ill with a sore throat, and died shortly afterwards when she was only twenty years old.

Robert Hume, born 10 July 1669, followed his older brother Patrick by embarking on a military career. We only know that he died of a fever in 1692.

Julian Hume was born on 16 August 1673. Grisell having married (and Christian having died in Holland), at the time of the Compt Book, Julian was the oldest daughter at home. There are several references to her there, mainly when materials were bought for her dresses or when jaunts took place where she looked after the youngest children. Of course, by the time the Compt Book was started, Julian was a young woman of twenty-one:

1695	6 Jan.	For – – els of blak creap for Julian and Ann at – – the ele	[blank]
	,,	For muslin for Julian and Ann	30 : 18 : 00
1695	11 Jan.	For creap for Julian	22 : 16 : 00
	2 Feb.	For tabi for Julian's bodis cofrin	03 : 15 : 00
	3 Jan.	Count of the money Julian got when she com in with the barns at Gunilkirk diner	04 : 10 : 00
		For the hors	00 : 18 : 00
		For a par glufs to hirself	00 : 18 : 00
		A par patns to hirself	00 : 16 : 00
1697	2 June	To Julian when she went to the wadin	01 : 09 : 06

Julian's younger sister Anne had for many years been engaged to Mr Hepburn of Humbie, and Julian herself was engaged to Sir James Hall of Dunglass. However, when the marriage settlement for Julian came to be discussed, a hitch developed and Patrick is reported to have said, 'What, is Sir James in pursuit of my daughter Annie? I have never spoke to her on the subject, and can say no more till I have'.[20] It seemed that Sir James Hall now wanted to switch his proposed marriage from Julian to Anne, and in due course this did in fact happen. Not unnaturally, Julian was highly incensed, and this was the start of a major upheaval in the family, the Charles Bellingham affair. George Home first got wind of it in Edinburgh on 19 January 1698: 'I went out after dinner and visited Jerviswood and his Lady. Going into their room I found her in great trouble, and to my astonishment the cause of it . . . she had got ane account that Lady Julian was privately married to one Bellinghame a young English fellow'. Julian had denied it when dining with her father, but was much out of countenance, which made him conclude there was something in it. From then on the diary is full of further gossip about the whole business. Her sister Grisell wrote to one of her friends in London, and the information that came back about his background was very up-setting — 'That his father was a poor man who had enough to live by a glasswork, of which he was overseer; that this blade and his elder brother, who was a captain in Lindsay's regiment, had formerly been in gaol for robbing on the highway, but had made their escape'. Small wonder that when George went to dine with the Marchmonts shortly afterwards he reports, 'I had not seen him nor my Lady since that business of Lady Julian's fell out; I see my Lady very much troubled'.

Julian had then to live in very straitened circumstances, and was the victim of unkind and slanderous stories for a very long time. She apparently told her nieces some years afterwards that she suffered more from these malicious tongues than from all her poverty. Lady Anne, who must have felt a strong sense of guilt at having precipitated the whole business by marrying Sir James Hall, 'before she died got My Lady her mother and Lady Julian reconciled, and My Lo: Chancellor promised her the same'. He certainly kept his promise, for almost immediately afterwards, in February 1699, he purchased for Bellingham the post of deputy governor at Dumbarton.[21] Although the reconciliation may not have been complete, Patrick did not alter the financial arrangements for Julian's future, which remained the same as for his other daughters. Bellingham died young and Julian was left with two daughters, Jane and Charlotte, who both grew up in due course and got married. Julian certainly did her best to make amends once she was a widow, and when her father was persuaded to give up living at Redbraes and moved to Berwick in 1717, she went to live with him and looked after him until his death in August 1724.

Alexander, third son of the Polwarths, was the one who eventually succeeded his father as the second Earl of Marchmont in 1724. He was born on 1 January 1675, and was known in the family as Sandy. While they were in Holland he spent two or three years at the University of Utrecht studying philosophy and civil law. His elder brother Patrick said of him when writing from Europe to his father in February 1695, 'he is a pritty good musitian and plays well upon the flute, which I am glad off, it is a pleasant and innocent divertisement and much properer nor either hunting or halking . . .'[22] After returning to Scotland with the family, he continued his law studies in Edinburgh. It was at church in Edinburgh one Sunday in 1695 or early 1696 that he was attracted by a young lady. Asking a friend, Mr Cleyland, who she might be, he was told, 'Faith, Sandy, you are a good marksman, she is the best fortune in Scotland'.[23] It turned out that Mr Cleyland's mother was a great friend of the lady's mother, the latter being a formidable character, Anne McMurray, Lady Campbell of Cessnock; and said he, 'The Gray Mare is the better horse in that family!'[24] So Sandy called on Lady Cessnock and apparently made a very good impression. Her eldest daughter, Mary, having run away to be married (for which she was disinherited), she was particularly determined to avoid a repetition of this with her other two daughters, Margaret and Christian. So Sandy adopted the strategy of not mentioning either of the daughters on his first visit, though Margaret, the older one, was the one in whom he was interested. Having been told that Margaret fended off all suitors, as another part of his strategy he arranged to meet her and her sister at the house of a mutual friend, Mrs Dundas, and to pretend that he was Mrs Dundas's lover. When this plan went wrong he enlisted the help of his young sister Anne. She invited the Campbell girls to the Chancellor's Ball on New Year's Eve in 1696. From that time a close friendship developed between the two families, and Margaret's father, Sir George Campbell of Cessnock, who had been the lord justice clerk until 1693, was easily won round. In the words of Lady Anne Purves, 'He thought that Sir Alexander Hume, a Second Brother, who, tho' he had great prospects from his profession and from Government, yet would cheerfully take the name of Campbell, and bear his Arms. On these terms everything was agreed upon'.[25] The only remaining obstacle was now the lady herself, who was not prevailed upon actually to marry him till 29 July 1697.

His marriage helped greatly towards his progress in the legal profession, and on his father-in-law's death in 1704 he obtained his place on the Scottish bench, and was also styled Lord Cessnock. Financially the marriage was also a great help to him, as he acquired his wife's family Ayrshire estates at the same time. Politics became an absorbing interest to him, and he soon played an active part in the Scottish parliament, representing first Kirkwall and then Berwickshire, and supporting causes that were dear to the heart of his father. He became a privy councillor and a lord of exchequer, and the death of his brother Patrick in 1709 gave him the right to the title of Lord Polwarth. Made lord lieutenant of Berwickshire in 1715, he obtained some experience in military matters, but the main new development in his career occurred when he was sent as Ambassador to the Court of Denmark in 1716, giving up his seat in the court of session, which was then taken by his brother Andrew. From that time, as a diplomat he went from strength to strength, culminating in his 1722 appointment to the Congress at Cambray.

With hindsight we can see that the skills he showed in winning the heiress he wanted for his wife were very much those which stood him in such good stead later on. Although his wife bore him eight children, including twins (one of whom became the third Earl of Marchmont), she 'does not appear, even by her own daughter's account, to have been a very loveable person. A spoilt child from infancy, with an inordinate idea of her own importance, she had grown up a fair-haired, supercilious-looking woman, who never seems to have fitted into her husband's family. She is rarely mentioned in their letters, and her death does not seem to have caused great sorrow'.[26] As we have seen, Lady Grisell Baillie made most of the arrangements for the education of their children.

After the peak of his career at Cambray, things did not go well with the second Earl of Marchmont in the political infighting of the years that followed 1725. Heartily disliked by Walpole, he was, nevertheless, a man of high principle and a true son of his father, with very deep religious convictions and a strong affection for his native country. The death of two of his sons before his return to England deeply affected him (more so than the death of his wife), and he himself died in 1740.

Andrew was the fourth son of the Polwarths who survived to reach adult life, and in the Compt Book he is always referred to as Andra. He was born on 19 July 1676. Some years after the family had returned to Scotland from their exile in Holland, he, together with his older brother Alexander, spent some time abroad, and George Home's diary entry for 24 June 1695 reads: 'I went at night to my Lord Polwarth's and was there when his sons Sandi and Andrew, who came over with Holland's fleet, came ther'. The two of them had been studying law at the University of Utrecht, and they had now come back. On the same day the Compt Book shows that their mother 'paid for Sandi and Andras bouks from Lith'. And despite the fact that, as already indicated, Andrew apparently felt that his mother preferred her other children to himself, her Compt Book records many occasions on which she gave him money when he went, for example, to Edinburgh, Berwick or Kimmerghame. Of all his cousin Patrick's sons, it was Andrew whom George Home liked best. He is 18 when the diary available to us begins, and 29 when it ends, and the seventeen-year difference in their ages fitted in well with the uncle-and-nephew nature of their relationship. George reports that after dinner at the Chancellor's on 21 February 1698 'Mr Andrew told me my Lo: Chancellour had proposed to him a match with Mrs K. H. [probably Kattie Hall, afterwards Lady Pitcure]. He asked my opinion about it. I told him I had made a resolution never to give advice on marriages etc., yet finding he was very indifferent, I told him I could wish it were put off now, he being to go to London: that better occasion might fall in his way'. Andrew obviously welcomed this advice, and asked George to see whether his sister Grisell could be persuaded to use her influence with his mother to head off any further pressure from his father in that direction.

About a year later Andrew brings George in on another disagreement with his family. This time they think he has already married, or plans to marry, Lady Mangerstone [Manderston]. She was Katherine Johnston, (daughter of Lady Hilton of Hutton Hall), who had married the Laird of Manderston. The laird became ill, went to England for a cure, and died on 2 May 1698. The only child of their marriage died at Hutton Hall on 26 April 1699. Andrew confesses to George that he is very much in love with Lady Mangerstone, but has no design to marry her against his father's will. Andrew says, 'his father has of late lookt doune on him and treated him harshly: he is afraid of some ill instruments at home'. This time he wishes that his mother would intercede with his father on his behalf but doubts whether she will, he 'being the child she has shown least kindness to'. The following day George hears from her the other side of the story: 'She complained to me of Sir Andrew that he staid late out and neglected his business and frequented idle company and of his intrigues with the Lady Mangerstone'. George is asked to use his best endeavours to persuade Andrew to mend his ways. His sister Lady Anne's grave illness, however, soon pushes worries about Andrew into the background. But in November 1699 Andrew writes to say he longs to have George in town to have his assistance in another affair of the heart, 'his design of marriage with Mrs Betty Primrose, Sir James Primrose's sister'. What George's views on this project are, or what assistance he gives, we are not told.

On 18 March 1700 George and Patrick have a long talk about Andrew. His father has now very much toned down his criticism of his son. Apart from the fact that 'he runs too fast' he sees no fault in him save what was to be imputed to youth — as a little vanity, and liking for fine clothes. George himself adds, 'if he were married these things would soon go off'. By this time, indeed, Andrew is ready to marry someone approved of by the family — the relict of Sir William Douglas of Cavers — and a week later the hard bargaining over the marriage contract had begun. The lady herself, perhaps because she had been through it all before, proved a very tough nut to crack in matters financial. When it was pointed out to her that her prospective husband's father had already spent a great deal of money in buying him his post as commissary of Edinburgh, she remarked that obtaining that place for him 'was only instead of his maintenance in his Lordship's family, where he had not been for some time'. In the end Patrick gave way, and she got the jointure and other provisions she was demanding. Clearly she was not someone who was going to be pushed around, even by Lady Grisell Baillie who was accustomed to getting her own way in most things. Because she claimed she had been slighted by her future sister-in-law on a previous occasion, the diarist notes, on 2 September 1700 'Sir Andrew and I had some difficulty to persuade his Lady to call to-morrow at Mellerstane to see Lady Grisell'.

One or two interesting points can be added to supplement the saga of Andrew's marriage plans as seen through the eyes of George Home. First of all, the family's objection to his marrying Lady Manderston had nothing to do with her suitability on other counts (she was, after all, the daughter of a great friend of theirs), but arose entirely from the inadequate financial contribution she would have been able to make to the marriage settlement. To George this was so obvious and so praiseworthy that it did not seem necessary to mention it; and Andrew, though as deeply in love with her as she was with him, increasingly felt that his family's way of looking at such things was the right one. Moreover, she herself was well aware that because he, as only a younger son, would not be too well provided for, a match with him would be far from ideal from *her* point of view. This was partly why, to keep their love affair as private as possible, they met at the house of a friend of hers, widowed Lady Douglas of Cavers. And this brings us to the second supplementary point. Inevitably, in the end, the two friends would find themselves rivals for Andrew as a husband if not a lover, and Lady Anne Purves in her 'Anecdotes' cannot resist recounting (or inventing) a scene where Lady Douglas tells her friend Lady Manderston that Andrew is false to her.[27] We hardly need to be told the third supplementary point, that it was Lady Grisell Baillie, matchmaker extraordinary, who conceived the idea that Sir William Douglas's relict would be the ideal match for her brother Andrew, and who made it her business to convince all parties — her father, her brother and the lady herself — that this was so. And students of such matters will not be surprised that the two conspirators, Lady Grisell and Lady Douglas, should, after the deal was successfully completed, develop a hearty dislike for each other.

Andrew's marriage in 1700, of which there were two daughters, proved to be a reasonably happy one. After George Home died, and on the death only a few years afterwards of Robie, the Kimmerghame estates came into his hands in 1710. And on succeeding his brother in the court of session in 1716, he took as his title Lord Kimmerghame which, in view of his very close friendship with George Home, was particularly appropriate. He died in 1730 at the age of fifty-four. Less serious-minded than his brothers, he seems to have been well liked by everyone, and had quite a reputation as a wit.

Anne was born on 4 November 1677, at a time of great difficulty for the family. When the Compt Book was started she was a young girl of 17;

there were four years between her and her older sister Julian, and six between her and Jean, the youngest of the family. In 1695, among other entries in the Compt Book, we note that in January Anne had 'a creap' costing £21:4s and in June a scarf costing £2:8s, along with sundry other presents. We know that she acted as go-between in helping her older brother Sandy to get to know the two Campbell girls in Edinburgh, by calling at their home and inviting them and their mother to the Chancellor's Ball.

As we saw, her long engagement to Mr Hepburn of Humbie had been brought to an end when Sir James Hall decided to marry her instead of her sister Julian. His father, the first baronet, had been Lord Provost as well as M.P. for Edinburgh. His son succeeded him in the baronetcy in 1695. Anne's marriage to him took place in 1698, but did not last many months, for she died at the Dean, not far from Edinburgh, on 24 January 1699. Her health had been causing anxiety for a month or two previously, and a fortnight before her death George Home was told by her mother that 'Lady Anne past a worme a span and more long which I wish may produce some change to the better'. On the day of her death he described her as 'much regrated by all that knew her — the pleasantest, sprightlyiest young lady I ever knew. I went to my Lo: Chancellour's lodging and found him mightily afflicted . . .' It was at her deathbed that a reconciliation took place between her sister Julian and her parents over her marriage to Bellingham.

As in Anne's case, **Jean's** birth took place at a difficult time for her father, for now he was actively preparing to flee the country to escape probable execution. Born 23 March 1683, she cannot have remembered very much of what it was like to be an exile in Holland where, because of her age, she was another mouth to feed rather than an extra pair of hands. Back at Polwarth House in the 1690s, however, she came into her own, being eleven years old when the Compt Book begins. Traditionally, the youngest in a family often tends to be spoilt, and Jean was no exception to this rule. She was said to be her mother's darling (she called her Janie, sometimes spelt Janei or Jani), and was indulged to a degree which frequently caused her older brother, Lord Polwarth, to take a hand in trying to keep her in order. Her mother obviously regarded it as important for her to have someone of her own age to work and play with, so Anne Scott came to Polwarth House to stay for some time. Anne's mother was Grisell's sister Isobell, who had married Hugh Scott of Gala and had been very helpful to Patrick and his family during their troubles, so inviting her for a long visit was one way of repaying this help. Grisell took pains to ensure that, as far as possible, everything Jean was given had its exact counterpart in what was given to her visiting niece.

Going through the Compt Book, we find some items relating to Jani alone, and a longer list for the two girls:

— Dec 94	12 Els of worset stuf for a piticoat to An [presumably her daughter] and a goun for Janei	09 : 08 : 00
31 Jan 95	For Jani's wires, silk and nidls thimls	00 : 07 : 06
1 Feb 95	For crap for Janis Goun and paticot 14 eals at 16/– per eal	11 : 04 : 00

Then items for Jani and Anne Scott:

22 Nov. 94	12 els and a half of scarlat crep for my nice Anne Scot	17 : 00 : 00
	12½ ells for my Janei	17 : 00 : 00
29 Jan. 95	For Jani and Anne Scot for their lernin to shew with Mistress Camal [Campbell] 6 wiks	05 : 16 : 00
19 March 95	To fontan which cleirs him for Anni Janei Anne Scot last month and pays him for a month to com	20 : 06 : 00
22 May 95	To Anne Scot and Jani for the fidls	02 : 06 : 00
	To Mr [sic] Camal for Jani and Anne Scot quarter payment with 2 dollars she got before	05 : 16 : 00
17 July 95	To fontan for 5 month titcin Janei to danc	29 : 00 : 00
	To his titcin Annei Scot my nice 3 months and half the first month 3 dolers the rest 2 dolers	11 : 12 : 00
	To my nice and Janei for the fidlers	01 : 14 : 00

We know at this time Mr Fountain ran a highly successful dancing school in Edinburgh. Edward and James Fountain had some years earlier been granted the gift of Master of the Revels by the Burgh Council. The daughters of the Duchess of Hamilton also had dancing lessons from Mr Edward Fountain.[28] George Home tells us that Fountain, the dancing master, was found dead in his bed on 26 November 1695.

James Sandilands, Lord Torphichen, whom Jean married at the age of 20 in April 1703, was the fourth but first surviving son and heir when he succeeded to the title in 1696, and was served heir in 1698. He became captain in the Earl of Mar's Regiment of Foot in 1702, and was transferred some time later to what had been Lord Polwarth's Regiment of Dragoons (which after Polwarth's death was under the command of Colonel Ker), where he became a major. He had quite a distinguished military career and saw service both at home and overseas. He also held several political appointments at different times, was in parliament from

1704 to 1707 and, as would be expected of Patrick's son-in-law, voted for the Union with England. He and Jean lived in Calder House, the Torphichen family seat with John Knox associations, and had a family of seven boys and three girls. Jean died in 1751 at 68 and James died two years later in 1753.

Things did not go quite as smoothly for her cousin **Anne Scott**, who had spent so much time with her at Polwarth House when they were both in their early teens. She married seven months after Jean, her husband being a cousin of hers, Walter Scott of Raeburn. They had one son and three daughters, and then one of those tragic events occurred, all too frequent at that time, when her husband Walter was killed quite unnecessarily when he was only 24. On 2 October 1707, the day of the Head Court at Selkirk, he and Mark, one of the Pringles of Crighton, had a quarrel over dinner, and next morning fought with swords nearby, with fatal results for Walter, Mark apparently then fleeing the country, and the place where it happened afterwards becoming known as Raeburn's Meadow. Despite this tragic beginning to her married life, however, she decided not to spend the rest of her days as a widow and married a MacDougall of Makerston and, after he died, a Honie of Eccles.

CHAPTER 6

Lifestyle of the Merse Lairds

Who were the Merse lairds? They were the men who, by being the eldest son of a laird, or perhaps by marrying an heiress, or in another way, found themselves owners of estates with a mansion of sorts in that part of the Scottish Borders. Some had a large acreage of land bringing in substantial rents; others, like George Home, had only a relatively small estate and a very modest seat. There were many other possible differences. Was a particular laird politically-minded, did he aim to get or to keep the support of his fellows in sending him to represent them in parliament? Was he an absentee laird, a younger son perhaps, who had made a success in the law or in trade, had bought an estate, and left most of its management to someone paid for doing so? Had his lands been declared forfeit in his own or his father's time and, now that the forfeiture was rescinded, been found to have suffered irreparable damage and decay? Had he inherited a burden of debt from which it seemed almost impossible to escape? Were his tenants old-established ones who expected to carry on undisturbed paying him the traditional rents, or were they on so many years' 'tack', so that after then they could be got rid of or their rents raised? In these and very many other ways the position of one laird might not be at all the same as that of his neighbour in the next parish. All this is merely to say that, as with any other social category of people or families, generalisations are sometimes dangerous.

Making all allowance for such potential dangers, there are nevertheless many features of the lives and the lifestyles of these lairds in the Scotland of the 1690s which were common to very many of them. They were, after all, not magnates or nobles who had inherited vast landed properties, armies of henchmen, and the inbred expectation of control and leadership in national affairs. Nor, on the other hand, were they plagued by the kind of chronic insecurity and poverty to which so many of those lower in the social scale were subject. They were what Patrick, in his letters to Lord Melville, called 'those of middle rank', who had a considerable say in what went on locally, who aspired to have more say in what happened nationally, and who had for the most part enough spare time and resources to engage in such leisure pursuits as they had a mind to. They interacted socially mainly with folk of similar (or if possible higher) family background, as stands out from every page of George Home's diary, where those whose houses he visited, or with whom he went hunting, or passed the time of day in the coffee shops of Edinburgh, were all very much of a muchness.

There was another, and to us rather unexpected, respect in which all lairds were alike, and that was their virtually identical treatment for poll-tax purposes. Very few of the 1695 lists of pollable persons have survived, but a careful study of those that do shows every laird listed in them to have been rated at 'above £1,000 valued rental', so that he paid £24.6s. in tax. Blackadder, Stewart of Allanbank, Cavers, Swinton, Cunningham of Craigends, Sir Thomas Dalzell of Abercorn in Linlithgowshire, and even Kimmerghame, perhaps the least well-to-do of the lot, all appear in these lists in exactly the same terms.[1] It is fair to assume, therefore, that all those described as lairds came into that particular category, although if, of course, like Patrick, they had been raised to the peerage, their poll-tax liability was also raised in the appropriate way. It is people of this sort, then, whose ways of living we aim to describe in the present chapter.

If the size and condition of the family seat you had inherited or acquired was of some importance, there is no difficulty in showing how wide the range of sizes was in the Borders. Within Berwickshire alone, easily the biggest family seat in terms of its hearth-tax rating was Sir John Davidson's Castle of Thirlstoune in the parish of Lauder (45 hearths). Two other very large establishments on this basis were Sir Archibald Cockburn's house at Langtoune (23) and Sir James Don's at Newtoune (22), with Sir Robert Stewart's at Allanbank (19) and Sir James Cockburn's Castle at Duns (18) a little way behind. Amongst those at the other extreme were Kimmerghame (7), Alexander Trotter's at Charter Hall (9) and David Lockie's in Lumsdean (9). The Hirsel, to which the Earl of Home's family had moved some time earlier because their castle had been partially destroyed, was rated for only 8 hearths. So Polwarth House's 17 chimneys brings it into a middling-sized group along with Blackadder (16), West Nisbet (15) and Sir John Sinclair at Longformacus (15).[2]

For the particular type of entertaining found in the Scotland of the 1690s, however, the size of the family seat was not always as important as might be supposed. George Home, for instance, despite his small establishment and pathetically inadequate staff and facilities, seems to have had plenty of his friends joining him for dinner in his own house, and we often find him sending his man to borrow drink from a neighbour, or to buy extra supplies when guests arrived. As we all know, there are some social settings in which it is quite usual and acceptable to call and see your friends without previous arrangement, others where you do not do so unless you have been invited. Amongst the Border lairds the first convention applied, although there were of course sometimes specific invitations, usually for more important occasions. Not being able to lift a telephone and find out whether a visit would be convenient, or to drop a line in the expectation that it would be received the following day, meant that no one expected to receive advance warning. Nor was there any certainty about the time of day when someone would appear, for in many cases you called on one family when on your way to or from seeing another.

This must often have been highly inconvenient, but if you were at the receiving end you did your best to seem welcoming. Dinner was a midday affair, but on one visit to the Hirsel George Home reports that it was one o'clock when they came there: 'My Lord was at Burghame: my Lady sent for him. We got some meat: it seems they had breakfast when my Lord went away. My Lord came about three'. Again, this time at Polwarth House, 'I came as they were arising from table, but got my dinner'. At night it was beds rather than food that the guests needed, and even a large house might find its resources stretched to the limit when a whole coachload arrived. Many of the visitors were relatives in any case, and expected to have to share accommodation: 'Commissary Home and I were bed-fellows'. Kimmerghame being a much smaller establishment than Polwarth House, even his own sister had sometimes to be turned away to find a bed at Blackadder; while taking Robie into his bed to let visitors sleep in Robie's was very often necessary.

In Edinburgh, though one might be cramped for eating-space, everyone at least had a lodging to go back to at night, so the problem of insufficient beds did not normally arise. Every Merse laird, and his lady, enjoyed visiting Scotland's capital. And as it took a day's travelling to get there, it was best to stay for some weeks or even months at a time, even if your political or other commitments did not, as was sometimes the case, make this necessary. There was no question, however, of having both a town house and a country seat. Like Polwarth, Kimmerghame and all the other lairds, you merely found temporary accommodation, as well as stabling for your horses, and arranged for the transporting to and fro of whatever you wanted in the way of household equipment, food and drink, and a skeleton staff of servants. One or two of your relatives who had been left on their own probably lived in Edinburgh anyway, and could be of help in organising these visits.

Apart from all the casual calls to see friends and relations there were, of course, the usual special occasions, the baptisms, weddings and, above all, the funerals. These were times when great stress was laid on the overt expression of mourning at burials. It was essential, therefore, that those attending these events should be well equipped with mourning clothes. Throughout Grisell's Compt Book we find references to quantities of black crape and other black materials being purchased. In January 1695, for example:

It. for 3 els and a half of Blak cloath for my Lords cloths	
It. for 6 els of blak cloath for my manto and paticot at 13 pund 16sh per ele	126.00.00
It. for 4 els of blak bas for my undrcot	004.16.00
It. for muscorad 10 els for ther undrcots at 13sh the el is	006.10.00
It. for holand for my Lords granars and my hid sut	
It. for muslin for Julian and Ann	030.18.00
It. for Blak glufs	006.04.00

If the trappings of funerals were sober, however, the 'wyks' and those who attended them were not necessarily so. A very large amount of drinking and feasting went on, causing one contemporary cynic from south of the border to comment that Scottish funerals were merrier affairs than English weddings. On such occasions you went in your black coach if, like the Polwarths, you had one. Failing that, you might be able to share with friends the cost of hire. Foulis of Ravelston, when going to the funeral at Cramond of the wife of the minister there, joined with three others — Polwarth's son Patrick, Manderston and Sir Walter Seton — and they split the cost four ways, so that each only had to pay £1.11s.6d. to get there and back.[3] For funerals of high-ranking or wealthy people there was no expense spared, of course, and large numbers of people attended. But even where one might have expected only a small turn-out, this was not always the case. When Sir John Home's youngest boy David was buried in November 1702, George Home tells us that the neighbours of five parishes — Edrom, Hutton, Whitsome, Chirnside, Swinton and Duns — were all there at Blackadder for the occasion.

One type of special social event that has since disappeared was the wedding festivity known as the penny wedding. The special feature of this very old-established institution was that the guests paid for their food, drink and entertainment because neither the couple nor their parents could afford the expense; and any proceeds left over were supposed to go to the bride and groom. As time went on, the church authorities became increasingly antagonistic towards such gatherings, which they claimed were 'fruitful seminaries of all lasciviousnesse and debausherie', and tried to stamp them out by punishing those involved.[4] But then a momentary and rather confusing light is shed on the matter by a peculiar clause incorporated in an assessment of wages by the justices of the peace for the shire of Edinburgh in 1656: 'The Makers of Penny Bridals are not to exceed Ten shillings Scots, for a Man, and Eight shillings Scots, for a Woman, whether at Dinner or Supper'.[5] The justices appear to be concerned that certain people (and could these include the bride and groom?) were charging the guests too much at events which, if church enactments had been obeyed, would not have taken place at all.

Foulis of Ravelston records contributing towards such festivities on numerous occasions during the whole period of keeping his accounts from 1671 to 1707.[6] It is never, however, just 'a' penny bridal, but always some particular servant's (his own or a friend's), and often at their master's invitation. In the 1670s his costs are usually given as either £2.18s. or, if a contribution towards the fiddlers is included, £3.4s. He himself seems sometimes to have taken along with him his wife or his children or other servants. But, particularly in later years, the wording often implies that he did not personally join in these festivities, but merely sent the appropriate amount for the members of his party who might have been expected to go along. No doubt they tended to be boisterous affairs. Many other account books contain reference to them. Grisell Baillie, for example, records payments of £2.18s. in 1702 and later.[7]

Although to the Merse lairds and their ladies, ceremonies associated with the marriage of people in their own social circle were important, much more important were the plans and negotiations leading up to such events. For the boys and girls in a laird's family could not just be left to marry whom they pleased. In the case of your eldest son and heir, a marriage into one of the most powerful families of Scotland would clearly be very advantageous, or failing that with another of the Border landed families, preferably one of better standing than your own. The same went for your daughters and younger sons; and as in any case the latter were going to have to make their own way in the world, marrying a daughter of a lord of session would help to advance a legal career. Many fathers of that day claimed, of course, that their children had a free choice of partners. When an unsuitable choice was made, however, they were apt to take a less detached view, as when in October 1697 the Lord Advocate, Sir James Stewart, was said to have 'threatened to ruin James

Scot and his family if he marry his daughter', though in this case the threat was not sufficient to prevent its happening.

George Home himself, when only 17, had been at the centre of a rather bizarre marriage tussle which illustrates how little regard was paid to the wishes of the young people involved when the financial stakes were high enough. The Laird of Ayton had left his whole estate to his only child Jean, and because she was very young she was put in the care of the Countess of Home, who was to bring her before the bar of the privy council when she was twelve so that suitable arrangements could be made in the presence of her relations. Some of her kindred decided to 'jump the gun', abducted her just before she reached her twelfth birthday, took her to England for safety and sought what from their point of view would be the best offer for her hand. This group, sad to say, included our Patrick, together with the Lairds of Ninewells, Hilton and Kimmerghame. They decided to marry her to the Kimmerghame heir, George Home, and committed the cardinal folly of having the ceremony performed by an *English* minister. The privy council decided to take harsh measures against those who had so openly flouted statutory and other provisions, imposed heavy fines on the bride and groom and imprisoned them in Edinburgh Castle for three months until these were paid, besides fining some of the others. George's father found the whole business such a strain that his death very shortly afterwards is said to have occurred as a direct result.

Whatever George may have thought about the lack of choice he himself had been given at the time of his first marriage (and no hint of any of this appears in his diary), in adult life he certainly took a keen interest in helping to arrange the marriage settlements of many of his young kindred, almost as keen, one might say, as if his own children had been concerned. The matter often involved a great deal of hard bargaining, with one of the parties holding out for very much better terms than had originally been on the table. Every possible contingency had to be provided for, looking several generations ahead, and the final drawing-up of the marriage contract entrusted to someone as proficient in such matters as Commissary Home, a Writer to the Signet. If, in spite of all this, things subsequently went wrong, it was not for want of the greatest possible care and forethought on the part of the participating families.

With one or two exceptions, the children of tenants of a laird were not felt to be of high enough status, or to have sufficient in the way of expectations, to be worth considering as marriage partners for his own children. Indeed, comparatively little socialising between lairds and even the larger or oldest-established tenants normally occurred. However, there were naturally some occasions when dealings had to take place. One of these was when a new tenancy was involved and, instead of leaving the matter to your factor, it seemed better to handle it yourself. A typical 'tack' case can be quoted from George Home's diary in February 1696: 'I agreed with James Jaffrey for 710 merks [£473.6s.2d.] for the Westfield, with 24 Carriages and 12 Cainfowl — half hens and half capons'. One carriage, as explained in another chapter, meant providing a horse and a man to lead it for a day, to carry coal or lime or whatever the laird or his representative might direct. This, and any other obligations in services or in kind, were ultimately of course translated into their money equivalents, but in the Merse the old requirements lasted well into the eighteenth century. George Home felt sorry for his friend Baillie of Jerviswood because of his tenants at Mellerstain: 'The rent there, it seems, is low, his tenants being unwilling to go away, and looking on it as oppression if he remove them: they are all old possessors without Tacks'.

Lairds might, on occasion, pay part of the cost their tenants had had to bear when soldiers were quartered on them. This would be quite a heavy burden, and we know that one laird, William Cunningham of Craigends in Renfrewshire, gave his tenants this kind of help in June 1678: 'I allowed to Ninian Parker, at his rent-paying, as half of the burden he bare of the souldiers, £07.16.0. I allowed to Arch. Arthur, on the said account, the souldiers being there 28 days £08.8.0'.[8] George Home gives a vivid description in July 1698 of what this practice of quartering could entail: 'Whitefield tells me that the dragoons, quartered in Aitone and Aynmouth and Dunglasse, will have their Landlords to provide them in victualls and have abused those that refuse: that the poor people have been forced to agree with them at two pence a day and that they force those that refuse them to furnish them coal and candle'.

One annual task which all lairds like Kimmerghame either had to do themselves or have done for them by some responsible person was teinding. A tenth part of each year's crop of oats, barley and so forth on each piece of land had to be calculated, so that it could be paid to whoever owned the teinds in that particular case (the minister of the parish or a lay owner). It was one of those jobs that had to be done when late September came along, but conditions had to be right for doing it. In 1702 George notes on the twenty-fifth: 'Da: Robisone importuned me for teinding. I went out and viewed his corn, but found it wet yett. I teinded his rye'. If you were particularly hard-pressed, a reliable servant could do it for you: 'John Lidgate went out in the morning to teind'.

Apart from a few jobs like this, and periodically scrutinising and arguing about the estate accounts, the laird could often reduce to a minimum the work he himself had to do as landowner and farmer. If that was what he chose to do, how did he fill in the rest of his time? He might, like Patrick, George Baillie and others, occupy himself fairly fully in the arena of national politics; but only a limited number of lairds could be elected as commissioners to represent their shires in parliament. There was also public work to be done in the locality, and in some cases payment could be claimed (and might ultimately be forthcoming) as salary, fee or expenses. There was quite an assortment of public positions, usually with part-time rather than full-time duties attaching to them, to which those with the education of lairds, or the sons of lairds, could aspire. Anyone with influence in these matters was inundated with requests that the letter-writer or caller should be remembered whenever vacancies arose. If you had influence, it was expected that in using it you would give preference to your sons or sons-in-law, your other relatives, and friends, more or less in that order. Money as well as influence was usually needed, and the 'going rate' for obtaining a particular public position was widely known, and comparison easily made between the pay you might receive for carrying out the duties of the post with the financial cost in obtaining it. George himself, in November 1698, turned down an offer from his friend the Chancellor of appointment to a post Jerviswood had given up, since the £1,000 sterling asked for was more than three years' purchase of the annual salary of £300 sterling. Another point to be considered, of course, was that serious arrears in the payment of salaries for public service were the rule rather than the exception. Also the type of financial arrangement in filling a public position varied. The person with authority to fill it might merely, as in the case just quoted, offer it to a potential candidate for a down payment in return for the prospect of a stated annual salary. Or the prospective holder might have to strike a bargain to buy it on a tack or lease for a stated number of years. Or, as a variation of this last arrangement, there might be a roup or auction where the highest bidder for the tack secured the position.

In securing sinecures, visits to London could sometimes be a help. On one such visit by Sir Andrew Hume in March 1703, George Home reports with some disappointment that 'all he has done is to get his father a pension on the civil list; he has got for himself the collection of tunnage and poundage'. Expenses, real or imaginary, that holders of such posts could claim might also be an important consideration. And no one need think that care and ingenuity in making out such claims is a modern phenomenon, after hearing the diarist tell us of a meeting with some of his friends in one of Edinburgh's coffee houses in July 1700: 'We were together jangling and framing schemes of our allowances for expenses all the morning'.

There were, of course, some public positions where zeal in carrying out your official duties could lose you many friends, as George himself found when taking proceedings against those who had not paid their cess or land tax. And sometimes the time and trouble needed to be selected for the position you had in mind turned out to be so excessive as almost to outweigh the rewards. When, early in October 1702, he took the first tentative steps towards being elected as one of the parliamentary commissioners for his shire, George Home can have had no idea what a hornet's nest he was going to find. Already by the middle of the month he was writing to his uncle Lord Crossrig about the intrigues over the elections, and asking him to write around and gain support for him. When on the 23rd the matter was voted on, however, the outcome was still in doubt, with two of the candidates securing 28 each, Jerviswood 25, George and two others 21 each, and the last two 18 apiece. Five months later, Berwickshire was still unrepresented because of the deadlock, and someone suggested that all of the original candidates who were in Edinburgh should meet in a coffee house and resolve the matter, but the issue was still being hotly argued over on 3rd June when George, as a temporary measure, started keeping his diary notes in a little paper almanack which has since vanished. One would imagine that by this time everyone was heartily sick of the whole affair, and there is no further mention of it when the diary resumes in November.

Some lairds had a passion for litigation, and spent a great deal of their time and resources trying to obtain legal redress for wrongs they thought they had suffered. And as thieving was widespread, there was always the chance of being named as one of those to take part in an assize to determine the guilt and the punishment of anyone who was caught. Country houses seem to have been just as prone to break-ins in lowland Scotland in the 1690s as they are today. In August 1700 George Home records a spate of such events, including a burglary at Polwarth House, but makes the encouraging comment that 'they take nothing for the most part but eatables'. A few days later he reports that six of the culprits had been apprehended, 'all highland or north country boys not above 17 years old'. Sometimes, however, more professional burglars appeared. In September 1695 Captain Cockburn in Duns found some of the ale and brandy in his cellar was missing, and blamed his servants, but even after changing his locks the stealing continued. So his manservant and two other young men resolved to sit up in the cellar and await developments:

'In the night on Sunday morning ane opened the door and came in whom they presently seized. His name is John Crawford, a common fellow. Cavers had put him away when he was found stealing bread in Nisbet. His house was searched by the town bailiff and a great deal of cloth found that several litsters knew to have been theirs'. So Patrick, who was sheriff, called an assize and Crawford (who admitted having made special keys for the purpose) was found guilty and sentenced to be hanged before sunset. In the event this proved impossible because the Duns hangman had died, and a substitute could not be found at such short notice. However, a fortnight later a local commission confirmed the sentence, which was carried out eight days afterwards: 'The poor fellow . . . was executed this day'. Four years later another convicted thief had a lighter sentence, to be 'put in the Joggs and burnt on the cheek'.

Even after doing what he chose to do in managing the home farm and the estates, and in engaging in political activity national or local, part-time public employment, litigation and law enforcement, there must often have remained (as there certainly did in Kimmerghame's case) plenty of time for a laird to indulge in recreation. Starting with indoor activities, we know of two card games being played by George Home and his associates. Picquette was for two people with a pack of thirty-two cards, the low cards two to six being excluded. Ombre was played by three people with a pack of forty, the eights, nines and tens being excluded. In July 1699 'I was engaged to play at Ombre with my Lady Polwarth and her sister: I lost half a dollar'. The following January when at the Chancellor's in Edinburgh, George went in to Lady Polwarth's room and found the Duke of Gordon and the Countess of Argyll having a game of Ombre with her. Chess is, of course, often referred to. There were facilities for a variety of indoor pursuits, presumably on a commercial basis, in Edinburgh, where on 22 May 1695 it was recommended by the Burgh Council that an Act be brought in 'discharging the keepers of billiard tables kyle alies and bouling greens and shoola boards to allow any of the Colledgioners to play at any of the ordinar dyets of the Colledge . . .'[9] Dublin lotteries, it emerges from George Home's diary, go back a surprisingly long way in our history, for in November 1702 a friend sends him 'a list of the beneficial lots of the Dublin lottery in which I was ane advertiser', and he finds that for his seven crowns he has got ten shillings by lot number 68307. However, cautious as ever, he 'sent the receats . . . to Mr John Dickson desiring withal he might get information before he gave up the Receat (it is from one Robert Bruce, Goldsmith) to be sure there is no trick'.

To turn to outdoor sports: horse racing was obviously very popular, and Leith the most usual place for it; but more informal race meetings seem also to have been held elsewhere, as when on Tuesday 7 May 1700 we are told that 'Sir Andrew and Hiltone, and I know not who, have a race on Thursday at Bunkle'; and a race 'for a plate' took place at Cavertone one April. Foxhunting was evidently almost an obsession with John Carre, the laird of Cavers and West Nisbet. Many more of the menfolk hunted hares on less formal occasions, often with greyhounds. A great variety of birds were shot for sport and for eating. Dotterels, evidently quite a table delicacy, were regarded as fair game. In 'A Description of Berwickshire or the Mers', a paper with no author and no date, but probably written in March 1683, it is thought worth telling us that 'the Dotterills use about Bastenrig on the East hand and the Moristouns of Mellerstane Douns on the West; the last the 14th of April, and the first the 14th of May'.[10] George Home reports on 6 April 1703: 'Mr Trotter, Robie and I went out to seek the dotterells, we took the dogs with us'. Eating these birds is generally also recorded in the month of April. Fowling is mentioned in June; and when a visitor reported seeing ducks and teal one October, today's sporting conventions were not observed, for 'we went out with the gun but they would not sitt'. He makes a note to remember to buy a hood for his 'spar hawk', and when Cavers's falconer offers him a good sparrow hawk, 'I bid him bring it'. Today's Kelso citizens may be surprised to learn that they had a bull-baiting there early in May 1700. Sports more usually associated with Scotland, such as bowls and curling, were actively pursued. Golf is not referred to by George Home, and in the Edinburgh Burgh Records the first, purely incidental, mention of golf on Bruntsfield Links is apparently on 25 December 1695.[11] But there is, of course, plenty of evidence from other sources that golf was being played in Scotland well before that time. As we saw in Chapter 4, David Home, Lord Crossrig, when he was at College in Edinburgh in 1658, went out with other second-year students (semies) to a football match on the 'Borrow Moor'. Young Robie Home, as we have seen, missed his dinner to go to football on Blackadder Green on 13 April 1703; other diary references to its being played seem to be confined to 'fastings even' (Shrove Tuesday) when 'we had a footballing but they played till they lost the ball'. That day seems to have been appropriate for other sports as well. In Marie Stewart's Compt Book for 6 March 1640 six shillings were given to John Erskine 'to bye a cok to fight on fastings even'.[12] Complaints of violence at football matches have a familar ring about them today. At Kelso in 1716 an attempt was made by the authorities to outlaw it altogether: 'Forasmuch as there were several unallowable abuses, tumults and riots committed last year at the football . . . these do therefore prohibit and discharge the football from being played by any of this jurisdiction, either within the town or the precincts thereof'.[13]

There were, unfortunately, some outdoor sports less acceptable to us today being practised in Scotland in the 1690s. To start with a relatively mild example, George Home tells us how at Blackadder one day 'the gentlemen after dinner fell to tossing dogs in a blanket, which is a usual divertisement in other places, particularly among the Swissers. They got dogs at Greenloan. They are not as yet very dexterous'. Chambers, in his *Domestic Annals of Scotland*, records what was said in 1702 by an Edinburgh man called Machrie about a much more reprehensible sporting activity: 'I am not ashamed to declare to the world that I have a special veneration and esteem for those gentlemen, within and about this city, who have entered in society for propagating and establishing the royal recreation of cocking (in order to which they have already erected a cock-pit in the Links of Leith); and I earnestly wish that their generous and laudable example may be imitated in that degree that, in cock-war, village may be engaged against village, city against city, kingdom against kingdom, nay, the father against the son, until all the wars in Europe, wherein so much Christian blood is spilt, be turned into the innocent pastime of cocking'.[14] And also in the *Annals* we are reminded that not only did this pastime remain popular in Scotland throughout the whole of the eighteenth century, but that as late as 1790 the income of the schoolmaster in Applecross in Ross-shire included 'cock-fight dues, which are equal to one quarter's payment for each scholar'.[15]

Even worse was the kind of sport organised once a year by a secret brotherhood of so-called whipmen in Kelso, comprising farmers' servants, ploughmen and carters. They assembled in the market place in the morning mounted on horses, armed with clubs and wooden hammers, and dressed in their best clothes, and marched with music and drums to the common half a mile away: 'The first part of the performance, which was called *cat in barrel*, consisted of putting a cat in a barrel, stuffed with soot, and hung up upon a beam fixed upon two high poles, under which the members rode in succession, striking the barrel as they passed with their clubs or hammers. On the barrel being broken, the cat jumped down from the sooty prison, when it soon fell a victim to the whipmen and the crowd of townspeople assembled to witness the sports. A goose was next hung up by the feet on the beam, and the members then rode one after another under it, each trying to catch hold of the head in passing, till some lucky brother plucks off the head, and carries it away in triumph'. Horse races followed, and on their return to Kelso the day ended in feasting and drinking.[16]

Some leisure activities can be pursued either indoors or outdoors: music and dancing come to mind. When musical instruments are mentioned in seventeenth-century Scottish account books, it is usually for one of several reasons. First, because fees had to be paid when the children were learning to play, secondly when instruments were bought or had to be tuned or repaired, and thirdly when musicians were paid for performing. No points of particular interest arise in connection with the first two types of entry. The girls in the family were often taught music; and in the Compt Book, £1.16s. was paid 'for tunin the vergnels'. But rather more can be learned from looking at payments to musicians for playing. The two stringed instruments to which reference is sometimes made in that context are the harp and the fiddle.

The type of harp involved was the clarsach, of which two sixteenth-century examples are in the Royal Museum of Scotland: 'They are low-headed harps with one-piece soundboard of hornbeam, not a wood indigenous to Scotland', and other features apparently also suggest an Irish rather than a Scottish origin.[17] In the 1680s the Hamiltons employed a resident harper, Jago McFlahertie, but there is no evidence of such a person being permanently attached to the household of any of the Merse lairds.[18] Payments to harpers are, however, recorded from time to time, when they presumably provided the musical accompaniment to social gatherings of one kind or another. The earliest seventeenth-century references to clarsairs are both from account books of families of higher status than lairds. Two entries in the household book kept for Lady Marie Stewart, Countess of Mar, lack clarity. The first, dated 8 September 1638, records the payment of 6s. 'to twa hieland singing women at my Laidies comand', though whether or not their voices were accompanied is not stated.[19] In the second item for 21 March 1642, 12s. is paid 'to ane woman clarsocher who usit ye house in My Lord his tyme', the doubt being if this is a payment for rent or a payment for service.[20] Then in 1664 the official who was keeping household accounts for James Sharp, Lord Archbishop of St Andrews, mentions a payment of £2.8s. 'to a harper at his grace directioun'.[21] The Thane of Cawdor's accounts note in 1682 payments to a harper (always in the singular) varying from 10 shillings to £1.8s.[22] And in Grisell's Compt Book we find £1.10s. being given to 'the harpers' in May 1695. We have already noted frequent entries in the Compt Book of payments to the fiddlers when the young girls were having dancing lessons, and we also find, in the same weeks of June 1695, 'To Sandi and Andra to give the fidls

£2.18.0'. In the accounts kept by Cunningham of Craigends, in 1677 the 'violers' are paid 13s.4d. on one occasion and 12s. on another; and this term rather than 'fiddlers' is also used in the Hamilton accounts.[23]

It was not by any means unusual for friendly interchange of the types described to develop unexpectedly into violent quarrelling leading perhaps to someone's serious injury or even death. It was an age when violent quarrels were liable to break out amongst the menfolk at any time and without warning. Lairds and other gentry drew their swords or reached for their pistols at (if one may mix metaphors) the drop of a hat. From the instances that have come to light in the course of studying the lives of the Polwarths, their relatives and friends, a few examples will serve to show the kind of pattern such events tended to follow. For the details of one occasion when tragedy was the outcome we are indebted to George Wilson, the tailor who visited Kimmerghame to make clothes for George, Robie and the servants. He recounts how, on 6 June 1700, Sir George Lauder of Edingtone, coming from Duns, called on Laird Spence in Chirnside and took him to the alehouse, 'they being great comrades'. They fell out, and Sir George drew his sword; but it was only outside, when he came to his horse and drew out one of his pistols, that things got completely out of hand: 'He came up to Laird Spence and fired it close on him whereof he died immediately, wounded just above his left pap'. The onlookers were too afraid of getting the same treatment to do anything about it, and Sir George apparently made his escape; perhaps he was apprehended later.

It must have been even commoner for a violent quarrel such as this to stop just short of killing. George Home himself tells how, the previous April, two friends of his, Hundwood and Spot, following some difference at a game of picquette, grappled and pulled off one another's wigs: 'The company came about them, and Hundwood drew his sword, with which he might have killed Spot, but my Lord Home took it from him'. No doubt many other less hot-tempered gentlemen would have echoed George's remark in recording this event — 'I wish I had not been in such company'. Brawls amongst the lower orders could sometimes spill over and annoy those of higher rank. After describing one such incident in January 1700, George remarks, 'if such things be suffered, insolent rascals may be encouraged to affront gentlemen'. When his woman servant took exception to being called a 'land louper whore' by another woman, George took her to task for having complained to the minister about it, believing that there was little to choose between the two who had quarrelled — 'she is a very bad scolding creature, and the other an impudent, graceless slutt'.

The quarrel followed by a killing which had the greatest impact on those with whom *we* are particularly concerned took place, however, at the Hirsel on 26 December 1683. The lairds of Hilton and Ninewells had gone there for a game of cards with William Home, brother of the Earl who was away at the time. We are told that William Home and Joseph Johnston of Hilton were such close friends that they addressed each other as 'Billie', meaning brother. A dispute during the game was made worse by the accidental or intentional mischief-making of the Earl's sister, and William, in a violent temper, went to Hilton's room and stabbed him as he lay in bed, with fatal results. The culprit is said to have fled to England and died in poverty. The widow of the murdered man was Marie Douglass, Lady Hilton.

When such sensational events took place, it was not unusual for a tail-piece to be added to the story, in the form of a prophecy having been fulfilled. In this case, it said that some years before all this happened Johnston had taken exception to something in a sermon in Hilton church, and had physically attacked the minister, dragging him from the pulpit and wounding him slightly. The minister apparently gave vent to his indignation by an adaptation of Elijah's prophecy against Ahab: 'In the place where thou hast done this shall dogs lick thy blood'. This prophecy was claimed to have been fulfilled when, after the murder, Johnston's body was put into a temporary coffin to be conveyed to Hutton Hall; because of a snowstorm the journey had to be broken, and the coffin was taken into Hilton church where dogs were said to have lapped up blood leaking from it.[24]

Not all quarrels ended in physical injury or loss of life. One in particular could easily have formed the basis for a French farce. George Home reports on 29 May 1698 that one of his fellow lairds, Sir Alexander Home of Renton (fourteen miles north-east of Polwarth House), had died the previous Friday. Then on 2 June 'they tell me Sir Pa: Home and his Brother's relict are contending who should possess the house of Rentone'. The house, a fourteen-chimney one in excellent condition, was a much more desirable residence than Sir Patrick Home's own much smaller one at Lumsden, with only nine hearths.[25] The final diary entry relating to this, on 25 June, records that 'the processe between Lady Rentone and Sir Pa: Home being referred by the Council to the Session it was discussed yesterday in favour of the Lady. That Sir Pa: had no right to disturb her'. For once in his life George failed to give an adequate account of the extraordinary events that took place at this laird's funeral. It seems that Sir Alexander, who was estranged from his wife, Dame Margaret Scott, and their son, Robert, had made his brother Sir Patrick

Home, an advocate, his heir. When the laird was dying, Sir Patrick's wife, Dame Margaret Baird (her husband being in England) took herself to Renton, shortly to be followed by Sir Alexander's estranged wife, who though having a partial reconciliation with her dying husband, was nevertheless ordered by him to leave the house. Instead of doing so, she and those with her stayed on semi-secretly and, when Sir Alexander died and the funeral was under way, took possession of the house. When the funeral party returned there was inevitably a confrontation between the two women (and between Sir Patrick and the widow), each side claiming their legal entitlement to be the sole possessors of the house, and demanding that the others leave forthwith. There followed a whole succession of threats of violence, and abusive language, and then an extraordinary scene between the widow and Sir Patrick. She locked him out of the main chamber, refusing to give him the key of the door. He retorted by having the door broken down, only to discover that his bed in the meantime had been carried away and locked up elsewhere, where-upon he borrowed a bed from a neighbour. And the evening of the funeral ended with one set of contenders in the main room, and the other in the footman's room. The legal wrangle that followed dragged on for fourteen years, with a mixture of favourable and unfavourable decisions for both parties, though Sir Patrick was eventually confirmed as Laird of Renton.[26]

It comes as no surprise that superstitions were widely talked about in Scotland at this time. What is in doubt, of course, is how far people's actions were influenced by superstition, and how far the stories were merely repeated because they were interesting, and not because the person passing them on really believed them. In George Home's case, his policy in the diary is usually to record such stories without comment, but occasionally he voices disapproval when people modify their actions because of superstition; he thinks it quite ridiculous, for instance, to postpone proclaiming a forthcoming marriage on Easter Sunday because it was thought unlucky to do so on that particular day. In recounting one case of a prophecy apparently fulfilled, he takes a typically cautious line. Young Joseph Johnston of Hilton died while a student at the College in Edinburgh in January 1695. Some days afterwards, Sir John Home of Blackadder tells George of a conversation that had taken place between Thomas Pringle and young Abbey (now minister of Ayton) when they were out riding near Hutton Hall the preceding summer. Abbey, after explaining that his grand-uncle had been tricked by a previous Joseph Johnston into selling him the Hilton lands for far less than they were worth, and after also enumerating some of the disasters that had subsequently befallen the Johnstons (to punish them for what Joseph had done), went on to make a prophecy — 'And as for this young man, you shall see he shall not live till he be 25'. George's diary comment on hearing all this is a masterpiece of diplomacy: 'Whether the matter of fact be true that Mr Jos: got the lands below the value, I know not, having never heard it before. And what moved Abbey to speak so in relation to this poor young lad I will not determine: whether any fore-sight of the thing, or a heat and concern transporting him, which eventually came to pass; if it was this last it was very unwarrantable. But I am no judge of these things'. On Christmas Eve 1703 a no-comment horror story appears in the diary. At a wedding at Jedburgh a well-dressed woman whom nobody knew is said to have joined in the celebrations by dancing with the bridegroom and some ten other men, she not being seen again afterwards: 'And next day all that danced with her died'.

So far we have provided a picture of the life of a laird in the 1690s. But of course whilst he was engaging in pursuits of any or all of the types described, a great deal of work had to be done within the family home and its surroundings. No one, least of all the laird himself, expected him to worry about such matters — this was work for his servants and his womenfolk to see to. A major contrast between domestic life at the 'middle rank' level then and now is, of course, the vital part played by living-in servants. But if we ask what was the *size* of a laird's domestic staff, it is not easy to provide a satisfactory answer. It must have depended partly on the number of young children to be catered for, on the size of the family seat, on the preferences of the laird as to how he spent his money, on the availability of suitable staff in the area and on many other factors. All we can do is to list the number of living-in servants at the time of the 1695 poll tax in the households of the lairds whose particulars are available. Stewart of Allanbank and Carre of Cavers both had 19 domestic servants, but their sex-distribution was exactly opposite — 8 men and 11 women as against 11 men and 8 women. At Polwarth House a staff of 17 consisted of 13 men and 4 women. Sir Thomas Dalzell (Abercorn, Linlithgow) had 13: 9 men and 4 women. Blackadder employed 9: 4 men and 5 women; and Cunningham of Craigends 6: 4 men and 2 women. Kimmerghame had only 3, one man and two women. And Swinton, employing only one woman, clearly spent most of his time in the capital.[27] On the basis of information of this kind, it would be fair to conclude that a laird's household quite usually contained between a dozen and a dozen and a half domestic servants, the men including probably a butler, a groom, a footman and at least one cook, and most of the women being styled nurses or chambermaids. The justices of the peace made no bones about the wide range of work and of skills expected of what they called in 1656 'an able', and in 1708 'a strong and sufficient', woman servant. She was there for 'Barns, Byres, Shearing, Brewing, Baking, Washing and all other necessary Work, within or without the House'. The wording remained identical in the half-century between these two pronouncements for different areas of Scotland; and the maximum she might be paid was much the same (£13.7s. and £14) at the two dates also.[28]

When the daytime domestic tasks were completed there was a whole range of work connected with flax and wool to be done, and the winter evenings were fully employed in these. Carding and spinning of the wool and flax from the estate were done at home; later processes were done by the appropriate specialists. Grisell Baillie, the archetype of the laird's supervisor of household arrangements, codified in the instructions she drew up in 1743 the practice of a lifetime: 'Keep the maids closs at their spinning till 9 at night when they are not washing or at other necessary work . . .'[29] There was to be no waste; everything was to be weighed before being given out; premises from which anything could be stolen were to be kept locked. 'Take care there be no hangers on.'[30] Apart from specified allowances of basic food and drink, a menu for the servants is laid down for each day of the week, ringing the changes on broth, beef, herring, cheese and eggs. Such a strict régime may well have had something to do with the frequent changes of staff in the household. Between 1695 and 1704 Grisell Baillie engaged sixty servants of whom thirty apparently left within a year, and only about a dozen stayed more than two years.[31] The girls in the laird's family were also expected to play their part in the skilled household tasks that had to be done. These included sewing, where there is ample evidence that the shirts worn by the men were almost always made at home, and there was plenty of mending of bed and table linen as well as clothing.

The laird's family ate simply, except on special occasions. Oatmeal and peasemeal were used in a variety of dishes. For porridge (or pottage or hasty pudding) the meal was put into a pot of boiling water; for brose the water was stirred into the meal. With sowans the mixture of meal and water was left to go sour; when the thinner parts were drained off and boiled, a light pudding resulted which could be eaten with milk. Kale had the same basic constituents, but with greens as well, and groats and meat could be added to the resultant broth. Hasty pudding and kale were often eaten cold. And oatmeal was, of course, the main ingredient in the baking of bannocks, meal cakes and bread, all of which were made on the bakestone.

One of the busiest times of the year for the servants was late summer or early autumn, when preparations had to be begun to cater for the winter months when food would be difficult to come by, for both humans and animals. Shut up in byres, a very small proportion of the livestock survived these months; those that did were reduced to skin and bone, and were quite unfit for human consumption. So towards the end of summer most animals were slaughtered, and if necessary others bought for slaughtering. This was preparation for the 'mart' (carried out at Martinmas) when everything had to be cut up, and then salted in large tubs. Similarly, fish was purchased in quantity for salting — haddocks, herring and ling. One standby for food in the winter was the pigeons, but the number that individuals might keep was limited by law because they consumed other people's grain. There were the hens too, including those contributed by tenants as part of the rent. Most of these were also in poor condition, causing one English visitor to make the cynical observation that Scottish fowls were so thin that the breastbone of one could be used to carve another.

Though it is unsafe to generalise about the internal arrangements of lairds' houses, there are two or three features that we can be fairly sure about. In most of their houses the ceilings would be unplastered. The windows would be fixed, and where more ventilation was needed it would tend to be provided by opening a wooden lower section. Beds would in the main be closed rather than free-standing. The dining-room would only be used on ceremonial occasions, social activities taking place as a rule in one of the larger bedrooms. Carpets would be on tables, not on the floor. As to furniture we have a few guidelines. In December 1703, Grisell Baillie spent £3.12s. on a 'black arme rush chair', £4.16s. on two low rush chairs, £4.4s. on 'a rush bottomd eassi chair', £18 on 'a big bufft eassi chair with cushion', and £7.16s. on three footstools.[32] George Home's somewhat more spartan furniture arrangements have already been indicated in Chapter 3. In 1703 Foulis of Ravelston bought six armed 'cain chairs', costing £9.18s. each, and ten without arms, £4 each. But he decided to ask Mr Mowbray to make him a further eight without arms, and he also told him that the final payment would only be made when they were all better varnished.[33]

For our knowledge of the living conditions of the *ordinary* people in lowland Scotland at the end of the seventeenth century, we have to depend on the descriptions left by three English travellers — John Ray in the early 1660s, Thomas Kirke in 1679 and Thomas Morer in 1689.[34] John Ray, 'Ray the Naturalist', gives his impressions on reaching Dunbar after visiting Berwick: 'The Scots generally (that is, the poorer sort) wear, the men blue bonnets on their heads, and some russet; the women only white linnen, which hangs down their backs as if a napkin were pinned about them. When they go abroad none of them wear hats, but a party coloured blanket which they call a plad, over their heads and shoulders . . . The ordinary country houses are pitiful cots, built of stone, and covered with turves, having in them but one room, many of them no chimneys, the windows very small holes, and not glazed . . . The people seem to be very lazy, at least the men, and may be frequently observed to plow in their cloaks . . . They lay out most they are worth in cloaths, and a fellow that has scarce ten groats besides to help himself with, you shall see come out of his smoaky cottage clad like a gentleman'.[35] Thomas Kirke, a Yorkshireman, gives an even more depressing description in 1679: 'The houses of the commonalty are very mean, mud-wall and thatch the best; but the poorer sort live in such miserable hutts as never eye beheld; men, women and children pig altogether in a poor mouse-hole of mud, heath and some such like matter . . . The Lowland gentry go well enough habited, but the poorer sort go (almost) naked, only an old cloak, or part of their bed-cloaths thrown over them'.[36] Ten years after Kirke, that 'splenetic and perverse observer', had travelled there, Thomas Morer, minister of a London church, who was chaplain to a Scottish regiment, wrote what is generally regarded as the most reliable account: 'The vulgar houses and what are seen in the villages, are low and feeble. Their walls are made of a few stones jumbled together without mortar to cement 'em. On which they set up pieces of wood meeting at the top, ridge-fashion, but so order'd that there is neither sightliness nor strength; and it does not cost much more time to erect such a cottage than to pull it down. They cover these houses with turff of an inch thick, and in the shape of larger tiles, which they fasten with wooden pins . . . 'Tis rare to find chimneys in these places, a small vent in the roof suffering to convey the smoak away'.[37] Morer explains the absence of a thatched roof by the shortage of hay, making it necessary to use all straw as fodder for horses. On points where all three of these English travellers are in agreement, it is reasonable to assume that there is a measure of truth in the picture they present.

For several consecutive years in the late 1690s Scotland suffered wet, sunless summers and very severe winters — some Jacobites styled them 'King William's Ill Years'. Harvests were lost and farm stock sorely depleted, the resultant famine amounting to a national calamity. Archibald Allan, writing in 1900, gives us a vivid description of the disastrous conditions in the country in his *History of Channelkirk*: 'October 1698 — the terrible year of harvest failure, of wild winds, rains and snowstorms; when great part of the corn could not be cut, and people died in the streets and highways, some parishes losing more than half their inhabitants . . .'[38] Although so close geographically, England was better able to withstand extremely bad weather, her agricultural methods being on the whole more advanced than those of her neighbour. In Scotland, efforts were made to prevent hoarding, and there was a prohibition of the export of grain and a reduction of control on the import of foreign grain. But in spite of these attempts to ease the shortage of food, meal was priced so high that it was beyond the reach of many people. Thousands died of starvation, and there was often difficulty in burying the corpses decently. The nadir was reached in 1698, and among others the Polwarths did what they could to alleviate the distress among their workers. According to Lady Anne Purves, when the famine was at its height a round pond was dug on the estate, and porridge made in a large cauldron was carried out in washing tubs to the workpeople.[39] Sir Thomas Stewart helped in Coltness (Lanarkshire) by distributing money, some of which he procured from his brother, the Lord Advocate, and other friends.[40] But efforts such as these made small impact on the sufferings of the population as a whole, and many thousands left Scotland, emigrating to Ireland. Things did improve, however, and the year 1699 produced a bumper harvest.

That there was widespread poverty in Scotland, then, is not open to question. All that we learn of the matter from the keepers of account books, however, is what contributions for the poor they made at the kirk door, as well as the help they gave to individual victims of poverty. Sometimes the entries are uninformative — 'given in charitie', or 'to a poor frind'. But very often some detail is provided suggesting why the donor's heart was touched by the circumstances of the particular case. Monorgun, who kept Marie Stewart's accounts, provides some interesting examples in the 1640s.[41] Three shillings and fourpence was given to 'ane beggar who fained himself madde and had his wife lighter in the Raploch'; and two shillings 'to ane masterfull beggar who did knock at the gate, my Lady being att table'. Thomas Norie, a messenger 'who moanit his povertie to my Lady', received 26 shillings. Sometimes they literally sang for their supper, as when three shillings was given 'to ane lame man callit Rosse, who plays the plaisant' or 'blind wat ye piper' was helped, or twelve shillings went to 'ane blind singer who sang the time of dinner'. Or the money might be given for a very specific purpose, thirty shillings 'to ane chapman boy to begin his pack with'. The instances quoted by Cunningham of Craigends in the 1670s and '80s are equally varied.[42] The largest single amount, £2.16s., went 'to a poor distrest preacher who had a great family'; 8 shillings was given 'to a poor man once landward schoolmaster'. Very often the recipient produced a testimonial or 'testificat', as in the case of a broken family getting 14 shillings, as well as individual poor men and women, though 'a poor sea-broken German' was given six shillings without one. Those locally well-known hardly needed to produce proof: 'The woman that keeps the poor daft lad at Houston syd' received four shillings, but when alms went to the poor daft lad himself, one shilling was felt to be more appropriate.[43] In Foulis of Ravelston's case he often specifies on whose recommendation he is helping someone. At other times the name of the recipient is given: 'to a distrest man named middleton wanting ye nose'.[44] Where only their being distressed is recorded, men seem to have fared better than women, for within a week or so of each other a case of male distress was given seven shillings, while a woman merely got three. On journeys, and in towns, beggars were often so importunate that it became expensive to move about at all. Sir John paid 14/6 to 'the staffmen [who] kept away ye poor folk' when his son William got married.[45]

As one would expect, the Merse lairds and their ladies spent a good deal of time in Edinburgh, sometimes for business or professional reasons, and sometimes simply to take part in the social life of the town with their friends. As usual, visitors from England and elsewhere were apt to comment adversely on features of life in the capital which were accepted as normal by the local people. In the old part of the town buildings were tall, tightly crowded together, and many still constructed of timber, making fires a constant hazard. Streets were dirty and ill-kept. Sanitation was more or less non-existent as there was no proper supply of water. Slops of all kinds were hurled out of windows with a warning of 'gardez-loo' to passers-by. The unfortunate pedestrian not wanting to be caught unawares would retort with 'haud yer haun'.

Street water sellers provided drinking water drawn from wells with which the town was well supplied, and there were restrictions on water for general use. In such circumstances personal cleanliness was a near impossibility. Even for wealthy people it was extremely difficult to organise a bath. So the rich masked body smells by continual application of perfumes and essences, while the poor just had to put up with the stench of body and clothes. Bad odours and vermin must also have contributed towards making the inside of houses unsavoury. It is not surprising, therefore, that disease and infections spread rapidly, and if they reached epidemic proportions people fled to the country where at least the population was less dense, the air was cleaner and water more plentiful. It was not until the middle of the eighteenth century that Peter

Bruce, a Flandrian, provided the first system of water supply to the town by laying a three-inch pipe from the Comiston lands.

Illness was naturally a hazard to which all sections of the community were exposed; there were, of course, remedies of a kind available for those who could pay. Amongst the diseases most prevalent at this time were dysentery or 'flux', ague, fevers of all kinds, chin cough or whooping cough, and even malaria and smallpox. Practitioners of healing were, however, mainly concentrated in the urban areas. There was little money to be had from country folk, and road conditions discouraged visits being made even over short distances. So almost to the end of the seventeenth century people had to rely on their own resources, which were self-treatment, help from folk healers (who usually did not charge), healing wells, healing charms or astrology, although this last resort had more or less died out. 'Simples' were passed on from one generation to the next, most families having their own particular cures in which they placed their faith. A 'simple' was normally produced from a single or simple herb such as feverfew or comfrey. If this alleviated the trouble, that boosted its efficacy. If it did not, the simple was discarded and another sought. This was a relatively straightforward way of proceeding by comparison with trying to identify a harmful ingredient in some of the complex and nauseating prescriptions which the physicians offered at extortionate prices. Self-treatment was also practised by the better-off, and we get an insight into their remedies from the records in many diaries and day books. In accounts kept by Sir John Lauder of Fountainhall we find in 1673 an item, 'For everyman his own doctor, 2 shillings', a book which must have been the counterpart of the modern *Home Doctor*.[46]

Poor Law funds were supposed to ease the condition of the poor, but few areas did much. Most parishes tried to keep reserves of money in the parish chests, and the landed gentry were frequently being asked for contributions to these funds. But even when help was given from these sources it was mainly as money or food. After the foundation of the Faculty of Physicians and Surgeons in Glasgow by Maister Peter Lowe in 1599, and the Edinburgh College of Physicians in 1681, free clinics for poor people were held each week in both towns.

Physicians were held in great esteem, and by the 1690s they had abandoned folk remedies and were producing highly extravagant and complex prescriptions which, together with their high fees, enhanced their status. By this time physicians had graduated in medicine, often both in Scotland and abroad; they themselves, therefore, came mainly from well-to-do families. It is interesting that Scottish physicians favoured Leyden and Paris when studying abroad, in contrast to their English counterparts who were more prone to opt for Padua and Montpellier. Of all Scottish physicians in the 1680s and 1690s, undoubtedly the most eminent was Sir Archibald Pitcairne, and it is therefore appropriate to give a brief account of his life and work. Pitcairne's father had estates in Fife to which his son eventually succeeded; he was also a baillie of Edinburgh. Archibald was born in 1652. He studied at Edinburgh, Paris and Rheims, qualifying in divinity, law and medicine. On his return to Edinburgh he began to practise in 1680, and when the College of Physicians was founded a year later, he was in at the beginning of things, subsequently playing an important part in its development. At the age of 29, and with only one year of post-graduate medical experience, he became the youngest Fellow of the college. In 1692 he was invited to fill the chair of medicine at the celebrated University of Leyden. This was indeed a feather in the cap of the young Edinburgh medical school. He did not, however, hold this position long. His first wife had died, and his second wife, Elizabeth, daughter of Sir Archibald Stevenson, had been persuaded not to go to Holland. So Pitcairne returned to Edinburgh, where he had a house near the Tron Kirk. In 1695 he quarrelled with the College of Physicians and, together with his father-in-law, who was also distinguished in the medical field, he associated himself instead with the College of Surgeons.[47]

Physicians frequently gave their prognosis and suggested treatment by letter and, like others, Pitcairne used this procedure. Patrick consulted both Drs Stevenson and Pitcairne when he was unwell and, in 1712 when he was in some trouble, Pitcairne prescribed for him by letter giving advice on medical treatment and diet. He was to take some Poterius's powder in his milk, to bathe 'the back place' with materials which would be sent to him, and not to engage in hunting. This last warning seems unnecessary as by this time the patient was 71 years of age. As to diet, pork was advised, lamb and poultry were permissible, but care was to be taken to eat nothing that was too salted or in any way soured.[48]

It was not only in medical matters that Archibald Pitcairne was a man of stature. He was a pre-Enlightenment figure who in his lifetime amassed a library of some 1,500 books which, after his death, were sold to Peter the Great for £430 sterling, a large sum of money at that time. He also wrote poems in Latin which were highly regarded by his contemporaries. A jovial man, he enjoyed good company, but his wit and sarcasm provided weapons which he used effectively when he felt like it; these did not endear him to his enemies. As an episcopalian with overtly-expressed

Jacobite sympathies, his political stance was not a popular one in post-revolutionary Scotland, and got him into deep trouble on one occasion.

He wrote a letter to a friend in London, Dr Gray, in which criticism of the government was expressed. By some mischance this eventually found its way into the hands of the Secretary, and by an order signed by Patrick as Chancellor and others, he was apprehended and imprisoned in the Tolbooth. This was a very serious crime, one for which only a few years earlier many had gone to the scaffold. On 25 January 1700 he was brought before the privy council on a charge of venting and circulating false reports against the government. Pitcairne pleaded that the letter had been written when he was in his cups, that he had no recollection of either writing the letter or of its contents (though he did not deny that it was his own), and that he had no ill designs against the government. His father-in-law, Sir Archibald Stevenson, stood guarantor for his peaceable behaviour and paid a substantial fine. Pitcairne was freed after being reprimanded by the Chancellor. He lived to the age of 61 and was buried in Greyfriars churchyard in October 1713. His tombstone fell into disrepair and was restored in 1800, when the medical practitioners in Edinburgh at that time felt justified in carrying out one of his last wishes, even though slightly amended. He had left a jeroboam (two magnums) of wine with a merchant along with instructions that it should be opened 'at the Restoration'. As there was little possibility by that time of the Stuarts ever again sitting on the throne, they agreed that this Restoration would do instead. The jeroboam was duly opened and its contents drunk, doubtless with self-congratulatory relish.

At this time surgeons occupied a very different level in the healing hierarchy from the one we are familiar with today. Without academic training, they normally served an apprenticeship, and their earlier association with barbers did nothing to improve the regard in which they were held by the general public. Their work consisted mainly of extraction of teeth, blood-letting, setting of fractures, sometimes amputations, and care of worms and skin diseases, these tasks often being carried out under the instruction of a physician. Blood-letting was, of course, accepted as a universal palliative, and one which could be competently carried out by a person of lower status than a physician. One must remember that anaesthetics and infection-killing drugs were as yet unknown, and surgeons were faced with hazards such as infections and post-operative complications of all kinds. Nevertheless, their contribution towards healing the sick was an important one. Furthermore, patients who had to face an amputation or cutting of any kind knew what was in store for them, and would put off the treatment as long as possible. When they did face it, they could not have been easy to handle.[49]

By the end of the century barbers did very little medical work, but there was still a host of quacks, sometimes itinerant, offering remedies at a price to people in distress. The apothecary's task was to provide drugs, either his own prescriptions or those of the medical men. But physicians preferred to make up their own prescriptions; they did not like the apothecaries, nor did they trust them. If the prescription had to be written it was often in Latin, to prevent less literate persons making use of it. And although the physicians were antagonistic to folk medicine and to those who practised it, some of the remedies they themselves offered could be said to be anything but scientific. One really harmless medicine often recommended by medical men and widely advertised was Scarboro' water. A newspaper advertisement in October 1707 explains: 'There is just now come to town the Excellent Scarburray Water, good for all diseases whatsomever except consumption; and this being the time of year for drinking the same, especially at the fall of the leaf and the bud, the price of each chopin bottle is fivepence, the bottle never required, or three shilling without the bottle. Any person who has a mind for the same may come to the Fountain Close within the Nether-bow of Edinburgh, at William Mudie's, where the Scarsburray woman sells the same'.[50]

Two small points are perhaps worth adding before we leave this account of the lifestyle of the lairds. Although, as we have seen, they and their wives often bought imported articles instead of home-produced ones, they sometimes had a sense of guilt about this. When, in November 1703, George Home, for example, bought in Berwick as much black cloth as would make a coat and breeches, he remarks sadly, 'I would not willingly have done it but I could get no cloath in Scotland so thick as to trust to changing my cloaths at this time of the year so that it is a kind of necessity upon me'. On another occasion, however, when he asked a friend to bring him razors from Paris, as well as a pair of shears and some books, George does not seem to have had any feeling of guilt about the transaction. When they duly reached him on 7 July 1700, he paid 35 shillings each for three razors, £3 for a case to keep them in, and 30 shillings for the shears.

Then there is the question of manners, and a few examples can be quoted as illustrations. In September 1702 at Berwick, George records with more than a hint of disapproval the behaviour of Sir Thomas Dalyell of Binns 'who is a perfect Beau and came from his chamber in his night gown, though he lodged abroad as we did, and in that Equipage waited on the Ladies'. He was even more incensed when Sir John and

Lady Swinton called at Kimmerghame in June 1705 to collect Robie and stayed outside in their coach: 'I have rarely seen such breeding to come to a Gentleman's house and call for his sone and stay at the gate and not a word of himself. Looks as if I kept a boarding school, or seeking a quarrel'. He himself tried to keep to certain rules of conduct, as when attending the burial feast of Lady Cavers on 3 March 1702: 'There was a table with a great deal of meat, but being a neighbour I thought it fit to give way to others, so went not up it being in the room above the drawing room'. And as we struggle to find better ways of ending the letters we write than 'Best wishes', we could follow the example of someone writing to Patrick — 'My hearty service to all friends neglecting none'.[51]

CHAPTER 7

How People and News Got Around

How speedy were local journeys on horseback? Much naturally depended on weather conditions. George Home tells us that one day in July 1698 he came from Edinburgh at six and reached Haddington, nineteen miles away, 'about fourty minutes past 8, being obliged to ride hard because of a thick mist that came on'. Just over 7 m.p.h. may seem rather slow to today's motorist, but it was slightly better than on a November journey from Kelso to home three years earlier. On that occasion he obviously felt he had been going exceptionally fast, for he gives the position in some detail: 'From Kelso to Ednam I rode in 23 minutes, from that to Eccles in 33: to Mersingtone in 24, from that to Thomas Mitchel's in 29: from that home in about as much'. The distance is about fourteen miles and the time two hours eighteen minutes, so he was achieving only a little more than 6 m.p.h.

Of course no horse could be expected to keep up such a pace on longer journeys. If you lived in Berwickshire in the 1690s the long trip most usually taken was naturally to the capital. And as most of our information on the problems of journeying from the Merse to Edinburgh comes from George Home's diary, it seems best in describing the route to take Kimmerghame as the starting point. The three routes to choose from were all of roughly the same length, some forty-eight or fifty miles. Whichever you chose, and whichever form of transport you were using, on a journey of this length both the horses and their passengers needed a break for refreshment and a rest. Indeed, if you had not set forth until the afternoon, an overnight break of journey would be necessary. George and his friends usually baited (stopped for food) at Channelkirk (then called Ginglekirk), at Gifford Hall or at Haddington, depending on the route taken. What we might call the central route was not suitable for coaches. It involved going through Duns to Preston, a distance of some five miles from Kimmerghame, then proceeding as best one could across twenty-two miles or so of very bleak country to Gifford Hall, from where, after a break, there was a further twenty-one miles to Edinburgh. A second possibility was to aim for the post road. The first five miles to Preston was the same, but then instead of going north-westwards to Gifford you proceeded north-eastwards through Quixwood, Butterdean, Blackburn, Ecclaw and Fulfordlees to Cockburnspath, an important meeting point of post roads going south to Renton, and south-east to Coldingham and Eyemouth, as well as north to Dunglass Bridge and so to Haddington and Edinburgh. Those going from the Kimmerghame area to Edinburgh were more fortunate than people travelling north from Newcastle or Berwick by this route, for the latter had to cross the Pease Burn before reaching Cockburnspath, an extremely hazardous and precipitous stretch of road which often became so congested and dangerous that no traffic could get through at all. For the third means of getting from Kimmerghame to Edinburgh you started off quite differently, going west to Polwarth instead of north to Duns, continuing westwards to Channelkirk, some twenty-six miles from home, and when you had baited there, turning north-west by Soutra Hill to Dalkeith and on to Edinburgh. Coaches could, under favourable conditions, negotiate this route, as they could the easterly post road by Cockburnspath.

A typical journey in the summer by the westerly route took eleven hours, including the stop for a midday meal: 'I came from Edinburgh about 11, dined at Ginglekirk and came home about 10 at night'. Another summer trip, this time using the central route, took rather less: 'I left Edinburgh about 10 o'clock, bated at Gifford Hall and came home about 5 o'clock having halted a little at Dunse'. Looking only at journeys in summertime, however, makes it sound a much easier business than in fact it was. For really bad weather could play havoc not only with the time taken but with everything else as well. If the conditions made you lose your way, it was sometimes necessary to get help from a guide, and on several occasions this was done at Preston, where there must have been local people able and willing to give assistance of this kind. But even in this sort of difficulty, problems we are quite unaccustomed to could arise. Losing the way on one journey on Fogo Moor when returning from Edinburgh, George and Sandy 'called at a house there and with difficulty enough got a fellow to show us the road. They are generally afraid of being prest to be soldiers'. Late in January 1695 there was a particularly bad spell of weather when George urgently needed to go to Edinburgh: 'So I sent to my Brother [in Duns] to know what travelling he hears it is. John Murdo brought me word there was no going by the wester way, but that some were gone this day by the post road, but that it is ill getting to it'. It was on this occasion that, as we have seen in Chapter 4, he 'sent to Blackader for a loan of his black sword, and his cloakbag, saddle and maille pillion'. He set forth four days later: 'I took horse in the morning betwixt 7 and 8, being resolved if possible for Edinburgh. It snowed all the time as we went to Dunse . . . Capt. Cockburn told me I would have ill travelling, and advised me to get a pair of light boots . . . I went to Preston and ther took a guide, one James White. We had very deep snow, and very oft were forced to walk above the knees in snow'. Fearing to spoil his black mare he left her at Haddington, and hired a horse there for the remainder of what was clearly a very difficult and unpleasant journey.

Hiring horses could be a bit of a gamble as well. In October 1697 in Edinburgh George had arranged to do this for his trip home: 'When I came to the stable the two horses I had bespoke were so sad-like I durst not venter on them, so I sent for others, which made it ten o'clock before I came away. The horse I got was the worst ridden jade I ever crost, would many times stop and not stir till my man came up and whipt her up behind'. And overloading even a good horse could have disastrous results. In November 1699 his sister in Edinburgh told him in a letter that she was returning Robie's pony with Andrew Watherset, with some prunes and tobacco and powder for George's wig. But Andrew 'having ridden not only himself but another fellow with him on the pony, and having beside had my things on it, it fell in some water with them as it was no wonder and the things, particularly the tobacco and powder, are spoilt'. Then there was the problem of what to do if your horse became ill on a long journey. This happened to George on his way to Edinburgh in May 1702. After he had dined at Gifford Hall, his black horse took 'the batts'. They gave him ale and brandy, which did no good. Then the smith there tried to bleed him in the roof of the mouth, but, being drunk, did not succeed in making him bleed. 'I caused run an elsine thro' his nose which bled pretty well. All this did nothing, so I give him a pint [puff] of tobacco at the fundament which gave him great ease, so I stept on gently to the toune.'

There had been other and even more serious hazards in the troubled years earlier in the seventeenth century, when Royalist or Parliamentary troops thought nothing of simply commandeering teams of horses on or off the road, and coaches used to go in 'broken convoy' so that some at least might hope to reach their destination; but by the 1690s this particular risk no longer applied. But what about highwaymen? It may seem odd to those of us brought up on tales of Dick Turpin that in all the huge volume of George Home's diary there is no mention of any occasion when either he or his friends, on horseback or in coaches, were robbed on the highway. It must have been because there were not the rich pickings available, on the roads they used, to attract this kind of attention. One writer facetiously remarks that any highwayman seeking to ply his trade in Scotland at this time would probably have starved to death, through having to lie in wait so long before any traveller worth robbing turned up. But, as we shall see, there was the occasional mail robbery. And George himself did not often make long journeys entirely alone, usually being accompanied either by his man or by a friend or two; but this may have been more because he liked company, or to run less risk of losing his way, than for reasons of personal safety.

The journey from the Kimmerghame area to Edinburgh was not, of course, the longest that might sometimes have to be undertaken. There was the much longer trip to London, on which the diary provides no information, because this was one of the times when George Home kept his notes in a pocket book that has since disappeared. However, as guides to the route and the time taken going on horseback from Edinburgh to London, two examples of widely separated dates may be quoted. Twenty-two-year-old John Maxwell of Pollok has left a record of the first part of a journey from Edinburgh to London starting on 13 April 1670. He got as far as Dunbar on the first day, carried on to Berwick on 14 April, where he dined at the postmaster's, and thence to Belford. On 15 April he went from Belford to Morpeth, and on the 16th reached Newcastle, sleeping at Durham on the 17th and reaching Allerton to stay the night of the 18th. On Tuesday 19th he dined at Boroughbridge and stayed that night at Ferrybridge. On Wednesday 20th he crossed the Trent to a place opposite Marnam, and he reports being nearly drowned in getting over the river, by which time it was nearly midnight, but the record then ceases.[1] A fuller but much later guide is provided by an extremely interesting set of directions for a servant bringing horses from Redbraes to Ealing around 1737. Because of the unusual nature of the information it provides on the route to be taken and the places to stop at, it is worth giving in full:

1. Bait at Milnfield.
   Night at Whittinghame.

2. Bait at Morpath.   Mrs Smith's.
   Night at Newcastle.   Mrs Spratt's.

3. Bait at Whitesmoks.
   Night at Ferryhill.   Thomas Linn.

4. Bait at Darlington.   The King's Head.
   Night at Northallerton.   Mr Richardsone.

5. Bait at Borrowbridge.   The Crown.
   Night at Wetherby.   The Angell.

6. Bait at Ferrybridge.   Mr Whirrell's.
   Night at Duncaster.   The Angell.

7. Bait at Eellpyhouse.
   Night at Newark.   Sareson's Head.

8.	Bait at Grantham.	The George.
	Night at Stamford.	The George.
9.	Bait at Milton.	The Angell.
	Night at Bugdon.	The George.
10.	Bait at Baldock.	
	Night at Hatfield.	The George.

'From Hatfield or Barnet, which is 7 miles further upon the high road, take a guide to bring you to Ealing near Brintford.

All the journeys are very short. The 10 day is the longest, so they must sett out early.'[2]

To possess a coach of some kind became, in the 1690s, very much of a status symbol, and everyone who could afford the initial cost and the running expenses hastened to acquire one. Such a luxury was quite beyond George Home's reach, but he cheerfully accepted lifts in other people's coaches, and as a result on some of his journeys to and from Edinburgh he sat in a coach for at least part of the way. As befitted a passenger who could not aspire to own one himself, he noted in his diary the shortcomings of his friends' wheeled vehicles. Sir John Home having just returned from a visit to London, George went to Blackadder to see him on 1 July 1698: 'He came home in a Calesh he had bought, and two good-like mares'. But a fortnight later, after being given a lift in it to Hutton Hall, he 'found it very uneasy'. A few months later when he went to the High School Wynd in Edinburgh and saw the Calesh being mended, he comments drily, 'it has too many gimcracks about it'. As in the early days of motoring, breakdowns in privately-owned coaches were frequent, and there are many references in his diary to having observed, when he himself was on horseback, a coachload of his more affluent friends sheltering in a cottage or an inn while repairs were being carried out on their coach, or while they were waiting for a hackney carriage as replacement. Nevertheless, there is more than a tinge of jealousy in the diary entries recording the Chancellor going to a funeral or to the races in his Berlin, and of pride when he himself accompanies Jerviswood and his Lady to the races in their newly-acquired chariot, which, when he joined them going to Polwarth House a few months later, had mysteriously been demoted to 'chariotte'. Apart altogether from the status angle, a coach could be a mixed blessing, for as we have seen, some routes were not fit for travel by this means, and some weather conditions ruled it out also, as when in September 1702 'My Lo: Chancellour came home on Munday night or at least the length of Greenlaw and lay in Slaps, the water being so great they could not get thro the coach'. On the other hand, if you had gout and riding became impossible, wheeled transport might be the only alternative, as when in January 1703, staying at the Hirsel with his father the Earl of Home, 'My Lo: Dunglass is expecting a Hackney coach from Edinburgh, being troubled with gout'. Nevertheless, a long journey in a coach over rough roads, in the days before suspension problems had been mastered, must have been a very uncomfortable experience indeed. The particular difficulties resulting from the combination of bad roads and bad weather are highlighted in several graphic accounts of seventeenth-century coach travel given by Dr Rosalind Marshall in *The Days of Duchess Anne*.[3]

Those of George Home's friends whose coaches are mentioned in the diary — the Chancellor, Jerviswood, Blackadder and Swinton — were all fairly well-to-do, and such ownership must have entailed quite heavy expense. As to the initial outlay required, not much information is available. An advertisement in the *Edinburgh Gazette* for 13-16 April 1705, though not specific as to price, clearly implies that the cost will be considerable: 'There is a Fine Chariot lately come from London, with a pair of Harness to it, to be sold at a good Pennyworth: any person may see the said Chariot calling at Deacon Brotherston's harness maker in the Canongate or at Robert Lauder's without the Water-Gate'.[4] We know that the Jerviswoods, moving to London in 1714, did not take their coach with them (travelling there by stage-coach), but bought one in London for £55 sterling.[5] London is, indeed, thought to have been the place where most of the best-quality coaches were made — many of them in Long Acre — but there were several people described as Coachmakers in Edinburgh at this time. To be added to the initial cost, then, there would probably be the expense of getting the coach from London to Scotland. The Jerviswoods paid £5.3s. for this in 1699, but Sir John Home, when he bought a chariot when visiting London, brought it back to Berwickshire himself.[6] Harness might or might not be included in the price of the coach, but a much greater expense was that of the horses to pull it — Blackadder, when buying his Calesh in London, purchased, as we have seen, 'two good-like mares' at the same time. We do not know what they cost him, but in June 1695 the Polwarths paid £108 'to my Lord Rankiler for a galdin to the coatch' plus £1.10s. in drink money for his man. Repairs, as already noted, seemed to be frequently required, and these were likely to be expensive. Scott-Moncrieff observes, in editing Lady Grisell Baillie's accounts, 'the constant mention of purchase of glass for the chariot, and the frequency with which new wheels have to be got', the state of the roads being a major cause.[7] He estimates the keep of a horse for a year in the period 1692-1704 as under

£60. We can glean something from the Compt Book regarding some of the running expenses coach owners had to expect in 1694-95. The Polwarths had two coaches, their black coach and their Berlin. When they were in Edinburgh they brought the Berlin and its coachman from Polwarth House. Apart altogether from his normal wage, this meant paying for his bed in Edinburgh, costing £1.8s. a month, as well as a coach house for the Berlin at £3.18s. a month. (Thirty years before, the Archbishop of St Andrews had paid £2.4s. a month.[8]) On the question of repairs, all we know is that what seem to have been routine ones cost between £3 and £9 a time, and that when wheels were needed for the Berlin in May 1695 the bill was £30. In June 1695 'helpin mending the cotch harnisen' cost £12.12s. Material at 20 shillings an ell 'for the cotchman's bige coat' cost £9. And one must not forget how vulnerable and expensive the glass on coaches was; one of the first items mentioned in Grisell Baillie's published accounts makes this clear, for in November 1693, £60 was paid 'to a glass to a chariot'.[9] John, later 2nd Duke of Argyll (1678-1743), was certainly not influenced by considerations of this kind in altogether rejecting coach travel (though he could well afford it), strapping the skirts of his coat round his waist, ignoring foul weather, and going everywhere on horseback.[10] On several occasions he used Polwarth House as one of his staging points on journeys south; he did this, for instance, on 23 October 1699.

What about the inns where weary travellers and their horses could eat, drink and if necessary sleep? The one at Channelkirk must have been something quite special, a place where you were most likely to meet your friends on journeys to and from Edinburgh, as when on 20 March 1695 George Home 'came from Edinburgh about 3 o'clock and to Gingelkirk that night. Swintone and his Lady were in the upper house: I visited them and Swintone came to my quarters and sat with me some time'. In addition, we know that it was sometimes patronised by Berwickshire visitors not journeying anywhere else, but just for its own merits. For in the Compt Book we hear that Julian took the bairns there for a meal, so it must have been both suitable for children and welcoming to them. At this distance in time, however, it is difficult to learn more about it, or even to discover just where it was sited. Archibald Allan's *History of Channelkirk* (1900) mentions Annfield Inn, on the old Edinburgh road, and two dwelling-houses opposite once used as a public house. He also quotes *Reminiscences of the County of Haddington*, published ten years earlier, where a more likely candidate seems to be 'The old hostelry or roadside public-house of Hunter's Hall or Lourie's Den [which] was on the south side of Soutra Hill . . . It is said that Prince Charlie's highlanders, on the march to England, stopped and got refreshments there. On its signboard there was the representation of a huntsman blowing his bugle-horn with the foxhounds around him, and the following doggerel lines of poetry:

> Humpty, dumpty, herrie, perrie,
> Step in here and ye'll be cheerie;
> Try our speerits and our porter,
> They'll make the road the shorter;
> And if ye hae a mind to stay,
> Your horse can get guid corn and hay.'[11]

It seems to have been noted in the late eighteenth century for gipsy fights and carters' squabbles — not the kind of place the people with whom George Home associated would have patronised.

So far we have talked about coaches in private ownership, but in Edinburgh particularly there had been coaches for hire for some time. In the Household Book of James Sharp, Lord Archbishop of St Andrews, on 21 September 1663 there is a payment of £2.8s. 'For ane hakney coatch from Leith to Edinburgh being late and dark'.[12] By the 1680s the council's regulations governing this were becoming both detailed and comprehensive. On fares, in October 1686 the hire of a coach from Edinburgh or Canongate to Leith was to be twelve shillings for up to three passengers, but four shillings more if there were four; and waiting time for the coachman was to be paid for at the rate of seven shillings per half-hour. The sides and floor of the coach must be reasonably wind and weather-proof. And coachmen, like carters, must provide a stated amount of 'graville or chingell' to repair the highway.[13] In July 1704 it was the dangers resulting from the furious driving of coaches that were causing particular concern, it being noted that frequently the drivers were either boys or at least not strong enough to manage the horses. So new regulations were introduced requiring all masters of coaches and coachmen in future to drive 'slowlie and softly and not violently'; and those under eighteen were only to be allowed to function as postillions, not drivers. The requirement about wind and rain was reiterated, and cleanliness was added to it; to enable transgressors to be identified, coaches were, as before, to have a number marked on the back.[14] Even more stringent regulations were introduced in September 1711. Unhired coaches could only stand in one place, below the lower end of Mill's Square, with their horses unbridled (equivalent to the 'for hire' sign on today's taxis). Anywhere else, horses must be bridled, to indicate that they were *not* for hire. Fines appropriate to all breaches of the regulations were laid down, including five shillings sterling and the servant to be publicly punished for refusing to hire the coach to anyone asking. The new scale of fares — all, of course, now in sterling — laid down sixpence as the rate for each coach-hire within the city and suburbs; waiting-time after the first hour was also chargeable at sixpence. The Edinburgh-Leith fares were now much more elaborate, summer being much cheaper than winter, and the time of day also making a big difference. Charges to any part of the country not exceeding twelve miles were also specified. Every driver must have a copy of the regulations in his pocket, and constables were there to assist them if necessary in obtaining the correct fare from their passengers.[15]

For longer distances, if you did not want to occupy a whole coach, but merely one or two seats in it, and if you could fit in with a timetable, the advertisements in the news sheets often provided the information you needed. In the *Edinburgh Courant* for 25-28 July 1707, for instance, an advertisement addressed itself to all those 'desireous to pass from Edinburgh to Newcastle or from Newcastle to Edinburgh or any part of that road'. They were told who to seek out in each of these towns, and informed that 'At both places they may be furnished with a New Coach and Good Horses every Munday and performs the whole journey in 3 days (if GOD permits) and sets forth by five in the morning. Each passenger pays 30 shill: ster:'[16] Once in Newcastle you might, of course, decide to travel on to London by sea — this seems to have been quite a common means of accomplishing that leg of the journey; back in 1664 *en route* for France, Crossrig rode to Newcastle, went from there to London by sea, and then rode on to Dover.[17] Or, of course, you could go the whole way from Leith to London by sea. In the *Edinburgh Gazette* for 30 March-3 April 1699 we are told that 'The Providence Paquet Boat, John Baptie Master, will sail for London upon the 12 day of this instant, goods or no goods. Whoever would transport themselves or good thither, may speak with the said Master at his House, at the Head of Burges Close in Leith the ship being now clear to take in goods'.[18] There was also, of course, the stage coach. In January 1699 George Home tells us that Jerviswood and his Lady had come from London to Newcastle by stage coach where a coach of the Lord Chancellor's met them and brought them to Polwarth House. Later, when they moved from Edinburgh to London in 1714, five places in the stage coach for that journey cost £22.10s. sterling, plus 2s.6d. for booking money and £2.7s. for excess luggage; only 20lb per person was allowed free of charge.[19]

We have seen how people travelled around. How did news get transmitted? Newspapers in Scotland originated because the authorities in 1661 were anxious to counter what they regarded as false news which was being spread by opponents of the régime. This, at least, was the avowed motive behind the decision of the privy council to authorise Robert Mein to produce a weekly news sheet, *Mercurius Caledonius*. Mein was a man of many parts. He had followed John Mein (who had first held the position in 1649) as postmaster in control of the Edinburgh Letter Office, but along with many other Scotsmen connected with postal affairs had been dismissed in 1655 by Cromwell's compliant president of the Scottish council, Lord Broghill. However, he was reinstated in the position after the Restoration, and busied himself establishing new postal links with other parts of Scotland and with Ireland. He was also a merchant, and in 1666 asked the Burgh council for permission to take on a second apprentice to train in public postal affairs and so qualify through that specialism as a freeman of the burgh. Perhaps because Mein himself had too many irons in the fire, *Mercurius Caledonius* ceased publication soon after having been launched, and a gap of some nineteen years followed before the first number of the *Edinburgh Gazette* appeared, headed 'From Tuesday the last of November to Tuesday 7 December 1680', and this once-a-week paper certainly lasted for at least four issues, the National Library of Scotland having what appear to be the only copies of these very early *Gazettes* that have survived. Up till now it has been believed, on the authority of Chambers' *Domestic Annals of Scotland*, that there was then a gap of almost a further nineteen years until James Donaldson relaunched the *Gazette* around January or February 1699.[20] However, in this as in many other respects, George Home's evidence enables us for the first time now to put the record at least partially straight. For he adds this note at the end of a letter he wrote to Patrick on Thursday 26 October 1693 from Kimmerghame: 'Pray my L° let this give my humble service to My Lady, Mrs Julian, Anne and Jean. I have restored a Gazette I very innocently stole last day knowing nothing of it till I found it in my pocket when I came home'.[21] So the *Edinburgh Gazette* must have been in existence at least five and a half years before its supposed relaunching in 1699, and thirteen (not nineteen) years after it was thought to have ceased publication in 1680. Moreover, we now know that the *Gazette* was also still being published between October 1693 and its 'resuscitation' in 1699, from information in the diary itself, for on 26 January 1696 George went to a coffee house in Edinburgh 'to see [not hear] the news', and he records having seen *Gazettes* at Polwarth House where 'I got them all read' on 31 March 1698, while he himself 'got 2' the following April. And there is also evidence in the diary of *competition* at a much earlier date than had previously been thought; for on 12 January 1696 George reports having a copy of the *Edinburgh Flying Post*.

Something approaching a relaunch (though after only a very short, not a nineteen-year, interval) seems to have taken place when James Donaldson, who had been a merchant in Edinburgh, then an officer in the Earl of Angus's regiment who had been badly wounded at Killiecrankie, obtained from the privy council the exclusive right to publish a newsletter, which was again called the *Edinburgh Gazette*, its heading proudly proclaiming, as before, 'Published by Authority'. For how long it then ran we do not know, but issues with dates in April and June 1705 have survived, and we also know that there was again competition from the *Edinburgh Flying Post* and from an even more serious rival, the *Edinburgh Courant*. At all events, on 6 March 1707 Donaldson, under the title *Edinburgh Courant Reviewed*, explained that the *Gazette* had become unprofitable as a result of this competition *and* of its policy of delaying publication of news items until they had been authenticated. This policy he proposed to modify on restarting the *Gazette* on 25 March 1707 on a twice-a-week basis. How long it then survived, again we do not know, though an issue appeared on 2 September 1708. It is doubtful whether it was still running when the *Courant* had the good fortune, after the death of its editor Adam Boig in January 1710, to acquire as its new editor a month later no less a person than Daniel Defoe.

The particular issue of the *Gazette* forming a loose paper between the pages of Grisell's manuscript account book can be taken as typical, and a brief description of its contents will give some idea of what news sheets of that time contained. It is Number 7, from Monday March 20 to Thursday March 23 1699, a single sheet measuring 12 by 7½ inches, printed on both sides by James Watson in Craig's Close. No price is indicated (which seems to have been the universal practice); but in the 1705 issues we are told where to buy it — the Exchange Coffee House. The first item on the front page is a proclamation asking persons who are willing to undertake duties as commissaries and paymasters of the Forces to appear at a specified date and time so that a suitable choice can be made. There then follows a series of overseas news bulletins, the places from which news is reported in this particular issue being Cadiz, Madrid, Philipsburg, Brussels, Paris, Milan, Warsaw, Dresden, Ghent, Liège, Cologne, The Hague and Basle in that order. This takes up considerable space, and does not leave much room for news from London. From Edinburgh, after recording the arrival and departure of ships and what they were carrying, and that parliament is adjourned to the 14th of June, several other items are thought worthy of inclusion.

First, a woman said to have murdered a girl some time previously in the Potter-row was brought to trial, but the evidence against her not being clear, further proceedings were put off until 10th April. Then it is noted that some gipsies and robbers were seized and committed to prison, together with a woman from Dumfries for murdering her child. The last Edinburgh news item is really an apology from the *Gazette* itself: 'In regard the Honourable Directors of the Indian and African Company have signified their Displeasure at the Contents of that Letter which was inconsiderately inserted in our last concerning the Settlement of the said Company. 'Tis hoped that none will lay any further stress on the said Letter than as a private person's Information to his Friend, of what he heard at Random on that subject, how ill forever grounded or expressed'. Donaldson was, indeed, put in prison at the instance of the privy council the following June for printing several things in the *Gazette* which were not truths, and for which he had no warrant.

In what little space is left after all this, advertisements are printed. To start with: 'STOLN, upon Munday the 13 of March out of the Lord Chancellour's house in Niddry's Wynd, a pair of large Silver Candlesticks, of weight 44 ounces the two, being 22 ounces the piece, having engraven upon them a cypher of PM with an Earl's Crown above it. Whosoever can find them shall have a sufficient Reward'. Whether they were ever found we do not know, but this advertisement is clearly the reason why this particular issue of the *Gazette* got caught up in Grisell's Compt Book. There is a similar item to finish the advertisement section: 'STOLN, on Tuesday last from James Miller Coppersmith in the Cannongate, two or three Copper Kettles, about 3 or 4 gallons each, several peices of old Copper and Brass, some forged Iron work, and a Light coloured cloth Coat, with some other Cloaths. Whoever shall give notice of the above mentioned goods (so as they may be got again) to James Lindsay, servant in the Flanders Coffee House near the Cross, shall have three Dollars reward'. In between these reports of stolen goods, a stolen 'Blew-gray Mare about 14 hands high, eight years old, a slough over her near Eye . . .' and 'LOST in the Cannongate . . . a Black Spaniel Dog with a Collar about his neck . . .' For the mare 'a sufficient reward' is offered, for the spaniel a dollar.

As to books, a short description of the Isthmus of Darien is reported to be in the press; an auctioneer advertises an auction due to take place some weeks later, so that prospective sellers can still have particulars entered in the printed catalogue to be made available to prospective buyers; and there is an appeal for old manuscripts, charters and ancient writings to be taken to the Advocates' Library, either as gifts rewarded by honourable mention in catalogues, or for sale with payment to the seller's satisfaction. A house, garden and orchard near Edinburgh are to let. And finally the White Paper Company of Scotland, having brought their manufacture to great perfection, have considerable quantities of Imperial Writing, Printing and Packing Paper available at 'their Ware House at Heriot's Bridge in the Gras Mercat'.

One type of advertisement surprisingly missing from this particular issue is the cure-all, but this omission is remedied a few years later when many appear: 'The most successful Plaister for Curing all sorts of Gouts', 'The Sovereign and never failing Eye Water and Salve which infallibly cures all Pearls, Bloodshot, dry and Watering Humours', and 'The most Famous Odentologick Tincture which in a few Moments perfectly Cureth the Tooth-ack, how Violent and Intolerable Soever, not only by removing the pain but it maketh a true and resolute Cure . . . keeps good for several years and may be carried anywhere by Sea or Land'. Strangely enough the same price, half a crown, is quoted for each of these remedies. A different class of customer is aimed at when giving notice 'to all Noblemen and Gentlemen who have a mind to build a small Turky Bagnio or Humum, for Sweating and Bathing, after the Turkish Fashion' to enquire for Mr John Valentine at the Chirurgeons Bagnio in the High School Yards. And we are down-market again with 'the famous Spanish Balls, which do effectively remove all Spots and stains out of all silk, woolen and Linnen cloaths'. An unexpectedly early mention of Britain's national beverage is found in the *Gazette* for March 30 to April 3 1699 — 'John Coventry, who lived several years in East India, hath gotten per last ship from thence a parcel of very fine Imperial Tea, and some preserved cloves'. Travel and transport (including hearses and mourning coaches), not mentioned in the issue we have examined in detail, frequently appear a little later, as do by 1707 the sale and mending of musical instruments, where 'Ralph Agutter of London, lately come to Edinburgh, Musical Instrument-maker, is to be found at Widow Pool's, perfumer of gloves, at her house in Stonelaw's Close, a little below the steps; makes the Violin, Bass Violin, Tenor Violin, the Viol de Gambo, the Lute Quiver, the Trumpet Marine, the Harp; and mendeth and putteth in order and stringeth all those instruments as fine as any man whatsoever in the three kingdoms, or elsewhere . . .'

An altogether different kind of advertisement appears with distressing frequency from 1699 onwards: 'John Irons, a Soldier in the Regiment of Fuzeliers commanded by Colonel Archibald Row, deserted on Saturday 18 March from Dysert in Fife with his commerade's Cloaths and Linnen, his own Red Coat, Cape, Sword and Belt'. Two guineas' reward and reasonable expenses are offered for information on his present whereabouts leading to his arrest.[22] Detailed descriptions of what some wanted person looked like and was wearing are sometimes given, as in the issue of Thursday December 21 to Monday December 25, 1699: 'Alexander Leitch of Colkipen, formerly a Drover, a slender Man of middle stature, Pockmarked, Flaxen Haird curling a little, his Eyes gray and full, his Wrists smal and hard, he wears an upper Coat of natural black Wooll, a Weast-Coat with a high Neck and Buttons of a kind of Berry, topped with Silver, a High-Land Laced-Band about his Neck, a little Blew Bonnet on his Head, a Broad Sword, and a pair of Pistolls, one of them with a round Butt, indented with Silver both Butt and Barrel, Run away with Ten Thosand Merks, most of it in Gold; he has along with him a Boy carrying a Bagg, whose upper Coat and Bonnet are much like to his own; whoever can secure the said Alexander Leitch shall have Thirtie Pound Sterling Reward'.

There is, as we have said, no indication of the price charged for individual copies of the *Gazette* — perhaps it varied according to where you bought it. That it was either felt to be expensive for what it contained, or hard to come by because of scarcity of copies, is shown by George Home's diary entry for 4 April 1698, which records that Lord Polwarth sends his copy to Captain Murray at Duns, who passes it on to Cavers, who then gives it to George Home. We know that some years later, in 1725, the second Earl of Marchmont's factor paid 3½d. sterling for two newspapers. And we do have some guide as to what a year's subscription cost, at least when Edinburgh Burgh Council were the buyers. For it is on record that, on 5 February 1690, they had been paying William Mein the postmaster £10 sterling for newsletters 'delivered be him to the Lord provost and the Magistrats each post day . . .' However, 'they will receave noe more newes letters from him in any tyme coming seing they will be served at ane easier rait . . .'[23] This 'easier rait' proved to be £6 sterling, since on 4 April in the same year a new 'generall postmaster', John Blair, was allowed this amount annually for providing the newsletters and gazettes formerly furnished by William Mein.[24] This provides further evidence for the view that the *Gazette* or its equivalent must have been on sale in the 1689-90 period, since the council would hardly have paid two people in succession for services they were not in a position to perform.

Although George Home and his friends were avid to get a sight of the *Gazette* as soon as it came out, they obviously found its news coverage unsatisfactory. Time and again after reading it he observes that there was no news of any note therein (e.g. on 6 July 1699), and this may well have

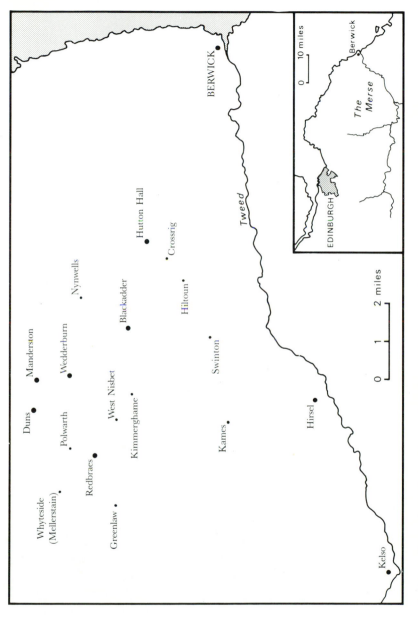

1. Map. A section of the Merse showing the relationship between seats mentioned in the text (adapted from Timothei Pont's manuscript map, from the Blaeu Atlas, 1654).

2 may 96 connt of resets at pole swit Neias

3 It from Ellon Bronn in peterur of hir swit ...
16 It from Iacndrs bronn of theint of Bleichs bank
18 It from Robin Iacndrson of ... mile rent
19 It from Duned smith of pole swimuns rent
   It for we ciltren pole work

There is one attempt ... furnished to my Lord
... by Alexander Biggar at the Gregounr ...
aug: 30. and sept: to nichull 1696 ...

b £57: 12:

2. Facsimile of a page of the Compt Book, showing Grisell's and her daughter's handwriting.

3. The home of the Polwarths. From an old picture at Marchmont. At different periods the house was styled Redbraes, Polwarth House, Redbraes Castle (illustration is from Margaret Warrender, *Marchmont and the Humes of Polwarth*).

4. Grisell Kar, aged about 18, by Scougall, c. 1660. Probably a marriage portrait (by kind permission of Miss N. J. Tweedy Bratt).

5. Grisell Kar, in middle life, attributed to Medina the Younger (private Scottish collection).

The Lady Grisell Kar, wife of Patrick Earle of Marchmont &.
Lord high Chancellour of Scotland. An.º Dñi 1698. Ætatis suæ 55.

G. Kneller E. ques pinxit.   I. Smith fecit 1699.

6. Grisell Kar, Countess of Marchmont, aged 56, from a painting by Kneller
(National Galleries of Scotland).

7. Patrick Hume, 1st Earl of Marchmont, aged 57, from a painting by Kneller. The crowned oranges can be clearly observed (National Galleries of Scotland).

8. Patrick Hume, 1st Earl of Marchmont, aged 79, by W. Aikman. Regarded as one of Aikman's finest male portraits (National Galleries of Scotland).

9. Lady Grisell Baillie, aged 44, by Medina (National Galleries of Scotland).

10. Anne Hume, artist unknown (National Galleries of Scotland).

11. Andrew Hume, aged 13, artist unknown (National Galleries of Scotland).

12. Jean Hume, aged 12, by J. Scougall (National Galleries of Scotland).

13. David Home, Lord Crossrig, aged 61, attributed to Medina the Younger
(University of Edinburgh).

14. Lady Margaret Hope of Hopetoun, in her mid-forties, by Medina, 1694 (National Galleries of Scotland).

15. Sir Thomas Kar of Cavers, attributed to John Scougall. Grisell's father
(National Galleries of Scotland).

16. John Carre of Cavers and West Nisbet. Probably the portrait referred to by George Home in his diary (see Chapter 3, p. 34). This suggests that Scougall was the artist and that the date of the portrait was 1696.

been partly because of the extreme care an editor had to exercise not to include anything likely to upset the authorities, and partly because of the over-zealous withholding of news, as already mentioned, until it was authenticated. Whatever the reason, we know that George Home himself, for example, placed much more reliance on the foreign news he received regularly in letters from his friend the Laird of St Ebbs, whose source seemed to be leakage from the postal authorities in Berwick; in return, George periodically sent him presents, often in the form of books in which he had expressed an interest. And for home news, Patrick and his many political contacts in Edinburgh formed a prompter and more reliable source of information on what was really going on than did the *Gazette*. Rather late in the day (the last day of December 1703, in fact), his attention was drawn to a still better source of authentic foreign news, when a friend sent him by John Lidgate, his man, the October issue of the *Monthly Register* or Memoirs of the affairs of Europe (Vol. 1 no. 10) which, it seems, he writes in his diary, 'began in January last — it gives ane account of what occurs in Europe every month'.

Since letters played such a vital role in the dissemination of news of all kinds, it is important to understand how they were transmitted in Scotland at this time. If you were a private individual, trying to ensure that the letters you had written reached their destination as quickly and as safely as possible was almost a daily problem. If a relative or friend happened to be on the point of going to the place, you hurried up and wrote only a brief letter so that, in our terminology, it 'caught the post'. If it was a really urgent letter you sent a manservant with it, but gave him instructions to bring some necessities back from the shops on the return trip, to make his journey more worth while. Then there were the carriers, usually several in every place of any size. Though their main activity was the carrying of goods, they were glad to take small parcels and letters as well. If the route to be traversed was not where an official postal service was provided, there was no problem. But even on a post route a letter to accompany a parcel could be sent by carrier; if, for instance, you were a physician, all you needed to do was to send a routine supply of pills with each of your letters. Moreover, the restriction was often ignored in any case. A carrier who was anxious to extend his business might offer a particularly attractive service, and George Home reports that 'one Robert Haliday in Fogo, who carries ordinarily for Nisbet folks, has promised to come here about my letters and bring the answers coming'.

Apart from special arrangements only available to the privileged few, such as letters on burgh council business being conveyed by messengers acting on instructions, the main alternative to the methods already described was, of course, the postal service. Starting as the King's post and only gradually made available to the general public, the service was naturally at first confined to trunk routes, as it were, and it was to these that, as we have said, the state monopoly was restricted in the early days. It was also to these routes that many other provisions, such as allowing free passage to the post, providing horses if required, and so on, applied. In Scotland a key figure in postal history was Sir William Seton of Kylesmuir, made master of the posts by the privy council in 1615, who carried out some improvements in the face both of opposition and unlawful competition from outsiders, but whose more ambitious plans could hardly be fulfilled in the troubled years that followed. After the Restoration, however, when Robert Mein regained his position as postmaster in the Edinburgh letter office, Mein was also given responsibility for instituting or re-instituting a whole range of postal routes both within Scotland and between Scotland and Ireland. His son William, who for a time, as we have seen, was under contract to supply the council with newsletters, used his position in the Edinburgh letter office to hold up mail from Ireland, and was sent to the Tolbooth by the privy council in October 1689. John Graham, a very conscientious postmaster general whose £1,000 a year salary was insufficient to meet his expenses in travelling to establish new postal centres, ran into debt, and on his death John Blair (an Edinburgh apothecary) took over the position, not on an annual salary but on a seven-year tack or lease, the terms of which proved much more advantageous to him. He seems to have succeeded in extending postal services to most parts of Scotland without financial loss to himself by the time of the Post Office Act of 1695. Henceforth the Master of the General Letter Office in Edinburgh, to be entitled His Majesty's Postmaster General, an office 'to be let to tack by the Lords of His Majesty's Treasury and Exchequer', would be in control of a national public postal service where the scale of charges for the carriage of letters (varying with distance *and* with the number of separate sheets) was laid down in the Act itself. The circumstances in which letters might be sent by other agencies without infringement of the state monopoly were left much as before, so that the use of carriers, express delivery and so on continued, though prosecutions for any actual illegality became more numerous as time went on. On the express delivery exception, George Home reports that, one day in November 1697 in Edinburgh, having heard that Patrick was 'going to send away a flying packet', he hurried back to his chamber and wrote a letter to go with it. The very opposite of express delivery was presumably 'Aiken the footpost' whom he occasionally patronised, though such a person was, of course, part of the official postal service.

Speed and safety were both, naturally, of prime importance. Although as now, the authorities quoted examples showing how expeditious the service was — reports of English parliamentary proceedings sent from London on a Saturday were said to reach Edinburgh by the following Thursday — there were widespread complaints of slowness. And robbing the mail was not unknown, as when in 1690 the postboy (a 44-year-old) carrying his postbag was intercepted by two masked men brandishing pistols when proceeding from Cockburnspath to Haddington, who bound him and tied him to his horse by his feet.

No less important than speed and safety could sometimes be confidentiality, and here the public postal service was held in particularly low regard. Confidentiality was indeed a perennial difficulty. With us, jokes about postmen reading all postcards or steaming letters open with the kitchen kettle are only told about remote country areas. In seventeenth-century Scotland you could be almost certain that, if entrusted to the post, your letters would be read in transit. So if they were going to contain any comments on political or other sensitive matters you took precautions in advance. Someone you could trust delivered a key letter to the person with whom you regularly corresponded, in which there was a code to be used in interpreting all subsequent letters. Each prominent political figure would in future appear in your letters as some harmless relative, friend or village character, whose utterances, or the opinion you might hold about them, could not possibly be used by the authorities as an excuse for taking proceedings against you.[25]

The confidentiality of a letter was, indeed, given scant attention even in circumstances where, one might have thought, higher standards should have applied. On a September Saturday in 1702, George Home was in the company of friends at Polwarth House, amongst whom were Sir Patrick Home of Renton and his son John. John, accidentally and without being aware of it, dropped a letter in the dining-room which Marchmont's son, Lord Polwarth, apparently picked up, read, and then dropped again. True to the conventions to which we are accustomed in opera on the stage, George decides this is too good an opportunity to miss: 'I chanced to see it and took it up. While I was considering whether to give it to his sone or read it, because I fancied it might be some thing about the matter in hand, My Lord Polwarth came and told me of the thing (not knowing I had the letter) that he had found it and read it'. Nor did either of them have the excuse of not knowing whose letter it was, being clearly 'backt for Sir Patrick Home of Renton, Adv.'

Envelopes were rarely used; you simply folded the sheets, put a seal on them, and wrote the particulars of the addressee on the back. There were, of course, no adhesive stamps. Letters sent in Scotland before 1693 normally had no handstamps to indicate place of origin, markings usually being handwritten and sometimes giving the price payable for transport, but not the means used. The Bishop mark (originally devised in the 1660s by Henry Bishop) began to be used in the Edinburgh Letter Office in August 1693 at least on mail for England. It was oval-shaped and gave the day and month, but not the year of posting.[26] On the question of cost, Sir Hugh Campbell, the Laird of Calder, receiving regular correspondence from his eldest son in London, always paid five shillings per letter when lodging in Edinburgh in 1689; and when a few years later his son was in Aberdeen, the rate from there to Edinburgh was three shillings.[27]

CHAPTER 8

New Beginnings

The particular combination of factors in the 1689 situation was almost a textbook recipe for ensuring the worst possible government of Scotland. First, you had a newly-installed King knowing nothing of that country (he never set foot on its soil at any time), dependent on advice from a variety of sources, preoccupied with military campaigns overseas, fearful of doing anything to offend powerful interests in Scotland's more important neighbour, England. Secondly, there were a number of old-established landed magnates prepared to go to almost any lengths to further the interests of their families and supporters. Third, there was the return to the political scene of a group of exiles, intensely suspicious of those who had stayed behind and collaborated to a greater or lesser degree with the now dethroned Stuarts. Fourth, there existed a fatal division of political power and influence between Edinburgh (where the privy council, parliament and the general assembly of the Church held their meetings) and London, the permanent home of the court, and the temporary one of every Scotsman angling for high office or indeed for any kind of preferment. One could hardly have designed a better setting for weak and vacillating government, chronic political uncertainty, intrigue and double-dealing.

Not to fish in these desperately troubled waters was, however, to ensure your indefinite exclusion from any say in what happened to Scotland, your district or your family. And Patrick, deprived for so long of the opportunity of exercising his skills as a political animal, and furthering the causes which had necessitated his going into exile, could hardly be blamed for availing himself of the opportunity. Moreover, like the other exiles, he had every reason to hope for more and more tangible rewards for having so steadfastly supported the House of Orange. By the time the first session of the Convention Parliament began in June 1689 — with the Duke of Hamilton and Sir John Dalrymple in Edinburgh holding key positions and obstructing each other at every turn, while Secretary of State Lord Melville seemed bewildered, ineffective and out-of-touch in London — the stage was set for Patrick to try his hand at political manoeuvring. On the surface he tried to give the impression to the Secretary that he was a loyal and devoted supporter of the new administration, as we can see from one of the letters he sent him from

Edinburgh.[1] It is dated Thursday 27 June 1689, and the first thing to strike the reader is its inordinate length, no less than 2,500 words. Patrick's speeches were often said to be too long, and his political letters showed the same tendency. The tone of the letter can be illustrated by quoting a couple of sentences: 'I had and have some reputation here among the honest men, especially those of midle rank; and I thank God it has still encreased hitherto. As I made use of it what I could for the publick good, so I did for your Lo. in particular'. So, in giving him an account of the debates that were taking place, Patrick was at pains to point out how Melville's actions as Secretary had been twisted by his enemies so as to appear obnoxious to his true friends, and how misunderstandings and dangers of this kind could be avoided in future by pursuing the policy outlined in the letter. The writer was steadfastly acting a friend's part, 'but sure it broke me up by day and night; I slept as little as any in the city'. And he himself was worried about his own enemies at court in London deliberately distorting *his* speeches and voting behaviour in Edinburgh to his grave political disadvantage. He spoke of the great discouragement 'of being mistaken by those I was struggling to serve, as I judged by my wife's letters' (she was in London at this time).

From very early on in its deliberations, however, this first session of parliament was in fact dominated by the highly organised opposition group known as the 'club', and in this activity Patrick was a prime mover. The strategy and tactics of the club were indeed so successful that the administration was virtually paralysed, an outcome greatly helped by the extreme unpopularity of the Dalrymples, and by Hamilton siding with the opposition whenever it suited him. The result was deadlock — court proposals could not be put into effect, acts voted by Parliament were negated by failure to secure the necessary royal assent. Parliament had to be adjourned, and in the interval before its next session the activities of the club reached their peak in the drafting of, and securing of seventy-two signatures to, an address to King William asking him to give his assent to all the acts that the adjourned Scottish Parliament had voted. Needless to say Patrick was not merely one of the signatories, but had played a major role in the whole affair. He had reason to feel embittered about his treatment up till then. The forfeiture of his estates had still not been legally rescinded, and although while in exile he could claim to have been just as helpful in advising the future King as other Scotsmen like Melville and Dalrymple, the seat he had been given on the privy council could hardly be said to match the rewards they had received.

Patrick, along with several other disgruntled politicians, decided to use the opportunity of parliament no longer being in session to see what a visit to London could achieve, not so much in furtherance of club objectives as towards the fulfilment of some of his own. He went there in the autumn of 1689, and though we do not know in any detail how he conducted his campaign, he was clearly satisfied, by the time he returned to Edinburgh in January 1690, that his rewards for past services would now at last begin to come in. He had, in a very real sense, been bought off as a leading member of the opposition by promises of future benefits on which (justifiably, as it turned out) he placed full reliance. But it was part of the deal that he should not publicise his change of sides. From that time forward, however, he supported the administration, and did all he could to persuade those club members who had worked most closely with him (Forbes of Culloden, Dempster of Pitliver, Monro of Bearscrofts and Drummond of Riccarton) to do likewise. The face-saving aspect of his change of sides was made the easier by Melville being given the post of commissioner and therefore the management of the session of parliament beginning in April 1690; for Patrick had always, both in public and in private, claimed to be a Melville supporter. And Melville, after the ineffectiveness he had shown in 1689 as Secretary operating from London, proved a much better strategist in his handling of affairs in Edinburgh in 1690, if only through making such sweeping concessions to presbyterianism that he could hardly fail to succeed in breaking up the rather disparate interest-groups of which the 1689 opposition had been composed. Then, one by one, Patrick's rewards at last came in. Before the year 1690 was out the forfeiture of his estates had been legally rescinded, he had been made sheriff of Berwickshire and, to him most important of all, had been elevated to the peerage as Lord Polwarth. His letter to Grisell telling her of this last development is dated from London 13 January 1691.[2] The letter begins 'My dearest', but in the course of it he calls her 'my heart', the same term of endearment used by his father when writing to his mother more than forty years before.[3] 'His Majesty said a while ago that before he parted for Holland he would put a mark of his favour upon mee whereby I might know that he is resolved to support my family; I could not guess what he meant, but at Christmas he explained it and gave me a gift of pension of 400 £. sterling by year to be doing with, as he expressed it, and a patent to be Lord Polwart, with an addition of an orange crowned in my armes'. He goes in some detail into the question of precedence on formal occasions, and tells her that 'you and my daughters take your place frankely before the ladys of baronets, Lords of Session, and all inferior gentlemen . . .'

Nevertheless, 'your way of liveing need not alter a bit from what it was; you keep a page, get a footman, and when you visit in foul weather . . . call a coach as you used . . . for we ar but a little step forward of our rank from what we were before, and so much the better, yet our place is not doubtful as before and ther is an ease in that'.

He takes the opportunity of a reliable person taking his letter from London to Polwarth House, to explain his latest views on two other family matters. As regards his daughter Grisell and her wish to marry Jerviswood, 'I must tell you I have other thoughts of his pretensions to my G. than I had formerly, if our neighbour be not concerned, which perhaps you can judge of by this time. You see how close you need to keep this letter, I pray do it'. What this meant was that though originally he would have preferred his daughter to marry another suitor, if that suitor had now in effect withdrawn from the competition, then Jerviswood (whose career prospects and financial position had now very much improved) would be quite acceptable. Another matter on his mind was a wife for his soldier son Patrick who was abroad: 'You know matches of great means ar not to be got there [i.e. abroad] and if I can here get a person of honourable birth, of sober breeding, of our own principle of religion, handsome and lovely, such as a young man may like for a bedfellow, with 10,000 or 8,000 £ sterling portion, wee need the less care for what disapointment the change of Court humour can give us, and to speake as it is, such a match cannot miss to strengthen our Court interest and make what we expect that way the more secure. My dear, I am hopeful God shall so bliss and prosper my honest and innocent design as you and I, my son, and all who wish well to us shall be satisfied in it. Therefor I desire you to discourse fully with my dear Patrick . . .'

Things no doubt looked bright to him, therefore, on his return from London to Edinburgh in 1691, to take part on Melville's side in the political infighting between him and Dalrymple. Whether parliament was sitting or not, there were meetings of the privy council to attend, and plenty to keep him occupied. And he could bask in the sunshine of now being a peer of the realm. Looked at from the standpoint of King William and his advisers, Portland and Carstares, who had to think of his future usefulness rather than his past services and loyalty, there was not as much to rejoice about. For however welcome his 'secret' change of sides from January 1690 onwards may have been, however sincere their promises of rewards both now and in the future, there was certainly at that time no question of giving him any major (or even relatively minor) governmental post. Viewed as a possible candidate for high office, Patrick suffered from three major handicaps. First, he was neither a magnate nor even a relative of one, so appointing him would do nothing to satisfy or even to please any of the powerful houses — Hamilton, Queensberry, Atholl, Argyll — the support of *some* of whom was increasingly recognised to be essential if the government of Scotland was not to be paralysed. Secondly, although he had been active in politics all his adult life, and had a small number of devotees like Forbes of Culloden, he could not be said to be the leader of any sizeable group whose votes the court could secure by giving him preferment. And thirdly, he lacked administrative experience. There had been a brief period after the church settlement of 1690 when, as Riley explains, 'the administration of the kingdom seems quite rapidly to have been drawn into the hands of a so-called 'secret committee', an inner clique of Melville, his sons and their anti-Dalrymple allies: Cardross, Ruthven, Polwarth, Forbes of Culloden and James Stewart'.[4] He had earlier been appointed a privy councillor, but a number of other possible candidates for office could also claim that. There was also the part he had played in planning the strategy of the club in its early stages. Nevertheless, as a potential holder of high office, his abilities remained very much an unknown quantity.

There were, of course, some points in his favour also. He was a staunch presbyterian, but not such an extreme one as to want the kind of persecution of episcopalian and nonconforming clergy calculated to cause alarm and antagonism in England. His loyalty to the revolution and to King William personally was unquestioned. And in addition there was nothing of note he could be accused of having done or of having failed to do, which potential enemies could use against him. The disadvantages of appointing him to high office clearly outweighed these advantages, however, and such preferment would certainly never have come his way but for the extreme disappointment of the King's advisers at how badly their successive attempts to secure the good government of Scotland had worked out in practice. The rivalry between the Melville and Dalrymple interests had been completely disruptive, and James Johnston and Dalrymple failed to work in harness as Secretaries either. Tweeddale as Chancellor had, perhaps unjustly, been made to take the blame for the Act establishing the Company of Scotland trading to Africa and the Indies, anathema both to the King and to powerful English interests. Added to this, the deaths of Hamilton in 1694 and of Queensberry the following year, and Atholl's need to keep in the background, meant relatively new blood representing those particular magnate interests. So in the reconstruction of the administration in 1696 Atholl's son and heir Lord John Murray was brought in as one of the

Secretaries, and Sir James Ogilvy, a man with some administrative experience who was unlikely to prove a thorn in Murray's (or anyone else's) side, as the other. Argyll was appointed to the treasury commission. Tweeddale, who admitted he was rather tired of it all, was eventually removed from the office of chancellor. Who was to replace him? It was decided to choose someone whose appointment would not actually offend any important interest, who was not a threat to anyone, and who could, it was hoped, be trusted to keep a low profile, to stick closely to the guidelines laid down for him, and not to indulge in an orgy of nest-feathering. So the choice fell on Patrick who, on 1 May 1696 became, against all the odds, Lord Chancellor of Scotland.

In the years before this totally unexpected elevation to such high office, Patrick's duties both as member of parliament and privy councillor had, of course, made it necessary for him to spend some months of every year in Edinburgh, and in doing this he was sometimes on his own and sometimes accompanied by his wife. One clue as to where in Edinburgh he stayed is provided by an entry in George Home's diary. Writing on 6 March 1700, he says, 'I dined with Mr Francis Montgomery and his Lady. They are now in Nidrie's Wynd in the house which was the Chancellour's'. This address was, as we have seen, given in the *Gazette* advertisement about stolen candlesticks in 1699. We do not know the sort of rent he paid, but George tells us on 29 January 1695, 'I sought a chamber in the stair where Ninewells lodges, in the back of the Court of Guard, and found one in Mrs Johnstone's . . . They ask 14 shillings Scots for it a-night'. A year later he was paying rather less — 'I payed Mrs Kessburn 52 sh.sterling for 52 nights' [i.e. 12 shillings Scots a night]. On this basis, the rental for a year would have been between £219 and £255, not unlike the £240 Lauder of Fountainhall had been paying as a yearly rental in 1673 (though two years earlier he had paid £320).[5] When, after their marriage, Lady Grisell Baillie and her husband settled for a while in Edinburgh, their yearly rental, as mentioned in Chapter 5, was £200, but when their financial position improved some years later they took a £400-a-year house.

The centrally-situated dwellings in Edinburgh were, of course, flats (hence the regular entries in the Compt Book for 'clinin the clos'). Graham, writing his *Social Life of Scotland in the Eighteenth Century* in 1899, gives a highly-coloured description of what they were like which is probably quite near the truth: 'In the flats of the lofty houses in wynds or facing the High Street the populace dwelt, who reached their various lodgings by the steep and narrow 'scale' staircases, which were really upright streets. In the same building lived families of all grades and classes, each in its flat in the same stair — the sweep and caddie in the cellars, poor mechanics in the garrets, while in the intermediate stories might live a noble, a lord of session, a doctor, or city minister, a dowager countess, or writer; higher up, over their heads, lived shopkeepers, dancing masters, or clerks . . . The dark, narrow stairs, with their stone steps worn and sloping with traffic, were filthy to tread on; and on reaching the flat where lodged an advocate in extensive practice, eyes and nose encountered at the door the 'dirty luggies' in which were deposited the contents which, as St Giles bells rang out ten o'clock, were to be precipitated from the windows'.[6]

Just as would be the case today, the advertising description of flats to let sounds very much more attractive than the reality. The three examples that follow, though they concern lodgings beyond the reach of Patrick in his less affluent days and of George Home throughout his life, are worth quoting; all were advertised in 1708.[7] The first is from the *Edinburgh Courant* 31 May-2 June: 'The Great Lodging lately possesst by the Duchess of Buccleugh in the Parliament Closs, consisting of Seventeen Fire Rooms with Closets and many other conveniences is to be set in haill or in part'. In the same news sheet, for 1-3 November, 'There is to be Sett a large Lodging at the foot of Fowls Closs consisting of eight Fire Rooms besides closets with cellars and garrets, and a convenient stable'. And in the *Edinburgh Flying Post* for 1-2 November, 'There is a lodging at the Abbay Hill to Set with Five Fire Rooms, Three Closets, a Good Seller under the Ground, a Brew House, Store House and a Stable will hold Twelve Horses'. One of the reasons, incidentally, for our not always being able to say exactly where the Polwarths lodged in Edinburgh in the pre-1696 period is that the address on letters they wrote from there is merely given as 'Edinburgh', with no further details; though when writing from home 'Polwarth House' is always stated. And the Compt Book is equally unforthcoming, for it merely says 'sins we com to Ednbro' or 'sent to Ednr' and never provides an address. If George Home's experience is anything to go by, however, they probably had a number of different Edinburgh lodgings at various times.

Turning back to the problems faced by Patrick and Grisell in the period immediately following their return from exile, the dominant one was undoubtedly shortage of money — they had used up virtually all their scant resources during their stay in Holland. When their plight was made known to those of their friends who could do so, assistance was soon forthcoming. One of these was Marie Douglass (the 'Ladykins' already discussed in Chapter 4), and on 30 November 1689 she wrote to Patrick, 'Your ladie to whom I have not time to write tonight writ to me this day fortnight showing me you and she intended to come away shortly and that you needed to provide yourselves of several things but would not adventure but as you had advice from me, I have layed down methods for sending you a bill of a hundred pound sterling which I intend to pay at Candlemas. Let me know if you need more'.[8] They must have received a great deal of financial and other help from the same quarter in the months and years before this, for when Grisell is writing to Secretary Melville on another matter at the end of June 1689 she says, 'The Lady Hilton is a person hes don mor for Sir Patrick and me, when we was in truble, than all the relations we had; and hath often venterd both life and fortoun upon our account'.[9] Then there was the problem of where the children could stay while Patrick and Grisell had to attend to things in London and in Edinburgh, and here Grisell's sister Isobel Scott was particularly helpful and had some of them to stay with her in Galashiels. By the end of 1690 Grisell herself was back in Polwarth House and able to assess the damage done during the years when the family seat and estates had been forfeited and granted to the Seaforths. For some of the exiled lairds the results of alien occupation of their lands had been quite devastating. Sir John Swinton, as we have seen, found the family estate denuded of its old timber and otherwise dilapidated.[10] Polwarth House and its lands do not seem to have suffered quite as badly as this, and by 17 September 1691, when the wedding of daughter Grisell and George Baillie of Jerviswood took place there, things were more or less back to normal. What sort of house was the family seat of the Humes of Polwarth? No one seems to know just when it was built, though an Inigo Jones influence in its design has been suggested as a possibility. It was quite a large and pleasant-looking building. All that remained in the 1890s were two back wings, the eastern one having originally held the kitchens and the western one the laundry.[11] For hearth-tax purposes in 1690 it was rated at seventeen hearths, a middling-sized mansion.

We know quite a lot about the change of name of the family seat from Redbraes to Polwarth House. When Sir Patrick Hume, our Patrick's father, wrote a letter to his wife on 8 March 1648 it was from Redbraes;[12] but our Patrick wrote a letter dated at Polwarth House on 2 October 1682.[13] So somewhere between these two dates the seat of the Humes of Polwarth ceased to be known as Redbraes, as it had been up till then, and became known as Polwarth House; and it continued to be so called for the remainder of that century. Strangely enough Margaret Warrender, writing the history of the family in 1894, was quite unaware of this, and never uses the second name at all. And even more surprisingly, the editor of the extracts from Grisell Baillie's Household Book, published in 1911, talks of her having been 'married at Redbraes' in 1691 although this description had ceased to be used a long time before that; and although he never mentions the correct post-1680 name, it *is* used by Grisell herself on page 258 of the extracts, where she refers to 'taking Nany (Nany Christy, her cook] to Polwarth Hows' in June 1695. Her mother calls it by that name throughout the Compt Book, and so does George Home in the 1694-1704 parts of his diary. The diary, indeed, enables us to pinpoint exactly when it was decided to revert to the old name, but accompanied by 'Castle' instead of 'House'; for early in April 1704 George Home reminds himself that henceforth the term Polwarth House must no longer be used, the new styling being Redbraes Castle. And from that date onwards Patrick's letters from home all have this revived and more imposing address at the top. It may seem odd that when the name Polwarth had been used by the family for at least twenty years, and probably much longer, 'House' was not simply replaced by 'Castle' and the desired improvement in status achieved more simply. But there was a reason for this, which was that the ruins of *another* Polwarth Castle on a different site were still to be seen, so Redbraes had to be brought back to enable the term 'Castle' to be introduced.

The setting was a delightful one. The house stood, in Margaret Warrender's words, 'in a . . . sheltered situation, at the top of a steep bank facing the south and was approached by a noble beech avenue . . . and on the sunny slopes in front lay the garden. The box-edgings of the old flower-border have grown into a tall hedge, and the long rectangular lines of clipped yews are now large single trees'.[14] On the Polwarth estates a number of quarries were worked. Peat was in fairly plentiful supply, and was used as fuel by most people, only the relatively wealthy using coal, which was very expensive as it had to be fetched a long way. Robert Home, the local minister, writing his report for the Statistical Account of Scotland about a century later, reveals something which must have been so commonplace that no one else had mentioned it: 'The village of Polwarth is situated on very wet, and even swampy ground, so that in almost every house they have a hole dug to collect the under water, which requires to be often emptied in wet weather; and yet the inhabitants are very healthy, being neither subject to rheumatic nor aguish complaints'.

To put Polwarth House and its estates in the *social* context of the locality in which it was situated, we are extremely fortunate to have manuscript poll-tax records from 1695 of the two relevant parishes, Polwarth and Greenlaw.[15] These two are amongst the very few records of this kind surviving either for Berwickshire (where the others are for

Ayton, Edrom, Eyemouth, Swinton, Hutton and Lauder), or for any other part of the Borders or the rest of Scotland. As an added bonus, partial 1690 hearth-tax records have also survived for the same two parishes; though in the case of the hearth tax, manuscript material is also available for a number of other Berwickshire and for Roxburghshire parishes.[16] The only *printed* records of this kind relevant to the present study are those for two Edinburgh parishes, Tolbooth and Old Kirk, edited by Marguerite Wood and published by the Scottish Record Society in 1951 (who have also published more recently, in 1981, some West Lothian hearth-tax records together with county abstracts for Scotland).

Had Margaret Warrender known about and used these manuscript poll and hearth-tax rolls for the parishes of Polwarth and Greenlaw when she wrote her book on the Marchmont family in 1894; and had the same happened when Robert Gibson in 1905 wrote Greenlaw's history, *An Old Berwickshire Town*, it would have made a very great difference to the value of their two studies. The particular types of information contained in these tax rolls can be briefly explained. To begin with, the lists of pollable persons provide an official record of all the adults (and some of the children) living in these parishes at that time. In some measure this amounts to a population census, and as nothing of that nature is otherwise available until nearly a century later, the central importance of these lists can easily be seen. And they not only give us a head-count, at least of adults; they also tell us what these adults did for a living, or whether they were spouses or grown-up relatives with no paid work. Nor is this all, for they also provide some indication of their range of income. And as a supplement, the hearth-tax rolls give some guide to the relative size of different families' living (or living and working) quarters. The reason why this information was recorded, or can be derived from the particulars given is, of course, because of the nature of the two taxes. As noted in Chapter 1, the tax on hearths enables us, in a rough way, to assess the size and importance of the buildings concerned, much as we might use today's rateable value taken from lists available for the public to consult. The poll tax was graduated, and took some account of ability to pay, so that information bearing on that aspect of the matter had to be collected and recorded in order to assess the poll tax payable in each person's case. The minimum rate of tax (if you were a pollable person) was six shillings Scots, and this applied to all spouses irrespective of the status of their husbands, and to other adults with no source of income. The treatment of under-age children for tax purposes being rather peculiar, the safest plan is not to use that particular information for our needs. The tax treatment of living-in servants, however, provides invaluable data on what they earned. For the tax they were due to pay was to be calculated as one-twentieth of their annual fee and bounteth (the latter meaning shoes and clothing provided by the master, but not including liveries). In other cases, the tax graduation provided a rather looser link with income or social standing, which varied somewhat from one parish to the next, but familiarity with the conventions being employed soon enables one to translate the data into usable terms. It can be seen, therefore, that the information provided by these two sets of rolls for these two parishes is so wide-ranging, so generally reliable and, for the usable categories of people, so complete, that no adequate picture of the social and economic structure of the inhabitants of Polwarth and Greenlaw in the 1690s could possibly be given without them.

An analysis of the 1695 poll-tax data for the parish of Polwarth, roughly equivalent to a population census, shows 64 households living there with 192 adults (104 men and 88 women). One reason for the small discrepancy between the numbers of the two sexes is because of the inclusion in our figures of apprentices, who were always male. The commonest description of the pollable persons listed was 'servant', by which was meant a living-in servant paid a yearly fee; there were 56 of them in the parish — 35 men and 21 women — another reason for the slight preponderance of men in the total population of the parish. Seventeen of these servants, incidentally, were in Polwarth House itself. The next most frequent description, other than 'spouse', was 'cottar', of whom there were 30, 21 men and 9 women (the latter presumably being widows). Other agricultural categories represented were hinds (7), herds (1) and gardeners (1). There were 5 weavers (with 2 apprentices), 6 'sutors' (cobblers), 2 shoemakers (who had 3 apprentices between them), 1 tailor, 1 wright (with an apprentice) and 1 smith. Eight people were described as 'tenants', 3 of whom — David Smith, Robert Old and Robert Fairbairn — were fairly substantial ones. All but 30 of the 88 adult women in the parish were only charged the minimum poll tax of six shillings each, because they were either spouses or women given no particular status category. At the other end of the poll-tax scale were Lord Polwarth, paying the appropriate £40 odd, his two adult sons counted as being at home at this time (Alexander and Andrew), taxed at £34.6s. each, David Smith, tenant in Polwarth Mains, paying £3.17.6 and George Holiwell the minister, rated at £3.6s. It may seem odd that, even though Polwarth was only a village, there were no butchers or bakers listed, but one reason was that in these respects people in the area were either reasonably self-sufficient, or else they could afford to go further afield to buy just what they wanted.

The parish of Greenlaw had three times the population of Polwarth, which was basically a village with the laird's house, as against a market town with a number of surrounding small settlements. Greenlaw parish had 208 households in 1695, with 578 adults, 301 of whom were men and 277 women. As before, the commonest description of the people listed was 'servant' and of these there were no fewer than 158 in the parish, 94 men and 64 women. Cottars numbered 59, 36 men and 23 women; and there were 22 hinds and 17 herds. As many as 67 of the men polled were described either as tenants or as heritors (excluding those given this description together with a craft, who have been counted with their fellow-craftsmen). Some of these had quite high-valued rentals — four of them £394 or over, four more between that figure and £212, eight more between the last figure and £106. There were, as in Polwarth parish, more weavers than craftsmen of any other kind (15, one having an apprentice), followed by 7 tailors (3 apprentices), 4 smiths (1 apprentice), 3 masons, 3 wrights (all with apprentices), a shoemaker and a dyer (both of whom had apprentices). Again, it may seem even more surprising than in the case of Polwarth that no butchers or bakers are mentioned, there being a market town in this parish. Another strange omission is that of alehouse keeper, for we know of at least one in Greenlaw town — Robert Brounfield, from whose wife, Grace, Grisell Baillie bought substantial quantities of ale in 1707.[17] The explanation is not, of course, that some tradesmen escaped being listed and paying their poll-tax, but simply that the trade was for some reason occasionally not added after the head of the household's name. Like Polwarth, Greenlaw had its kirk and therefore its minister; but it also had something that a mere village normally lacked, a notary. The position in respect of millers is slightly confusing. Three people are *described* as millers — George Wilson at Slaigden Mill, William Wood in Greenlaw and John Ovens in Halyburton. In addition, James Thomson is the principal tenant in Castlemilne and Tenandrie, though he is not described as a miller and seems to have kept too large an establishment to be one. So there were certainly three, and may possibly have been four, mills operating in Greenlaw parish in the 1690s.

So the stage is now set for viewing Grisell's Compt Book, which she started keeping (though there are loose papers of earlier date) in November 1694, nearly four years after her husband became Lord Polwarth, and eighteen months *before* he was so unexpectedly made Lord High Chancellor of Scotland. By a curious coincidence the earliest surviving volume of the manuscript of George Home's diary also begins in 1694; the poll-tax records we have been looking at for Polwarth and Greenlaw were compiled only a few months later. From around 1694, therefore, we are no longer groping our way in comparative darkness, but have a flood of light provided by a combination of three unique manuscript sources — the Compt Book, the Diary, and the Lists of Pollable Persons. The next chapter shows the kind of help the first of these can provide in showing what housekeeping was like at that social level in the Scotland of the 1690s.

CHAPTER 9

Housekeeping and the Compt Book

There are three special features of the Compt Book — that it was kept by an amateur and not by a professional, by a woman and not by a man, and that Dame Grisell herself had some unusual characteristics as an account-keeper — each of which deserves separate consideration. Take first of all the amateur/professional contrast, which can be brought out by looking at the earliest surviving account book of John Dickson, factor to the first two Earls of Marchmont, begun in 1724.[1] In that book, Dickson divides both expenditure and money received into a number of categories, each of which is kept quite separate from the others. Thus certain pages are devoted to house and land rents, and in those pages all the relevant particulars are recorded. On the expenditure side, one set of pages details items relating to the maintenance of the Earl's family and stables, another those concerning repairs to Redbraes Castle (the post-1704 name, as we saw, for Polwarth House), another the expenses of a particular funeral, and so on. By contrast, although in the Compt Book an attempt is made to deal with receipts and expenditure on separate pages, within these two broad categories there is hardly any subdivision, items merely being recorded according to the date of their happening or of their being recollected. And the detail, or lack of it, in each item depends on the mood of the moment rather than on any policy related to the uses to which the information will subsequently be put.

A second important feature of the Compt Book arises from its being kept by a woman. There seem, as noted already, to be only three other surviving seventeenth-century account books not kept by men in the whole of Britain. Two of those three, as it happens, relate to the Scottish Borders. Lady Grisell Baillie, the eldest daughter of our account-keeper, left records of this type covering the period 1692-1733, of which substantial portions have been reproduced in the volume published by the Scottish History Society in 1911. Dame Magdalen Nicolson's little manuscript book, relating to southern Roxburghshire in the period 1671-93, formed the subject of A. O. Curle's article in 1905, appearing in identical form in the *Proceedings of the Society of Antiquaries of Scotland* and in the *Transactions of the Hawick Archaeological Society*. For our purposes, however, it was necessary also to consult the original manuscript of her account book, which is in the National Library of

Scotland.[2] And the third and only other known case of a seventeenth-century account book kept by a woman relates to Furness in Lancashire. Sarah Fell was one of the seven daughters of Margaret Fell, a convert of George Fox's who, after her first husband's death, married the founder of the Quaker movement. Being George Fox's step-daughter gave Sarah's manuscript accounts a very special importance to the Society of Friends, resulting in the whole of them being published in 1920.[3] A team of research workers spent several years searching for information on all the people and all the transactions recorded by Sarah Fell for 1673-78, and the volume of well over six hundred pages resulting from their labours, and from the faithful transcription of everything in her manuscript, is a model of how archive material of this kind can and should be presented and interpreted for the benefit of future generations.

The Compt Book with which we are concerned, then, increases the number of surviving seventeenth-century account books kept by women from three to four. It should perhaps be explained that a number of account books *apparently* kept by women are not in their own handwriting and were in fact kept by someone else, as with Lady Marie Stewart's Household Book, for keeping which George Monorgun was responsible.[4] And this brings us to another special feature, or group of features — those peculiar to Grisell herself. Take first of all the question of handwriting, a distinguishing characteristic of which is that each letter is separated from its neighbours, while the space between adjacent words is often no greater than that between the individual letters of which the words are composed. And that is not all; the formation of the letters themselves is very strange. Thus 'a', 'o', 'e', 'i', and sometimes 'c' as well, are so alike that it is difficult to tell them apart, and the same holds good for 'u' and 'n'. Indeed almost the only letters where doubt never arises are 'l', 's' and 't'. Then there are two difficulties associated with her spelling. First, she quite often spells the same word differently in adjacent lines, and the same is true of her spelling of surnames. In the latter case we are fortunate to have her daughter's index to the Compt Book, which is in practice largely an index of surnames; for as Lady Grisell Baillie knew most of the people referred to by her mother, it seems sensible to follow the spelling in the index where it differs from that in the text itself. A second difficulty arises because the spelling of very many words is not the one to which we are accustomed. Here the explanation is not some idiosyncracy of Grisell's, but merely that she was spelling them in the way they were pronounced in lowland Scotland at that time. So that what may look to us like words misspelt are in fact the equivalent of recorded everyday speech, perfectly suitable for the down-to-earth business of keeping one's own accounts, but not used by the writer in correspondence or on more formal occasions. In the same way, the use of words that have since fallen into disuse is not peculiar to Dame Grisell. Here the volumes of the *Dictionary of the Older Scottish Tongue* are particularly helpful. For words in the later part of the alphabet, not yet reached by that dictionary, the recently-published *Concise Scots Dictionary* has been valuable. Altogether, despite the problems presented by handwriting, spelling and archaic Scots words, it has proved possible by intensive work over a period of time to discover the meaning of almost everything contained in the Compt Book.

Once having overcome the difficulty of deciphering Grisell's hand-writing, one attractive feature of the Compt Book is the homely phraseology in which much of it is expressed. Many examples could be given, but one will perhaps suffice. She realised that it was important always to have a receipt for money or goods handed over to anyone. Her name for this was a 'tikat', but this was not unusual, since the term 'ticket of receipt' was quite widely used in Scotland at this time. In one case, however, after providing Robert Lunham the candlemaker with 24 pounds in weight of tallow, and obtaining a ticket from him, she was subsequently unable to find it, and her entry recording this reads 'I fanci I have lost it'. A professional account-keeper would certainly not have explained things in these terms, but even in the context of accounts kept by the only three women whose records have survived — Grisell Baillie, Magdalen Nicholson and Sarah Fell — the phrasing is unique.

Other entries in the Compt Book form an interesting mix of formality and informality. For example, she refers to her children as Janei (or 'my Janei'), Anne, Julian, Andra and Sandi, and only when it comes to her eldest daughter does a note of formality begin to creep in. She had been married some three years before the Compt Book began, and appears as 'my dochter' or 'my dochter Jerviswood', never as 'Grisell'. What to us might seem an excess of formality is also found in all entries relating to her own husband, who is never 'Patrick', but always without exception 'my Lord'; where Patrick is mentioned, she is referring to her eldest son, not to her husband. When it comes to people who are not members of the family — and the account book contains mention of as many as 150 of these — a Christian name and surname are all that she considers necessary, occasionally supplemented by where they live or what they do for a living. With servants, it is either a Christian name alone, or the full name, sometimes adding their position in the household. Only teachers and a few (presumably important) tradespeople have Mr or Mrs preceding their names; and on the rare occasions when a medical man's name occurs, it is naturally preceded by 'Doktar'. One highly idiosyncratic feature of Grisell's account-keeping, not found in any other set of accounts, is that no columns of figures are ever added up, so that there are no totals to transfer, or carry forward, or compare. She clearly had no intention of recording total receipts or total expenditure, and indeed the form in which she kept her accounts makes it difficult for anyone else to engage in such exercises either, even after doing the essential simple arithmetic. Though all this detracts from the value of her record from a strictly bookkeeping point of view, it does not, of course, make it any the less important in terms of the significance in every other respect of the mass of material it contains.

Another unusual feature of the Compt Book is probably to be explained less by Grisell's personal predilections than by external circumstances. For it contains three types of subject-matter one would not expect to find in a lady's accounts or memoranda. The first of these three types of case unexpectedly falling within her province is the following:

Count of mil stons sold sumar 95

It sold to Jams Lomsdanne in farbarn mile 2 stons about 12 eincis thik the other 9	24.00.00
It sold to Samul Thomson on with thee kies on at 12 eincis thik at	14.00.00
It to Mr Eferhal on 12 encis thik at	14.00.00
It to Hutan mil 8 incis thik at	11.00.00

Not all quarries in the area were extracting stone of a quality suitable for being put to this use, but on the Polwarth estate there was one where the material they were quarrying had the necessary characteristics. What is surprising, therefore, is not so much that they had these products to dispose of, but that the details of their sale should be recorded in an account book kept by the lady of the house.

A second and equally unexpected type of transaction for such inclusion is the purchase of lime, essential both for agriculture and for building and repair work (including the pointing that constantly needed to be done), but hardly something coming within the housekeeping province as normally understood. Two loose papers were summarised in one sentence in the Compt Book and then thrown away, so all we know of them is that they listed '348 loads of lime carried from Lothian in summer 1696' and contained 'the names of those who carried it'. Because of the poor state of roads and tracks, the lime, like coal, had to be brought by packhorse. And if we guess that a horse load must have weighed between two and three hundredweight, and that it was not fetched in the shorter winter days, this means that between 700 and 1,050 cwt of lime a year must have been used at Polwarth House. Each of the larger tenants had, as we have already noted, an obligation to provide on a stated number of days (varying with the size of his holding of land) a horse and someone to lead it, but as there was coal and much else needing transport as well, for some of the lime-carrying people we should now call private contractors had to be relied upon. Although making such arrangements would normally, as with so much else, have been done by the laird or his factor, it is clear from the Compt Book that in the 1690s Grisell saw to this matter herself. In June 1695 there were entries 'to David Hamelton in part of payment of his bargn of leim' and 'to Johne Robison on the count of his bargon of leim', the cost per load sometimes being nine and sometimes ten shillings. Neither Hamilton nor Robinson was from the parishes of Polwarth or Greenlaw, so they probably came from Duns. Such bargains would need to be made quite frequently during the summer, and by undertaking this along with other activities normally done by men, together with similar arrangements for the carriage of coal, Grisell must have taken quite a load off her husband's shoulders.

The third type of material one would not have expected to find in a book of accounts kept by the lady of the house consists of details of daily wage payments to the workmen doing their regular and mainly outdoor work on the estate. It is clear from the wording used in these entries that she sometimes gave out the wages to the workmen herself, and sometimes through one of her servants.

Having glanced at these three unexpected types of entry in Grisell's Compt Book — the sale of millstones, bargains for the supply of lime, and details of the payment of wages to the outdoor day labourers on the estate — how are we to account for their inclusion? They are all matters normally handled either by the laird himself or by his factor. One possible explanation would be a gap of a few years between factors. We know that in the very early 1690s Robert Craw, described as 'my Lord Polwarth's Baillie', provided information for hearth-tax purposes; but there may have been an interval between his going and the arrival of John Dickson as factor in the late 1690s. And it may be significant that, out of the 150 different people referred to in the Compt Book, there is no mention of either of these two men or of anyone else described in these terms.

These, then, are the special features of Grisell's Compt Book, making it a rather different kind of manuscript from any of the others coming into the same general category. Every account book has its own peculiarities, but in her case the way she kept it, and the kind of information she recorded in it, have first of all had to be described before the help it provides in understanding domestic life in seventeenth-century Scotland can be appreciated. We can now proceed to analyse the contents of the Compt Book, bringing in at every stage relevant evidence from other sources, and making a broad division between entries where sums of money are *not* mentioned, and those where they are.

To begin our consideration of items where no sums of money are mentioned, three groups of these could be called inventories, of silver, of pewter and of 'furniture'. The count of *silver* on 20 November 1694 cannot have taken long to do. The items listed were 98 spoons, 13 forks, 11 knives, 3 tumblers, 1 tankard, 1 cup, 2 salvers, 2 rings, 6 salts, a sugar caster, a pepper caster and a mustard pot. One must remember, of course, that this was a family not long returned from exile, whose estates had been confiscated and whose fortunes were only now beginning to revive. The impressive hoards of silver, familiar to us from the records of many of the nobles and lairds of the period, had usually been built up over several generations, and could not be created in just a few years. Later on we find Patrick patronising the silversmiths of Edinburgh quite often, and having what he had bought suitably inscribed. It was the normal practice, whenever purchasing either silver or pewter articles, to trade in your old ones, and so have less to pay.

There are two counts of *pewter*, one from a loose paper dated 26 December 1691 and the other for 18 November 1695. The first speaks of the articles having been received *by* the cook, the second *from* someone who was probably the cook, so it looks as though an inventory was taken both when a new cook arrived and when an old one left. As the first count lists more types of article than the second, it is worth giving in full: 'Receaved by Wm Symenton Cook of pewter vessell from the Wardrob trenchers 35 Big dyshs 9 Mazarimes 6 Sole plates 3 ffrom the Romme below big dyshes 11 trenchers 48 one ashet-dysh one Ketle with the Cover ane other Ketle 3 pots 3 pans 5 spits 2 pair of Clips 2 frying pans 1 eggplate 1 brass scimmer 1 fleshfork 1 iron shovell 1 pair of tongs 1 large grater'. The nature of some of these articles can be explained. A masarin (the mother spells it with an 's', the daughter with a 'z') is a dish to be set inside a larger vessel; the Cardinal apparently had dishes of this kind. A sole plate is the dish in which the masarin stood (two pewter sole plates at an Edinburgh auction weighed 5½ lbs Scots between them).[5] The later inventory includes four 'sasers', dishes for holding sauce. Trenchers were the general-purpose dinner plate, hence their large number, 35 + 48 in the first inventory, 61 in the second. In this latter case Grisell had begun to write 'trenchers' but blotted it out and called them plates, perhaps suggesting that the old term for them was already on the way out. Many slightly earlier account books speak of 'timber trenchers', reminding us that, in the last quarter of the seventeenth century, wooden plates and dishes had only fairly recently been replaced by metal ones. The pairs of 'clips' referred to are hooks. And the 'wardrob' is, probably, the name of a particular room, not an article of furniture.

A count of furniture (in Grisell's terminology) means an inventory of *beds, bedding and table linen*. The longest such list, dated 20 November 1694, provides great detail in respect of categories, but she did not get round to recording the numbers in each category. The list begins with feather beds, bolsters, cods (pillows), pairs of blankets and half blankets. It then goes on to distinguish four kinds of table cloths — 'damis', 'dornik fine' (a good-quality linen cloth, originally from Dornick in Flanders), 'ordner' ones, and round ones. The servits (napkins) are also given in descending order of quality — damis, dornick, fine, 'servits for ordner use', and 'cours servits'. 'Touls' are damis, 'small dornick', or 'for ordner use'. Sheets are of three types — broad, narrow or round, but 'cod wears' (pillow cases) only of two, small or coarse. 'Cofrins' or 'courins' can be 'chalander', 'shoued', 'rund' or 'hare'. Then there are mattresses (a number being given for the first time: 2), and 'bolstrs sutable to the matresis: 2'. Finally, a 'stamped caliko tuolt', ending up with 'wonda courtins'. Eight days later she has a count of furniture sent to Edinburgh, when some quantities are entered. Twenty pillows and twenty pillow cases were sent, 17 pairs of linen sheets (broad and narrow), ten dozen napkins, six dozen towels, and other items without the quantity being specified, but a year or so earlier we are told that 21 round table cloths and 6 small ones had been sent to Edinburgh. We know more about the number of beds from a furniture count made on 8 May 1696 — there were 11 feather beds at Polwarth House and 2 in Edinburgh, with the same number of bolsters to go with them. There were also 9 'calf beds' at Polwarth House and 2 in Edinburgh, again with the matching number of 'calf bolstrs'. ('Calf' is a variant of 'chaff'). Forty pairs of double blankets are mentioned at Polwarth and 5 in Edinburgh. A few pillows are described as 'Inglis' and a small number as 'of my makin'.

The next group of unpriced items to be considered is not an inventory in the accepted sense. It reads as follows:

Count of lint and tou 20 Novr 94

It sent to Polwart of Lint pot up in half pouds	22 halfp
It sent to Grinla of Lint	18 halfp
It of lint kiped at hom	03
It of strekins to Polwart	13 pund
It of hardn to Polwart	10 pund

Novr

18 It of my doutrs Lint sent to Maldiston	11 pund
It to the strekins of this Lint sent ther	10 pund
It of the hardn of it sent ther	4 pund
It of bout Toue of hirs sent ther	11 pund

Transforming the flax grown on the home farm into linen cloth involved a whole series of processes. When the plants had ripened, they were pulled up by the roots. Then there had to be rippling, retting (steeping in water holes), scutching (breaking the bark), swingling (freeing it from its wooden particles) and hackling (combing the fibres, making them straight and smooth preparatory to spinning). All this was usually done in the home, though there was often a hackler (or heckler) in the village who would undertake that final stage of dressing. It seems probable that the lint that was made up in half pounds (Scots) ready to go to Polwarth, to Greenlaw and to Grisell Baillie in Maldiston (presumably Mellerstain) had been through all these stages of dressing. The 'hardns' were the coarser parts of the flax separated in hackling; so were the 'strekins', roughly intermediate (in coarseness or lack of it) between 'hardns' and the best lint. This is confirmed by the detail of what took place at the roup (auction) of the household goods of Andro Hog W. S. in Edinburgh in October 1691, when pairs of linen sheets fetched £4, pairs of 'straikine sheits' £2.8s., and pairs of 'harden sheits' £1.16s.[6] It is significant that though Grisell kept some of the lint for use at home, she did not do so in the case of either of the two coarser varieties. 'Tou' or 'toue' is a term used to cover all these coarse fibres separated from the lint when hackling took place.

Making the yarn into cloth was, of course, a job for the webster or weaver, and every village had one or more of them. Entries in the Compt Book about work done by them for Grisell mostly relate to woollen fabric. In November 1694 she paid £1.2s. to Thomas Angus, one of the weavers in Greenlaw, for 22 els of plaiden work, and £1.7s. 'to a weifer in Gordan for 27 els of plaidin wirkin' (plaidin being coarse worsted woollen cloth, not quite like flannel, and an ell being 37 of our inches). Quite frequently the weaver would be paid in kind, often with grain. From the weaver, cloth went to the fuller, and from him to the litster or dyer. In January 1695 the 'Litstr in Grinla' was paid £1.0.0 'for dresin my blou bad and rid scourin pladin, 27 els'. He must have been William Pearson, the only dyer in Greenlaw, who employed two domestic servants, and was training an apprentice.[7] The litster could produce more interesting colours on linen materials than on the woollen ones. But at this time Scots linen was not of good quality, the weavers being as yet unable to compete with the fine holland imported by those who could afford to do so, nor could they produce fine dornick and damask for towels and table linen.

Let us look now at some 'counts' (to use Grisell's term) of things to be drunk or eaten. It so happens that there is no record in the Compt Book of wine stored at Polwarth House, but on 21 June 1695 there is one for Edinburgh. Roughly half of it is 'Rid canarei wein' and the other half 'pam' [palm]. The bottles are of two sizes current in Scotland at the time, mutchkin (about ¾ pint today) and chopin (about 1½ pints), and there seem to have been 50 of the smaller size and 72 of the larger; a fortnight later some of it was sent to Polwarth House for drinking before the family's normal return to Edinburgh in the winter. Apart from four chopin bottles of brandy there does not seem to have been any other drink in the cellar. But there is a curious memorandum noting that '23 galons' (7⅔ of our gallons) of red wine were 'sent bak to John Sprenel', no reason being given for the return. Grisell also records that eleven bottles of wine were 'left out to my Lord when I am out of toun', but with no indication of how long that might be.

Besides baking and the brewing of ale, for both of which barm was bought at regular intervals, there is also an entry in the Compt Book about the making of cheese:

June 95   A Count of Chis
7 of June   I be gond to mak chis and on the 12 I had mead 5 in the mikel chesnort and tha day be gont to mak in a les chasnort.

There is also a brief entry indicating how an ox was shared amongst the household: 'The ox was broken upon the 27 of November 1697 in 21 pieces for the table and 10 pieces for the servants table and the head'.

As would be expected, the Compt Book reports numerous transactions relating to meal. Large quantities of oats were grown both on their own land and on the land of tenants, and most of the crop was turned into meal by Robert Knox in Polwarth Mill or by the two millers in Greenlaw parish, Jean Young in Slegden and James Thomson in Castle Mill. Both oats and oatmeal formed a widely-used currency, tenants paying part of their rent in this way, and payments of many other kinds also being made in whole or in part by this means. When oatmeal was delivered at Polwarth House from one of these local mills, the Compt Book records how much of it went to supplement what was already stored in the 'Arke' for the use of the house, how much was put aside to be sent for use in Edinburgh, how much for making 'sourkaks' (a dough made of oatmeal, left until it fermented, then made into a kind of oatcake), and so on. Each time a milling took place it is noted down how much (usually about four per cent) of the product took the form of 'grots'. Apart from weavers and others being paid for work done by receiving some of the oatmeal, there are cases where the meal may have been a gift to someone. When, for example, it is put on record that two firlots (roughly three of today's bushels) were 'to the Lady Law', it looks like a present. The same lady is the subject of an equally mysterious entry in Grisell Baillie's published Household Book — in November 1694, £1.10s. is noted 'for cariing the Lady Law's chist'.[8]

We may not know exactly why both Grisell and her eldest daughter should apparently have gone out of their way to help Lady Law on these two occasions, in November 1694 and May 1696; but we can briefly say who she was and why she would be especially grateful for help at that particular time. She was Jean Campbell, who had married a wealthy Edinburgh goldsmith in 1663. In 1683 he had purchased the estate of Lauriston, but in the same year died on a trip to Paris, leaving his widow with the problem of trying to secure repayment from those who owed him money. She had, however, more serious problems arising from her son John who, settling in London after his father's death, got into financial difficulties, his mother coming to the rescue in February 1692 by buying from him the Lauriston estate he had so recently inherited from his father. This naturally left *her* in a very poor position, which was made the more tragic by the next development in this extraordinary story, when John fought a duel with his rival in a love affair, killed him, was thrown into prison, escaped in January 1694 and fled the country. No wonder friends like Grisell and her daughter did what they could to help at such a time. They were not to know, of course, that Lady Law's erring son, John, would a few years later become an internationally famous financier, whose exploits over the Mississippi scheme and the control of the finances of France are legendary (even though on his death in Venice in 1729 he was once again in poverty).[9]

Returning to the subject of oatmeal, though a great deal of it must clearly have been used by the family and their servants both at Polwarth House and in Edinburgh, there is evidence of some wheaten flour being employed in their home baking as well. The Edinburgh baker Grisell patronised was Adam Keir in the Old Kirk parish, whose household consisted of himself, his wife, their five children, an apprentice, and as servants two men, two women and a boy.[10] From him she regularly bought white flour when in the capital, but equally regularly 'a dich of tarts' and occasionally 'a venisen pasti'. We do not know what she used the flour for; in most weeks the purchase of bread is also mentioned, both when in Edinburgh and in the country.

So far the Compt Book entries we have looked at have not had sums of money attached to them. We can now move to the types of entry for which account books are best known, where prices or money amounts are given. And we can begin by looking at the different groups of people with whom Grisell had financial transactions, starting with the tenants. But a word of warning is necessary at the outset, for even in account books people do not fall neatly into the categories designed for them, but often play a number of roles. Take the case of Robet Lunham (whose surname is also sometimes shown as Lownam or Lounan). He was a maker of candles, of soap and of tar, and there are numerous entries of payments for selling these to Grisell. She did not always pay the full price, for there was sometimes a substantial offset in the form of tallow supplied to him by her. Also he had to pay her the rent of his house in Greenlaw, amounting to £4.10s. a year. Nor was this all, for he rented the Claydub outfield as well, and in addition had to pay her £4.10s. for an ox grazing on her pasture. In the modest house in Greenlaw where he carried on his business as candlemaker and soap maker, he lived with his wife Helen, a son Walter and some younger children, and he could evidently afford to have two women servants, each of whom was paid £14 a year.[11] Oddly enough, in the poll-tax return he is merely described as tenant of the house, no mention being made of his manufacturing and trading activities. But these must ultimately have proved remarkably profitable, for some thirty years later he appears in the manuscript book of John Dickson, factor to the first two Earls of Marchmont, as joint tenant with his son-in-law Patrick Trotter of the extensive lands of Greenlawdean and Broomhill, whilst still continuing to make on his own account annual payments for the rent of the little Claydub outfield.[12]

In looking at the tenants with all sizes of holding in the parish of Polwarth, one is struck by the contrast between the laird's mansion with its seventeen hearths, and the very small size of even the larger of the other dwellings. Mr George Holywell the minister, living with his wife, two children and three servants, has five hearths, Robert Fairburn in Woodsyde had three, and Polwarth Mains probably the same number, but apart from the special case of Polwarth Mill with two hearths, no other dwelling in the whole parish seems to have had more than a single hearth.[13] The most substantial tenant of the Marchmont family in the parish was David Smith of the Mains, whose money rental in 1695 was £204.13s. He and his wife Bessie had three sons and three daughters; there were eight indoor servants, four men and four women. Next in importance was Robert Old (whose surname Grisell not unnaturally gives as Auld). He and Jean Old (who had been a Fairbairn) had two sons and one daughter, and employed four servants, two men and two women. Then came Robert Fairburn (or Fairbairn) in Woodside, paying only £70 a year in money rent, married to Agnes, and living with them one daughter and also his son and daughter-in-law and five servants (four men and one woman). After this there was Robert Knox, paying a money rent of £35 for Polwarth Mill. With a wife but no children living at home, there were five servants (three of them men). There was also, however, an undermiller George Thomson with his wife Christian and one woman servant. Apart from George Manderson in Blaigden (with a wife and three sons) paying £15 in money rent, and Margaret Grieve, apparently on her own, paying about the same, the other tenant-householders in Polwarth parish paid only twelve shillings as their poll tax, so their money rentals were probably £5 or less. They included tailors, weavers and smiths, but the only one whose trade skill was made use of at Polwarth House seems to have been Thomas Whilas the wright; Grisell notes on the last day of the year 1694 that she has 'counted all counts with Thomas Whilas procidin this day' but forgets to enter the amount involved in the money column. The wright (who, in addition to the types of work suggested by such a name, did what is now done by joiners and carpenters) lived with his wife Margaret together with an apprentice and a woman servant.[14] Grisell did, however, buy butter, chickens and ale from a number of the wives of the smaller tenants in the parish; the men, unless they were practising a craft, did unskilled work for daily wages on the home farm.

We have looked so far at the parish of Polwarth, but there were also, of course, some large and some small tenants of the Polwarths in the parish of Greenlaw. Thomas Brack in Bellsheill had a valued rental of £335, for instance, while James Reidpath and his wife Agnes, who rented Parks Walls and Old Greenlaw, could afford to pay a manservant of the same name £32 a year, a very high figure for Berwickshire, and they had three other servants living in as well. Then there was another fairly substantial tenant, Alexander Henderson and his wife Margaret Craw in Broomhill, as well as William Polwarth and his wife Isobell Drysdale in Eastfields, and also Isobell Dickson in Hardins; cheese and butter were bought from both of these last two women, and linen was purchased from Isobell Dickson as well. However, the main acquisition of lands in this parish did not take place until after Grisell had stopped keeping her Compt Book, and to extend the list of tenants further would add little to the examples already given.

The rent required from tenants in Scotland at this time included, of course, a number of other things besides money. There was victual in the form of grain or meal, the amount of which might or might not vary with the success of the harvest; vicarage and teinds, originally intended for church upkeep, and always in the latter case varying with the harvest, were payable to whoever had the right to demand them; the kain element was a fixed amount of cheese or number of fowls, specified as hens or capons; and the service element, the provision on a stated number of days of a horse and someone to lead it for carrying lime or coal or anything else that might need to be carried. There were also a number of other irksome requirements, such as having to take your grain to one particular miller to be milled, even though you would prefer to have the job done more cheaply elsewhere. And on top of all this was the burden of taxation, including hearth tax and poll tax, and the obligation to accept having soldiers quartered on you. Indeed, almost the only advantage of being near the bottom of the socio-economic scale was that you thereby escaped most of these burdens.

The people described as hinds, herds or gardeners were not strictly speaking tenants, for the house-rent they would otherwise have had to pay formed part of their annual wage. They were all, of course, highly skilled. The hind was supposed to know everything about husbandry and to be able to plough, to sow, to stack and to perform all other agricultural tasks. A whole hind kept an able fellow-servant, making it possible for the ploughing to be done by the two of them. A half hind was supposed to have the same skills as the whole hind but did not have a fellow-servant living with him and helping him. The duties of the wives of hinds of both sorts, as laid down in the wage assessment made by the justices of the peace for the shire of Edinburgh in 1656, sound extremely onerous: 'To shear daily in Harvest, while their Masters Corn be cut down. They are also to be assisting with their Husbands in winning their Masters Hay and Peats, setting of his Lime-kills, Gathering, Filling, Carting and all other sort of Failzie [manure] fit for Gooding . . . the Land . . . all manner of Work, at Barns and Byres, to bear and carry the stacks from the Barn-yards to the Barns for Threshing, carry meat to the Goods, from the Barnes to the Byres, Muck, Cleange and Dight [clean up] the Byres and Stables, and to help to winnow and dight the Cornes'.[15] Nothing is said as to how, if all this is to be done, the bearing and looking after children, not to mention other household needs, are to be fitted in. The whole hind is to have a convenient dwelling house and a kailyard, specified quantities of oats and pease, ground sufficient to sow stated amounts of oats and barley (the seed to be provided by himself), and certain rights of pasture. The half hind is also given a dwelling and a kailyard, but with only half the entitlement of the whole hind in all other respects (save for a small 'augmentation' of two forlets of oats). Hinds, servants and wives are to have their meat for their work at harvest but not at any other time.

The herd, like the full hind, was to have a fellow-servant to help him, but was also to provide his master with a daily shearer for cutting his corn at harvest time. Nothing regarding his wife's duties was laid down, but his wage, in the same form as in the hind's case, was to comprise a dwelling and kailyard plus specifications of the other three types. Gardeners, whose conditions were not laid down in the assessment, seem in practice to have had, in addition to a house and kailyard, an annual money wage with some additional payments in kind, and also provision in many cases for an apprentice. On the basis of the poll-tax descriptions, there were three full and four half hinds, one herd and two gardeners living within the parish of Polwarth in 1695, though some of them may have been employed by the larger tenants and not by the Polwarths. The full hinds and their wives were Will Dods married to Isobell; Thomas Sanderson married to Janet; and John Davidson married to Janet. The half hinds were Robert Williamson (Margaret), George Whitehead (Katherine), William Young (Isobell) and Thomas Stemson (Margaret). The herd was Alexander Redpath (Agnes). One of the gardeners was Peter Brown (Alison), the other Finlay McCracket, who was a widower living with his daughter and his son.[16] It was clearly this gardener's son who was meant when the Compt Book noted receiving £7.4s. 'from young finla for gusbris and corns' in October 1695.

In its consideration of agricultural workers hired by the year, the Lanarkshire wage assessment of 1708 differs in several important respects from the Edinburghshire one of 1656. First, the words 'hind' and 'half hind' are not used. The skilled worker is now simply described as 'a domestick servant man or inn servant who is able to perform all manner of work relating to husbandry', but the duties specified are much as they had been in 1656. Secondly, the maximum payment is now given wholly in money terms. He is to have yearly for fee and bounty '£24 Scots at Whitsunday and Martinmas by equal portions'. A younger manservant, 'commonly called a half lang', is to have on the same basis £16 Scots, and 'boyes or lads' £8. The corresponding 'strong and sufficient woman servant for barns, byres, shearing, brewing, bakeing, washing . . .' £14; and a 'lass or young maide' £8. And the same rates are to be payable when serving masters who have 'no labouring of land'. A third difference is that no mention is now made of living quarters and a kailyard, nor are the duties of the hind's wife set out (although there is an oblique reference to them). Daily rates for shearers (all *with* meat and drink) are six shillings for men and four for young men, five shillings for women and three for young women.[17]

Near the bottom of the social and economic ladder come the cottars. This term, though used in the poll-tax return, where people are recorded as being in a particular dwelling, is not used in the Compt Book at all, where the same men are spoken of collectively as workmen. And this is, of course, what the justices of the peace for the shire of Edinburgh in 1656 called the "Common Work-man or Labourer who works for daily wages' and who was not to be paid more than six shillings without any meat and drink (or three shillings if meat and drink were provided by his employer); and this was to be 'diminished' when the outdoor working day was shorter in winter. As with other wages, this rate, which figured again when the Lanarkshire justices drew up an assessment in 1708, seems to have been adhered to generally throughout lowland Scotland at the time. There were some eleven men coming into this category whom Grisell records as having herself paid, or sometimes given by way of Patrick Allen, the six shilling rate. All eleven were married, and lived in the parish of Polwarth, paying annual rents of around £4. Because the children of cottars did not count as 'pollable persons', size of family is not known.

In interpreting the following data from Marchmont records it must, of course, be borne in mind that although we only know the number of days in the year they spent working for that particular family, these day labourers must at times have worked for some of the larger tenants as well. They also had certain other opportunities of making extra money, however little. For we know that their wives sometimes sold chickens, ducks, eggs and butter to Grisell, and probably to other people as well.

And in late July virtually all of them brought her six or eight pounds weight of wool (eight or eleven of our pounds) and were paid £1.4s. for the smaller and £1.15s. for the larger amount.

The other information it has proved possible to piece together from a variety of sources can now be given for each of these day labourers in turn. The work John Allen did for his daily wage when working for the Polwarths was variously described as building stone work, mending dykes, thatching, 'at the shearing' and 'at the haystack', and the number of days in the year he was so employed averaged about 180 in the three years from November 1695 to November 1698. In July 1713 an agreement was made with him to be 'working oversman' in a quarry, still at the six shilling Scots daily rate, but possibly with the prospect that this rate would also apply in the winter and that he would be more continuously employed. Alexander Hunter worked at the south quarry besides helping to mend dykes, but in the same years his annual number of days working for the Marchmonts averaged only about 60. He and his wife Janet lived next door to Christopher and Isobell Redpath; he also worked on the estate, but for three times as many days per year as his neighbour. Two of the other daily workers were also neighbours. Patrick Whitehead (married to Beatrice Grieve) lived next door to John Johnston, and both of them averaged between 200 and 230 in the days they worked each year for the Polwarths. John Taylor (married to Jean Jaffray) was employed by them for roughly the same number of days as the last two, but more of his time seems to have been spent in serving the masons and less in other work. John Turnbull (whose name is sometimes given as Trumble or as Thornhill) worked about 260 days on the estate. Two men who may have been related to him and his wife Janet — as except for them there were no other Turnbulls in the parish of Polwarth at this time — were living-in servants in Robert Old's house (John Turnbull) and with Robert Fairburn in Woodside (Robert Turnbull). For the remaining regular day labourers we do not know how many days a year they worked. James Jaffray (who may have been the brother of Jean Jaffrey, wife of one of the other daily workers on the estate, John Taylor) was employed a good deal in 'building at the kitchen'. James Manderston (or perhaps Manderson) was mainly engaged in cleaning ditches and in quarry work; he was married to Isobell Hogg. David Sheill, married to Elspeth Brown, may have been the brother of Isobell Sheill, who had married Patrick Brierson the weaver; what makes this the more likely is that this weaver's apprentice was another David Sheill. And finally James Currie was married to Katherine Redpath, who was probably Christopher Redpath's sister. Inter-marriage was obviously just as common at this social level as it was amongst the lairds. It took place, however, within a parish rather than a regional area, and without the driving force of dynastic and financial motivation.

Which brings us, in this survey of the different groups of people with whom Grisell had financial dealings, to the servants living in Polwarth House itself. If we ask what size of domestic staff was employed there, the answer is, as we have said, not entirely clear-cut. According to a loose paper transcribed into the Compt Book, drink money left by five visitors between 12 May and 5 June 1697, amounting to £103.12s., was divided between the following servants:

> John Lamb Master Household
> Robert Manderston Butler
> Henry Lyon Cook
> John Murdo Porter
> Barbara Day my Lady's Gentlewoman and Housekeeper
> Margaret Foord, Helen Home, Bessie Allan Chambermaids

There are several rather odd features about this list. First of all, a staff amounting to only four men and four women is only just over half the number given for the household in the 1695 roll of pollable persons, where twelve men and five women were named as servants, although their duties were not specified.[18] A second peculiarity is that we know the staff included both a footman and a coachman, yet neither of these is included in the 1697 list. The coachman might not be eligible for a share of the drink money left by guests, who perhaps had not been in his coach, but the footman certainly was. Indeed, evidence from many sources suggests that *all* servants shared in the distribution of drink money (e.g. 'mor to him aloued in his hand of drink mony that I gave out to the rest of the servants'). So we ought perhaps to take the 1695 pollable persons figure as a more reliable indication of the number of living-in servants. The Compt Book entries tell us something of the conditions attaching to the appointment of two members of staff. Bessie Allan, one of the chambermaids, had received in wages from 11 November 1694 to 9 November 1697 £14 and three years' rent of her mother's house (£18), so that she was being paid under £11 a year. And the fact of her mother's house rental being included in the arrangement may well be one reason why she is the only servant whose name appears in both the 1695 and 1697 lists. On 29 June 1695 'I agreed with John [space left blank] to be my Couk he is to have 20 pund Scots til Martimes and his part of the Drink mony and a grin Apron no advantig in the kitsion at al'. Although the cook was usually a man, 'Rebaka Boldry couk' is also mentioned; perhaps she was an under-cook.

One other manservant in the 1695 list receives a similar wage — Patrick Allen — and he and William Allen the younger, only slightly lower in pay, both seem to have been entrusted with the responsibility of carrying quite large amounts of money between Polwarth House and Edinburgh, and other places where my Lord happened to be. They also paid workmen or tradesmen and accounted to Grisell for what they had done. The last of the four better-paid menservants was Adam Marshall the coachman, and all of these went and stayed in Edinburgh as required. The same was true of Elizabeth Brysson, the best-paid of the women on the 1695 staff, to whom (until Robert Manderston the butler received it in 1696) most of the money 'for the euse of the hous' was given, and who had to engage in more transactions on behalf of her mistress than any other servant. Nothing to the discredit of any of these men or women, who were obviously felt to be loyal and trustworthy employees, is to be found in the Compt Book, but when Grisell was critical of a servant she noted the grounds of her criticism. The most frequent transgressor was John Tiler (whose name is spelt Taylor both in the 1695 poll-tax return and in Grisell Baillie's index to the Compt Book). In November 1695, for instance, 'John Tiler fotman he spnt of my Sandis mony he should bout hors drogs in Barnik', the sum involved being £1.13s. And in the previous July 'John Tiler fotman kiped of the ching of a doler £1.4s.', and this evidently jogged her memory that there had been 'mor before he kiped'. But only a week or two before, she had given £2.18s. 'to John Tilear fotman when his wife was brout to bad'. Then in June 1695 a payment of £9.10s. 'to Jamei Weat [James Wat] which cliers fer shns that half year he served after his Unchel chited my Lord with other sums'.

A very reliable picture of the financial position of living-in servants at this time in this area can be gained from a study of the 1695 poll-tax records for the parish of Greenlaw, where the annual wages of all 150 such people are given.[19] Taking the men, the range is a very wide one, from £32.16s. to £3, the last clearly being for mere boys. Roughly ten per cent of the men were paid £26 or more, a further nineteen per cent between £20 and £26, and a further twenty per cent between £14 and £20, so that nearly half of them were getting £14 per annum or over. The highest wage for a woman was £16, and twenty per cent of them were in fact paid that top rate. The lowest wage was £4, implying that a young girl was more use in the household than a young boy, and in fact only a mere three per cent were paid as little as that. Half of them received a wage of £13 or over, so the commonest wage for women was not much lower than that for men, though the top rates for a small proportion of men were much higher than the top rates paid to women. But the money wage was not all that living-in servants received. There was also 'bounteth', which always included two pairs of shoes per year, costing £1.10s. to £2 a pair, and sometimes old clothing, even an old hat; though if a livery was provided, that usually remained the property of the employer. Much more important, however, was drink money. It is very hard to assess what financial benefit this brought to most servants, but certainly in Polwarth House and other places where visitors frequently came to stay, the effect of sharing out the drink money they left must often have doubled the money wage received for their employment. To the visitor, the need to leave such tips when staying with relatives or friends meant quite a substantial addition to travel costs, for even an overnight stop entailed £6 or so, while on quite a short visit £30 or more was expected. In 1671 Sir Gilbert Elliot of Stobs and his family paid some twenty-two visits to Craigmillar, Nidrie, Cockpen, Darnhall, Dryden and elsewhere, leaving sums totalling £169.5s., the 'going rate' then, probably being a good deal lower than it became a quarter of a century later, and the houses they stayed at perhaps having fewer servants.[20]

We can now turn to entries where the interest lies in what Grisell had to pay for the goods and services she got, rather than from whom she bought them. For it goes without saying that some indication of the value of money in the Scotland of the 1690s is needed if the implications of many of the figures quoted in this book are to be appreciated.

Before 1914 it was customary, when presenting historical material of this kind, to offer the reader a simple guide by saying that the Scots pound of the period being considered was roughly equivalent to X of today's currency, but such guidance is unsatisfactory on two counts. To begin with, it presupposes that the price level will remain the same in the future, so that for someone reading the book or the article fifty years later the multiplier will still be the same. And it also implies that the relative value of different goods and services has remained, and will continue to remain, constant, which is clearly not so. To meet this second difficulty we now, of course, use a cost-of-living index, and over relatively short periods of time this is a very useful aid to understanding. If, for example, we were dealing with life in the latter part of Queen Victoria's reign, it might just be possible to make up, however roughly, some kind of working-class or middle-class cost-of-living index to make money values at that time meaningful in terms of the cost of living today. But in the two preceding centuries the whole structure of economic and social life in Britain had changed so radically as to render any such index quite valueless, so it would be pointless to attempt to construct one. This does not mean, however, that no guidance can be given. What we *can* do is to provide a list of certain fairly standard individual goods and services for each of which there is a rough counterpart today, and to quote the prices in Scots currency of that time that were being paid for them in southern Scotland. It is, of course, very easy to quarrel with the inclusion of almost any single item in such a list, by pointing out that ordinary folk were so poor in those days that it was far beyond their reach. Such a criticism, though valid on the face of it, misses the point of the whole exercise, which is merely to show, for someone living in that time and place who was lucky enough to have any financial resources to spare, what would have been the *relative* cost of obtaining a variety of fairly standard goods and services.

To help us to discover what food, drink and household necessities cost, we are very fortunate in being able to consult the original manuscript of Dame Magdalen Nicolson's Account Book, covering the eleven years 1681-92, which contains a large number of such prices.[21] Then for 1694-7 there are many entries of this kind in the Compt Book, and for 1702-14 in Grisell Baillie's Household Book.[22] Where accounts were kept by men, there naturally tend to be very few items of this sort, and although Lauder of Fountainhall's material for 1670-75, Foulis of Ravelston's for 1672-1707, and Cunningham of Craigends' for 1674-77, provide valuable evidence for the prices of other things, the only common consumables whose cost they regularly record are drink, tobacco and snuff.[23] From these and other sources, then, a fairly reliable picture has been built up of prices in the lowlands of Scotland. And unless some indication to the contrary is given, the prices quoted can be taken as applying to the whole of the twenty-six year period 1681 to 1707, and in the case of drink, the longer span from 1672.

Before going on to quote these prices, one complication has to be dealt with. The Scots pint was equivalent to three of the pints we know today, and the Edinburgh Tron Pound (in which the material in our account books can be assumed to have been expressed) weighed substantially more than the pound we now use. For the purpose of what follows in this section (and *only* in this particular section) all prices will therefore be expressed in terms of today's pints and today's pounds in weight and *not* in the units in use in Scotland in the 1690s. So that, for example, when we know that butter was being sold in Greenlaw for five Scots shillings per Scots pound, this will be shown instead as three shillings and eight pence in Scots currency per pound as we measure weight today.

Ale made with malt and barley was the drink universally consumed by all classes at all times of day, breakfast included. As it was usually brewed at home, price information can only be given when it was purchased away from home, and here something between sevenpence and eightpence was usually charged for a pint, Preston ale being slightly dearer and mum beer (brewed from wheat instead of barley) a good deal more expensive. Much of the ale was bottled, and if new bottles were bought by the gross in Leith, the cost remained constant over the period 1697 to 1706, at two shillings and three shillings each bottle for the mutchkin (¾ of a pint today) and the chopin (two mutchkin) sizes respectively; the price of corks varying from 14 to 24 shillings a gross. Wine, usually without any designation, ranged from 6/8 to 13/4 per pint over the years 1672 to 1707; where its origin was specified, it tended to be rather more highly priced. Brandy could be had for 9, 10 or 11 shillings a pint for much of the period, though prices as high as 17 shillings were sometimes charged in the latter part. Sack was more expensive, but remained at a constant 12 or 13 shillings from the 1660s to the late 1690s, again tending to rise and sometimes reaching the 19-shilling level; it was often bought for quasi-medicinal use (e.g. with herbs), and then it tended to be rather cheaper. It should be mentioned that the price of imported wine was not always left to be determined by the free play of demand and supply. The Edinburgh Burgh Council, for example, laid down on the last day of December 1697 the maximum amounts per pint that might be charged for the best sack (14/8, reduced to 13/4 a year later), canary (12 shillings) and claret and white wines (10/8).[24] The avowed reason for imposing these limits was that wines of all sorts were to be had in great plenty and more cheaply than before.

Tobacco prices show considerable variations, at 6, 9, 10, 12 and 17 shillings a pound from the 1680s to 1707, the trend being generally upward. Pigtail tobacco cost only half as much as this; it is variously described as being for the workmen and 'to boil . . . for to rub the young horses'.[25] Pipes were, of course, very cheap, costing only twopence or threepence each; they were sometimes bought by the gross. Snuff, bought only in fractions of an ounce at a time, cost from £2.1s. to £2.7s. an ounce.

When we come to bread, we face some difficulties. For one thing, in many families oatmeal-based products, rather than bread as we now have it, formed the staple article of diet; for another, where it was baked at home no price information can be given. Nevertheless, many households in which accounts were kept did make regular purchases of bread, and these are sometimes stated in usable form, as when Dame Magdalen Nicolson records '3 Jany '88 To Tam Ansliy baxter in Jedburgh for 7 doson of brid had got thrie months befor 9.0.0'.[26] It would seem reasonable to infer from this that the family bought some 6½ loaves a week, at a cost of roughly two shillings and three halfpence per loaf. During the whole five years of her account book she hardly ever paid more than two shillings. Prices rose towards the end of the century, and in the years 1697 to 1706 they ranged from three shillings to five shillings and sixpence, a wheat loaf quite often being specified. If rolls were bought, eight shillings a dozen was sometimes paid. As in the case of bread, butter and cheese were often made at home, though on the evidence of the account books that have survived, they seem quite often to have been purchased as well. The price of butter, as several commentators have noted, stayed surprisingly constant over quite long periods, at between 3/8 and 4/9 a pound for fresh, and ninepence or a shilling less for salted. Foul butter, used for lubricating coach wheels and various other purposes, was naturally cheaper still. Prices for cheese, including Irish cheese, varied from two to three shillings a pound. Coarse cheese could be had for 1/7, and Cheshire cheese is recorded at five shillings a pound in 1699. As with many other foodstuffs regularly being bought, the price of eggs is constantly given, but often without any number being specified. Dame Magdalen Nicolson does, however, record quantities, and in her part of the Borders prices stayed virtually static from 1661 to 1692 at 1/4 a dozen, only rising a little at the very end of that period.[27] We know that in Edinburgh and St Andrews in 1664 eggs were regularly 1/6 or 1/8 a dozen; by the early part of the eighteenth century 2/8 was the more usual price. Prices paid for hens, ducks and geese ranged from 3/4 to ten shillings, and only for capons was it necessary to pay more than this. Pigeons, partridges, moorfowl, rabbits and hares often did not have to be bought; but where it proved necessary, the price was as variable as one would expect from the variety of people who might want to dispose of a pair. The price paid for beef, veal and mutton is often given, but hardly ever in a form enabling easy comparison with today to be made. We know that when a ham weighing sixty pounds was bought in Leith in 1699 the price per pound was 3/8, but usually all we are given is the cost of a roasting pig, not a meaningful price to us now.

When it comes to fish and shellfish the situation is a little clearer. Oysters, bought by the hundred or half hundred, are found to cost £1.4s. to £1.12s. a hundred in the 1690s. Prices of fresh herring varied a good deal depending on where they came from, when, and whether they were to be salted for the servants or eaten by the family straight away. If they were for salting, and bought by the thousand, they could cost as little as £4 for that quantity. If bought by the half hundred, the bill could be proportionately higher, at fourteen shillings. Haddock, bought by the half hundred, were also twelve or fourteen shillings for that number. There are isolated Edinburgh prices for lobsters at 3/4 each.

Sugar, even though the availability of honey was a help, was a very essential commodity, and was sold in a variety of forms. If we limit our figures to two types of sugar, fine and coarse, the position was that in the 1690s the better quality cost from 6 to 9 shillings a pound, and the poorer 5 to 7 shillings; by 1702 these prices had risen significantly to 14 shillings and 9 shillings respectively. Salt, always a necessity, was required in much larger quantities by households of that time, and the unit needed for price comparisons is the imperial gallon. When it was wanted for general use and bought locally, its price in the 1690s lay between 1/10 and 2/6 a gallon. When coarse salt was required in bulk for preserving meat, fish and so on for use in the winter months, a visit was made to the salt pans, where it could be obtained for about half that price. Grisell notes, for example, that in June 1695 5 forlats (32 gallons) of salt was brought to Polwarth House from the salt pans.

Prices for locally-grown fruit and vegetables are so variable as to make it difficult to present them in any useful way. Imported oranges and lemons were, however, bought by well-to-do households in Scotland in 1676-78, and the price usually paid at that time was from 8 shillings to 14/6 a dozen for oranges, and around £1 for lemons. By 1709-10 the price in each case had risen to £1.10s; buying 30 dozen at a time for making drink, however, they could both be had at 15 shillings a dozen in 1714.

Two non-food commodities figuring in almost all household accounts are candles and soap. Sir James Nicholson in Cockburnspath regularly made bulk purchases of candles in the 1660s in Duns and in Haddington at threepence per pound.[28] Thirty years later Grisell, again buying in large quantities, was paying Robert Lunam of Polwarth fivepence a pound. For small purchases the price was predictably a good deal higher. Dame Magdalen Nicolson, buying only one or two pounds at a time, paid from 3 to 4 shillings a pound over the whole period 1681-92; and evidence from other sources shows this also to have been their price in the 1660s. By 1707, however, the cost had risen very substantially — Lady Grisell Baillie, buying in large quantity from Agnes Smith in Kelso, and from Greenlaw, paid 3/8 a pound for cotton-wicked candles and 3/3 a pound for common rag-wicked ones.[29] Soap presents diffi-culties all of its own. Castle soap was clearly of very high quality (we know it was used when shaving), being bought in very small quantities at a time, and between 1691 and 1699 the price varied from 9 shillings to

11/4 a pound. Soap bought only a pound or so at a time, and sometimes described as white soap, cost Dame Magdalen Nicolson from 3 shillings to 4/6 in the 1681-92 period.[30] When Lady Grisell Baillie in 1707 bought 50 pounds weight of soap from Thomas Chato of Kelso over a period of three months and paid 4/4 a pound for it, this may also have been what we would call toilet soap.[31] Kitchen soap (sometimes called crown soap in Grisell's Compt Book) was bought in very large quantities at a time and much more cheaply, but an insuperable difficulty arises in trying to determine its price, for the unit of quantity used in the Compt Book and several other accounts is either the daill (usually 18 daills at a time were bought) or the firkin (small barrel), and neither of these units can easily be translated into modern terms. In the 1690s, 18 daills of such soap cost between £5.15s. and £6, and a firkin cost from £9.10s. to £11; if a small barrel held between 8 and 9 of our gallons, the price range for this kitchen soap would have been 21-28 shillings a gallon.

With the types of goods described so far it has been difficult enough to present prices in a form suitable for even rough comparison with their present-day counterparts. When we move to articles of clothing or household furnishings the task becomes impossible. To know, for example, what a laird and his lady in late seventeenth-century Scotland paid when they bought gloves, shoes or stockings is important information in its own right. But for the purposes of the present section there is clearly no valid basis of comparison with buying nominally the same articles today, for the materials of which they are made, their expected lifespan and almost everything about them has changed too radically in the intervening period. And the same holds good for kitchen utensils (who has plates made of wood or of pewter today?), and for the furnishings of the house; we can, it is true, quote prices paid for sheets or blankets, but no clear indication of *size* is ever given, and only a very rough guide to quality. And with materials, though the price per unit of length is given, the width is not.

It might have been expected that grain and precious metal prices would have figured on our list, since on the face of it both of these seem important in estimating changes in the value of money. The explanation for their omission is different in each case. Although official prices of the different grains are available, the *actual* price at which grain changed hands in Berwickshire alone varied so much from one month to another in the same year, and from one transaction to another even in the same month, as to make it seem an unreliable yardstick for our purpose. In the case of silver prices per ounce, of which there are examples from valuations of property and other sources, doubt exists as to which of two widely-varying Scots units of measurement was being employed in specific statements of value, and it therefore seemed best not to use them.

Another type of evidence of the living costs of the families of lairds in the Scottish Borders in the 1690s is provided by a particularly interesting entry dated 1 April 1691 in the manuscript of Dame Magdalen Nicolson's Account Book (not mentioned in A. O. Curle's article): 'I agreed with my son for taking me and Magdalen Scot. I should give him 3 honder mark for myself and 2 honder mark for Magdalen Scot in the year and if I go to Edr and stay a month or 2 or 3 it should be discompted as also Magdalene if she go to Edr it should be discompted to me also'.[32]

The son she speaks of must have been her stepson William who had succeeded his father (her husband) on his death around 1680. This stepson had married Elizabeth, eldest daughter of Sir John Scott, first baronet of Ancrum, and it seems probable that the Magdalen Scot (or Scott) mentioned was a younger sister of hers. We know that Magdalen Scot was a very close friend of Dame Magdalen's, and when the former was in Edinburgh they exchanged foodstuffs sent from Roxburghshire, with currants, raisins and nutmegs as well as fabrics and gloves sent from Edinburgh. Dame Magdalen and she had obviously decided in 1691 to join forces and live in one of the Roxburghshire houses (perhaps Woolee) — they may both have been widows by then — but they still intended to spend a good deal of time in Edinburgh. Dame Magdalen was clearly going to pay her stepson William for board and lodging for *both* of them, though why the figure should have been different for the two of them is not clear, unless perhaps the cost of servants was to come out of Dame Magdalen's 300 marks a year. At all events, 500 marks (£333.6s.8d.) seems to have been felt to be a reasonable board-and-lodging figure for two people of their social level for a year.

We can now move from prices of goods to prices of services; but before discussing the evidence as to what wages for different kinds of work were in fact paid in the Scottish Borders in the 1690s, something must be said about justices of the peace, who had certain functions in relation to wage levels. The office of justice of the peace did not exist in Scotland until the Stuarts, in the early part of the seventeenth century, sought to introduce a system which had, in their view, worked very well in England. There were, however, too many traditional vested interests in Scotland able to frustrate the implementation of the new system, and it was not until early in the eighteenth century that the justices really began to function as their counterparts south of the Border had been doing for so long. One of their duties was to draw up, publish, and enforce maximum wage rates, and though in Scotland there was little hope of taking proceedings against those who accepted or offered more than the maxima laid down, justices in some areas did in fact sometimes fulfil the first part of the programme by promulgating a set of wage rates.

Only two such assessments have survived for the seventeenth or early eighteenth centuries, and we have already referred to them in this chapter when discussing the duties and terms of employment of hinds and others working for the Polwarths.[33] Both these assessments, as we have seen, are very detailed; and they seem to be almost exactly the same in the scale of wages they lay down. It is therefore worth looking at the earlier assessment, noting at the same time any respects in which the later one differed from it. For though legal enforcement may in practice have been out of the question, the rates resulted from detailed discussions as to what was felt to be desirable (only, of course, on the employer's side) at the time. And there is every reason to believe that the views held in the Borders would have been much the same had any assessments for those areas survived. In the present section only *daily* wages will be discussed, yearly wages having already been looked at.

We have already noted how it is made clear in the assessments that the daily wages to be described are only to apply in the summer, defined as from the first of March to the last day of September, except where work is possible by candlelight, in which case the summer rate can continue to apply. In all other cases wages are to be 'diminished' in the winter months. The 1656 assessment fails to define the extent of this diminution, but in Lanarkshire in 1708 a reduction by one-sixth is specified. For each daily wage two rates are given, one where the worker has to bring his own meat and drink, and a lower one where the employer provides him with it. The basic wage is that for the 'common workman or labourer', who, as we have seen, is to have 6 shillings Scots per day without meat and drink, and 3 shillings if the employer feeds him. Moving from this basic wage to the best-paid craftsmen, the mason is to have a mark (13/4) or half a mark (6/8), and the wright 12 shillings or 6 shillings. A thatcher of houses came next; he was to have 8 shillings or 4 shillings in 1656, but this had been raised to 10 shillings and 6 shillings in 1708. The 1656 assessment provided for the case of an inferior class of mason called a cowan (who had not served a regular apprenticeship, or could only be trusted with drystone walls), who was to get the thatcher's rate; but no provision was made for such a category of worker in 1708. A barrow-man (called 'borrow-man' in 1708) was only to get the labourer's wage. The remaining worker, the tailor, was in rather a special position, since he normally lived for a while in his employer's house, 'getting his meat' while plying his craft. In his case fourpence a day was deemed sufficient. Piece-rates as well as daily rates are laid down in the 1656 assessment for a mason, a 'sklater', a wright, a shoemaker, and even a maltman, but the only such provision in 1708 is for the ploughwright making a plough (13/4 in 1708, 20 shillings in 1656). Women are not included in this list, but they do appear in yearly payments, and for daily harvest work; and if married to hinds their duties are, as we have seen, specified.

From the wide range of daily wages for work of many different kinds mentioned in the account books consulted, and covering the period 1670 to 1707, it can be said that there are not very many cases where *less* was paid than the rates just quoted, though Grisell Baillie reports paying only 5 shillings a day to labourers at Mellerstain from 1709 to 1714.[34] Women employed in tasks such as weeding received 4 shillings a day; they never seem to have been paid either less or more than this. Maximum wages (and this, of course, is what the assessed rates were supposed to be) rarely seem to have exceeded the figures given. The main exception is the thatcher, who was sometimes paid 13/4 a day. Men described as gardeners seem to have had a daily wage of 6, 7 or 8 shillings a day. The broad correspondence between actual daily wages paid and the maxima laid down by the justices in these two surviving assessments half a century apart must have been due to the unwillingness of employers to pay more, and to the availability of men with the requisite skills at these rates. It certainly had nothing to do with any legal sanctions. And although (except for the Mellerstain example just quoted) there are relatively few cases in our account books of labourers receiving *less* than six shillings a day, the differential between the basic rate with, and without, meat and drink can be used to show how grossly inadequate such a wage was for a man with a wife and children to support. For if the 3 shillings difference reflects the bare minimum of what food and drink for a man for a day actually cost, then even on the totally unrealistic basis of working 365 days a year, living rent free, and having no other expenses whatsoever, a labourer could only just provide subsistence for himself and his wife. In any meaningful sense, therefore, the 6-shilling daily wage for unskilled work current in Scotland during the second half of the seventeenth century was a wage far below subsistence level.

At the other extreme of payments for services, the cost of a home visit from a doctor was always considerable, but seemed to vary slightly according to what the particular person receiving the visit felt like paying. Foulis of Ravelston regularly paid Dr Stevenson and others in Edinburgh £11.12s. a visit in the early 1670s. But by 1702, £14.14s. (a guinea at that time) was what he almost invariably gave him, Dr Pitcairne and several other doctors, occasionally raised to a jacobus (£15.6s.).[35] In 1695 Grisell Baillie gave Dr St Clair in Edinburgh £11.12s., the same as Foulis of Ravelston had then been paying.[36] George Home gave Dr Stevenson five ducadoons (£18.10s. at that time) when he was near Kimmerghame and visited him in 1704; and this is exactly what Foulis of Ravelston gave Dr Dundas for a visit in December 1702, paying him with the same coins.[37] George Home's payments to Dr Abernethy in 1695 were five rex dollars (£14.10s.) for one visit; but a few weeks later for a similar call he was given six rex dollars (£17.8s.). However, when he went to Polwarth House in that same year, he was paid only £12 for a visit. Summing up this rather confusing picture, one could say that quite a usual fee for a home visit from the 1670s to the mid-1690s was £11.12s. (and sometimes more if the doctor was a personal friend), but by the early 1700s, £14.10s. or above was needed, and the amount could be as high as £18.10s.

One of the relatively minor irritants of life in Scotland in the 1690s was the shortage of coin to use in ordinary transactions. This should have been no reason for the chronic delays in, for instance, paying the wages due to living-in servants. But it did make for difficulty in meeting substantial bills. When the Polwarths bought a large quantity of headsuits and other clothing in Edinburgh on one occasion and the bill came to £495.19s.2d., there was written on the back 'given in money £389–16', the balance being made up by tendering five guineas (£60.10s.), a quadruple (£39), and a half-sovereign (£8.2s.2d.). It sounds as though that time the lack of suitable coins worked out to the purchaser's disadvantage, to the tune of £1.9s. A similar instance occurred on 10 May 1703 when Foulis of Ravelston gave William the coinage to pay Mr Scougall the remainder of his bill for pictures. The items given were '½ a luidore, half a croune, a dollar, and two 14sh 6d peices, and is in all £37–18–6'.[38] Paying the doctor was another cause of difficulty, for he was always given coins of high value, depending on what you had laid by for the purpose; yet you neither wanted to under-pay him nor to ask him for change. Then there was the problem of coins that had been clipped. English halfpennies that had been maltreated in this way could only be exchanged by George Home in 1696 by losing twopence on twenty-eight — 'Captain Cockburn offered me a shilling ster. for my clipt fourteen pence halfpennies'. Counterfeiting went on as well, despite alarmingly stiff penalties. In the diary in 1704 we learn that 'there came over two fellows from England pretending to buy cows'; they paid for them in coins that proved to be counterfeit, were apprehended and were sent to Edinburgh. When anything of this sort happened, those responsible were usually said to be not from the locality but from as far afield as possible.

Every account book records purchases of clothing, and in this respect Grisell's Compt Book was no exception to the rule. A surprisingly wide range of materials available for making the clothing worn by Scottish lairds and their ladies is mentioned in seventeenth-century account books. Making allowance for oddities in spelling, it is interesting to note how many are still in use today:

Baz	Flannell	Muslin
Brocade	Gause	Silk
Cambric	Grogrin	Tabbie
Crape	Holland	Tafity
Dornik	Linnine	Velvet
Damask		

Others are either obsolete or are now put to different uses:

Alamod,	a thin, light, silky material used for mantles, hoods and linings for rich garments.
Antherine,	a kind of poplin.
Bustine,	stiffening, a kind of fustian.
Camlet,	could be made of wool or silk or a mixture of the two, and was used for clothes and coverings of all kinds.
Dimity,	strong cotton, usually white.
Farandine, or	
Ferrandine,	wool, handsome and colourful.
Galloon or Galloune,	narrow ribbon or braid of silver and gold silk thread, used as a border trimming.
Lutestring,	silk material, used for petticoats and ribbons.
Muscarad,	used for petticoats.
Plaidin,	coarse woollen cloth.
Sarcenet,	fine, soft silk not unlike alamod.
Temming,	fine worsted with a glazed finish, used for waistcoats and petticoats.

Fine goods and trimmings, galloon, braids and ribbons were usually bought in Edinburgh, which was, of course, the centre of fashion. Silk and various types of these ornamentations were purchased by the drop — 16 drops being equivalent to one Scots Tron ounce. In the Compt Book Grisell Baillie enters some items of expenditure for 1694 which she found on a loose sheet of paper; among the materials is '4oz. 13 drops of black silk fringe at 38/- per oz. £9.' Quality materials which were bought abroad were, as in our own time, liable for customs duties. Silks from Italy, lace from Flanders and fine Holland for shirts were items which were much in demand, and ladies who could afford to do so would take every opportunity of asking visitors to these countries to bring them back a supply. It was common practice to wash the material, or to have it made up and to wear it, thus avoiding duty by familiar methods. Lairds' sons, who were often abroad studying, looked on cheating the customs officer as good sport, and would bring in fancy goods in this way for themselves and their friends.

Most housewives were very economical in the care of their clothing, which was seldom discarded until no further possible use could be found for it. In household accounts of the period there are constant references to clothes being altered, turned, patched, or renovated in some way or another, and very commonly being made down for the children or given to servants. In Grisell Baillie's accounts we find entries for gowns 'ternin', altering, 'making up my old goun' and so on. If they did not make their own clothes, or only some of them, a sewing woman was employed for some days or weeks at a time, and it was also quite usual for ladies to have their clothes made by a tailor. In the early 1690s Dame Magdalen Nicolson employed the tailor on his rounds; he stayed for a season, and fashioned the cloths into garments. From the Compt Book and other manuscript evidence we know that the Polwarths patronised an Edinburgh tailor, Mestr. Lapearle, and ran up sizeable bills with him. When George Home, who had no woman in his family, brought a tailor to his house, his rate of pay was the usual 4/- a day, together with his board and lodging.

At home, where they were fairly secluded, the women may not have taken great trouble with their dresses, although they did love bright colours. We have evidence of this in the Compt Book from the payments to the litster (dyer) for carrying out the commissions he had been given. And when Patrick was Chancellor the ladies in the family naturally spent more on clothes when they were attending formal and social occasions in the capital. Again on a loose paper some of their purchases in 1696 are detailed as follows:

Ane headsuit and Ruffles	£106
Ane other headsuit and Ruffles	77–12
For Cumbruck 10 els at 3 gilders per el	30
2 els Lace at £3–5 per el	6–10

7 els at £2–5 per el	15–15
For a Cravat and a pair of Ruffles	46–18
It. For a headsuit and Ruffles	44–17–2
It. For a headsuit and Ruffles	80– 2–0
Summe £407–14–2	
Given in money £389–16–0	
For a Cravat and Ruffles	£ 88– 5–0
Payed for the things bought in all	£495–19–2

This was a time when ladies wore their hair swept high on the head, with curls at the side of the face falling to rest on the shoulder. Sometimes there were further elaborations of short, curled fringes. Hats disturbed these styles, so to preserve the arrangements various types of headgear were devised — the commode, the headsuit and wired hoods — all of which, being free of other garments, were easily removed. All could either be bought or made at home, and we find entries for the latter practice when wire and catgut were bought, or when a woman was paid for dressing a headsuit. In the Compt Book an entry for 1694 reads 'A Commod wyre and catgutt 16/3; 2¼ ell fine gause at 48/- per ell £5–8– 0'. The frames were lined with muslin or cambric, and covered with some delicate fabric, alamod, lutestring or sarcenet. Lace and ribbons played a most important part in all costume at this time, so the headsuit was well adorned with ruffles, knots and bows. This fashion persisted into the eighteenth century. When Margaret Rose, daughter of the Laird of Kilravock, was married in 1701, she had ¾ ells of camrick for a headsuit, and 9½ ells of lace for trimmings and ruffles to it.[39] In 1710 the two daughters of the late Sir George Broun of Colstoun at a ball in Edinburgh wore gowns and petticoats of antherine, and headsuits of white ribbons.[40] And in the same year Lady Baillie bought headsuits for both her daughters on the occasion of Grisell's marriage.[41] Petticoats were other accessories to which importance was attached. Skirts were tied up or tucked up, so that petticoats — often more than one — could be shown. It was customary, therefore, to have them trimmed almost as elaborately as the gown itself.

In matters of dress the lairds made the same distinction as did their ladies between private and public appearances. At home they tended to be slovenly, going about until late in the day in dressing gowns which were often in poor condition. If they wore underwear it would be rough, of harden, or perhaps flannel or plaidin. Soft slippers on their feet, and some kind of cap on the head would complete their attire. Men wore caps night and day to cover their baldness, and probably also for warmth. For the well-dressed man or lad, fashion dictated the wearing of a wig; these necessitated shaven heads, and were both cumbersome and uncomfortable. So it was customary for the wig to be discarded at the earliest possible moment (the counterpart of women kicking off shoes which hurt their feet), and to be replaced by a cap. There was a variety of wigs one could choose from. Periwigs made with long, good-quality hair were expensive; on 17 August 1705 Sir John Foulis of Ravelston paid 'To George Gordoune for a new long piriwig 7 guineas and a half' (£106.10s.).[42] Whereas his bob wig (plain with no queue or tail at the back, and meant to look like real hair) and his dress wig each only cost him 1 guinea (£14.4s.) in the previous year.[43] There was also the more serviceable campaign or travelling wig and several other variants. Men were enormously fussy over their wigs, as to whether the hair was the correct colour, or if the curls were sufficient in number and in good order; wigs were constantly having to be sent to the barber to be dressed or repaired. Sir John once paid 'the barbour lad for . . . dressing my wig ye ratts did eat'.[44]

When they ventured from home and family, men could, if they chose, be as flamboyant as women in their dress. They wore long, belted coats with ample skirts, which had to be fastened with buttons, and even 'sad coloured' ones could be made gay with silver and gold loops and buttons. Breeches were buttoned at the waist, and had side pockets for fobs; the materials used varied according to the needs of the occasion. Waistcoats, also worn long, gave considerable scope for extravagance in colour and trimmings. They could be made as sumptuous as you liked. Rich materials were further enhanced with gold and silver lace and buttons, and even simple holland could be made ornate when points (bows) of ribbon or lace were applied. Cravats, which were simply loosely tied scarves, were more ornamental than practical by the 1690s. Choice of material for these could range from gold and silver cloth or lace to fine muslin or linen edged with lace frills. Grisell Baillie's accounts for 28 February 1696 show

	£ s d
For a muslin cravat	14–16–0
2 ells muslin for a cravat	6– 0–0
2 ells muslin for a cravat	4–16–0[45]

Coarse material was used for underwear, and it was not often changed, so it was common practice to have detachable fronts and cuffs in the form of ruffles made up of finer linen. Probably for warmth, both men and women wore separate understockings which were kept in place by garters. Great attention was paid to gloves and shoes; the latter could be trimmed with buckles, and ribbons made into roses. Ladies also decorated their shoes and slippers in this way. When involved in out-of-door activities men wore jackboots, and women had pattens or clogs for wearing in bad weather. Men's hats were normally three-cornered, commonly made of beaver, an economical material which could be turned when necessary. From several accounts we see that hats from Caudebec in France were fashionable. The Laird of Calder bought himself '1 fine Godbeck hatt' for £4.10s. in 1672 (Foulis of Ravelston paid the identical amount in the same year for the same type of hat), and later he had '2 French codbeck hatts' for £7.4s.[46] In 1696 George Broun of Colstoun in East Lothian bought two Coudibeck hats which were of wool; unfortunately no price is given. Then in 1713 Sir George purchased a Carolina hat.[47] Was this perhaps an early version of the Dallas type of headgear with which we are familiar today?

When children were young, no distinction was made between the sexes; boys were dressed in petticoats and gowns until they were five or six years of age. When they were eventually promoted to wearing masculine clothes, these were more or less identical with those of their parents and older siblings. Trimmings were applied just as lavishly on the children's clothes as on those of their elders. Grisell Baillie spent generously on ribbons and laces, much of which was entered as 'for the bairens'. In 1646 the executor of a certain George Forrest of Haddington found himself responsible for two adolescent orphans, George and Jean Forrest, and having completely to reclothe them. It is interesting to note what was felt to be necessary in the matter of trimmings to their outfits.[48] George was sent to school at Tynninghame, and for him cloth costing 50s. an ell, and 5 yards of grey ribbon for points, were bought to make him 'some cloathis'. His summer suit the following year needed 6 ells of green material at 30/- an ell, and this was embellished with 'sax drop weight of grene silk to sew upon them perling quilk cam aff some of his mothers auld clothis', as well as 4 dozen buttons, and 5 ells of ribbons to make points for his 'breik kneis'. Many of Jean's clothes were made from old ones of her mother's, suitably trimmed and decorated with buttons and ribbons. We are told that she also had 6 ells of red ribbons and 4 of green for snoods and bells and roses.

CHAPTER 10

Crest of the Wave

Patrick had only been made Chancellor on 1 May 1696, but within a week or two the Edinburgh Burgh Council, hearing that he intended to avail himself of one of the 'perks' of office by moving into a suite of rooms at the Abbey of Holyrood House, started making urgent representations to him to live in the town instead. The case they made out was that of 'it being a great conveniency and ease to the leidges who resorts to the toun and to the inhabitants who have busines adoe with the Chancellar'.[1] So they appointed two of their number to try and persuade him to do as they asked, and offered to find him a convenient dwelling-house with necessary coach house and stables, and to pay the rent each year. Needless to say, the attraction of living in the Abbey was far too great, and the negotiations got nowhere. Undaunted, the Burgh Council tried again when his successor as Chancellor lost all his furniture in a fire there in April 1703 and had to move away until things were put right; but their efforts were no more successful in August 1703 than they had been seven years earlier.[2]

It took Grisell and Patrick some time after moving into their apartments in the Abbey to get all the furniture and decorations just as they wanted them. Over two years later, on 11 July 1698 (by which time young Patrick and his Lady had moved into the Abbey with his father), George Home gives an enthusiastic account of what had been achieved, though some things still remained to be completed, and the cost was obviously considerable: 'I went with my L⁰ Polwart to the Abbey where I see some furniture they had put up which is very fine: the hangings of the drawing room have silver in them and Chairs of Crimsone Damask, the Bed of State is very fine the Curtaine of Damask bleu and white and lined with green satine and orange fringes: I never thought bleu and green suted well near each other before. The chairs are of the bed, the hanging wer not up. Ther are also 2 cabinets 2 Tables 2 large glasses 4 stands all finely Japand. I see the Coach which is very fine and very high but they say the painting was spoilt in the ship but it is done up again tho not so well. My Lady has also a very fine chair Japand. They tell me they have spent 1200 l. more than their allowance'.

But before any of the plenishings were attended to, there were more urgent things to be done. 'Swipin the lums' was necessary; there were

171

twelve of them, and it cost four shillings each, as against only five at three shillings in their old lodgings. Then within ten days or so of moving to the Abbey, much that was essential for entertaining was bought:[3] fourteen water glasses at eight shillings each, twelve custard dishes at £2.8s. in all, eight dozen bottles ('with corks thereto') costing £15.2s., two brandy glasses fourteen shillings, and 'ane duzen of Laim [earthenware] Trenchers' £1.8s., while 'the Aile wyffe in Woodhall' had to be paid no less than £100. Three months later the following were bought:

2 dozen fine trenchers	£20. 8.0
6 big dishes, 4 mazarines, 4 ashets	£45.10.0
3 dozen fine metal trenchers	£39.12.0
1 dozen other trenchers	£10. 4.0
A little Monteith	£5. 0.0
A large flagon	£8. 8.0

In addition to all this, five pairs of green stockings were bought for servants costing £5.5s; the Chancellor and Andrew treated themselves to a hat each, the two costing £19.4s. A wig for Andrew cost £51, and a sword for Alexander was £30. Hadden the upholsterer was paid £28.16s. for 'furniture for the Bedds' and for 'dressing my beds'.

From the time of moving into the Abbey a special note was kept of expenses there, an account of disbursements 'in keeping the Lord Chancellor's house and of other expence of household and stables etc taken up and pay'd by Grisel Lady Polwarth'.[4] Beginning on 1 June 1696 a regular daily note is made of expenses directly connected with meals. Care has to be taken in interpreting this information, for no indication is given of the number of people who were eating these meals. In addition, some of the food was not paid for, because it came from Polwarth House. In one week in June, that contribution amounted to a wedder, a lamb and three capons, the next week three lambs, six capons, forty chickens and two pounds of fresh butter, but for many weeks nothing came from there at all. Then there would be isolated cases where a salmon, forty-two pigeons, two turkeys, three geese, or 'artichoaks and colliflowers' were recorded as being Polwarth House produce.

Two types of regular weekly payment are noted, usually on a Sunday. The first of these is for water; between fifty and fifty-five barrels a week were bought from the water man, initially at sixpence each but later at fourpence, two-thirds being for the kitchen and the rest for the porter 'and ye women in ye rooms'. The second regular weekly item is sweet herbs and roots from John Cockran the gardener, sometimes mentioning cabbage and kail as well, the cost being usually between £3 and £4. From time to time Holland sand is bought for scouring dishes (sometimes described as grey sand to scour the pewter), and there are payments of three shillings for 'pyps to my Lord at several tymes'. The food mentioned for a typical day's meal costs £5, and comprises a quarter of mutton (£2.6s.), eight chickens at four shillings each (£1.12s.), and 'ane side of Lamb to the servants' (£1.2s.). In a week when no special entertaining was being done, the cost of meals averaged about £46, including the regular amounts of water and sweet herbs. But items such as the £9.4s. 'given to ye carrier that brought ye canarie from Glasgow' appear as extraordinary expenses not forming part of the weekly food bill. On a Friday in February when 'my Lord and Lady and the young ladys and the gentlemen dined abroad' the cost of meals was only £1.3s., and occasionally (presumably for the same reason) fell as low as 12, 13, 17 or 18 shillings; on a 17-shilling day the only item mentioned is the 'two dozen haddocks to the servants' costing that sum, but we do not know for how many of them the haddocks were provided.

On a day when one of the special dinner parties (to be described shortly) was taking place, the cost of meals rose from the normal £5-£8 to £14-£30, the commonest dinner-party-day figure being around £20. The extra expense of the food involved seems only to have been about £3 per guest. In a week when one such party was held the food bill rose by £15 or so, but quite often two would take place in one week, usually on a Tuesday and a Thursday. The available figures do not enable us to estimate the extra cost of drink consumed. It must, however, have been considerable, for many consignments of wine from Glasgow are mentioned. Someone was paid £3 for cleaning the cellar, and £1.4s. was given 'to the man that easyed down the wines to the cellar'; and ten shillings was needed for 'a padlock to the cellar door'. Nor do we know what supplementary domestic staff were taken on, though the purchase of shoes for servants seems unusually frequent. Horses often needed to be hired to take servants from Edinburgh to Polwarth or vice versa; in May 1696, for instance, £5.3s. was paid for the cook and butler (presumably Robert Manderston) transporting themselves in this way. And when they did so, refreshment had to be paid for at the usual staging point, hence the payment of 'ane account at Ginnelkirk of servants coming and going'. Living at the Abbey seems to have entailed many more payments for carrying than had previously been the case — 'carrying the meat from the market', 'for carrying of 9 burdens to the Abbey', and so on. But some types of expense remained much the same; it still cost £3.18s. 'for 5 horses grassing 2 nights in Grange Park'.

Patrick's new importance — as an Earl, as Lord Chancellor living at the Abbey — certainly meant having to give more generously to all and sundry in Edinburgh at New Year. On 1 January 1701, for instance, we find this list:

To McLauchlan musician and his partner	£11.12.0
To the King's Trumpets	11.12.0
To the Cannongate Drumms	5.16.0
To the Town Guard Drums	2.18.0
To the Hoboyes	4. 3.6
To the poor boy that waits for and brings the letters	2.18.0
To Hugh Scot	14.6
To Isaac Blackwells son	14.6
To Lady Jean	14.6
To small hansells	1. 9.0
To the servant waits in the Signet Office	5.16.0
To the bedells in the New Church	3.14.0

Some explanation is required regarding the hoboyes (who also appear in Foulis of Ravelston's accounts when on 10 September 1705 he gave them £2.18s.).[5] These were the Town Waits. Fairly detailed arrangements were laid down for them at intervals in the 1690s. They were to play every morning (except on the Sabbath and humiliation days) from the first Tuesday in October until the eleventh of March.[6] Their number was to be four or at most five. From February 1690 onwards the instrument they were to use was the French oboe, but one of them was always to play the double curtle or bassoon.[7] And they were to have a livery consisting of a grey cloth cloak with black and white lace.[8] In December 1701 they claimed that these cloaks, though authorised, had not in fact been provided, so new instructions were given to ensure that they got them.[9]

Within a fortnight of being made Lord Chancellor, Patrick, aided by Grisell, had started to organise a special series of dinners, the main purpose of which was to try and achieve smoother working of the new administration than had characterised recent ones. This series of special dinners, about which we have fairly full information, numbered 55. They began on 14 May 1696 and went on at intervals until 11 August 1697. They resumed on 16 June but broke off on 21 July, when there was a gap until one or two took place in January/February 1698. They were held either once or twice a week during these periods. The number of invited guests varied from 3 to 13, but the two extremes of this range were highly exceptional. On 16 occasions there were 6 guests, and on 13 there were 5, so at more than half the dinners the invited guests numbered either 5 or 6. Some people were only invited to a single dinner, others were guests on many occasions. In all, more than a hundred different people were invited to attend one or more of these parties.[10]

There were clearly certain people whose views, religious or political, were so diametrically opposed to Patrick's, or whose past behaviour rendered them so suspect, that they would never under any circumstances have been invited to these functions. At the other end of the spectrum were close personal friends — Kimmerghame, Blackadder, Culloden and so on — but as all of them were frequent guests on many other occasions, they were only invited to a small number of these special dinners. On Friday 15 May all three of those just mentioned were guests at the dinner on that day, with five other suitably selected people to join them. Twice, when the guest of honour was a woman closely associated with the Polwarths, the others invited as members of the party had obviously been carefully chosen. The first such function was on Sunday 17 May 1696, when the name at the top of the list is that of Lady Hilton, widow of the Joseph Johnston an account of whose murder at the Hirsel thirteen years earlier after a game of cards has already been given. Her eldest surviving son Joseph had, as we have also seen, died just over a year before this dinner, so the next son Robert, now Laird of Hilton, accompanied his mother to the function, and two of the other guests invited to join them were both great friends — Blackadder and Commissary Home. Captain James Baillie, of the Edinburgh Town's Company, completed the party.

On Wednesday 18 November 1696 the guest of honour was Margaret, Countess of Rothes, widow of Charles Hamilton, 5th Earl of Haddington, who had died eleven years before when he was only 35. She had become Countess of Rothes in her own right on the death of her father in 1681. Also invited to this dinner were, not her eldest son John, Earl of Rothes, but her two younger sons, Thomas and Charles. Sixteen-year-old Thomas, the 6th Earl of Haddington, brought with him his eighteen-year-old bride Helen, whom he had married only a few months before. She was the daughter of the 4th Earl of Haddington, so it was clearly very appropriate to invite her widowed mother Lady Hopetoun to this dinner as well. Helen's brother, Lady Hopetoun's son Charles Hope, was also invited. Charles, the fifteen-year-old Laird of Hopetoun, was seven years later to become the first Earl. And the list was rounded off by inviting a few other relatives and friends.

Someone whom it would have seemed odd if Patrick had not invited to a dinner or two was Charles, 6th Earl of Home. He was, after all, the present representative of the longest ennobled family in Berwickshire, of the clan from which Patrick and so many of his closest friends were descended. The Earl was not, it is true, altogether *persona grata* with the authorities, and had recently been confined in Edinburgh Castle; but two dinner invitations need not be taken amiss. And as we have noted elsewhere, a closer link was to be established between the two families in a few years' time, when Patrick's son Lord Polwarth married as his second wife 'bonnie Jean o' the Hirsel'. As a courtesy, and to preserve good relations with the city authorities, whoever was current Lord Provost of Edinburgh was invited to one of the dinners. This meant that in June and July 1696 Sir Robert Cheislie was among the guests, and in November it was Sir Archibald Mure; while Baillie George Home, who was to be the latter's successor, was invited later. Then there were a number of people of distinction in fields other than politics whose presence would add interest to these occasions. One of the most interesting of the non-political people invited to these dinners was Sir William Bruce, who was in his seventies at the time. He had had a distinguished career as Scotland's foremost architect, perhaps best known for the restoration of Holyrood House after his appointment in 1671 to the post of the king's surveyor and master of works. In this capacity he designed the quadrangular building that was completed in 1679. Among other buildings for which he was responsible were his own house at Kinross, Moncrieffe House in Perthshire, Harden House in Roxburghshire, and also, as already noted, Hopetoun House in Linlithgowshire (the last better known for the Adam modifications carried out later).

Two other types of guest can be loosely described as non-political — ministers of religion and law lords. But such a description does not imply an entire absence of political leanings. For in many, perhaps in most cases, they would not have obtained their posts without being known to subscribe to the political beliefs of those in whose hands the power of appointment lay, or at the very least not to be opposed to them in any way. Three ministers were invited to the dinner on 7 January 1697, and a year later Patrick wrote, 'many ministers dined with me the time of the Assembly several days'. The invitations to law lords (two or three of whom were also members of parliament), unlike those of the ministers, are more widely distributed over the range of dinners, though on 17 November 1696 one was held exclusively for them. The names of the law lords first appeared in post-revolution Scotland, in a list dated 22 October 1689 of fifteen persons having a Commission for the College of Justice, all but three of whom came to these dinners in 1696-8. Home of Crossrig, who was one of them, has already been mentioned in his capacity as a close friend; he was invited to five of the special dinners. Another was Hamilton of Halcraig, who received no fewer than nine such invitations. Nearly as many were received by Maitland of Ravelrig, but by the time his eight invitations were sent he had already succeeded to the Earldom of Lauderdale on the death in 1695 of his elder brother Richard, so it was in that name that he appeared on the dinner lists. Murray of Philiphaugh attended five dinners, as did Campbell of Arbruchell (who was also an M.P.), but another law lord who was invited the same number of times was Lauder of Fountainhall (an M.P. as well as a law lord), a more interesting person from our point of view, for he not only kept a journal from 1665 to 1676 but also kept accounts from 1670 to 1675, long extracts from both of which were published by the Scottish History Society in 1909. His accounts, besides their value as such, are enlivened by his habit of periodically breaking into schoolboy French. Was this perhaps done to keep certain items private? We know that someone was paid to teach his wife writing and arithmetic; we do not know whether she was able to read French. At the time of the dinner parties to which he was invited he was fifty, living in an eight-hearth dwelling in Edinburgh with his wife Marion, four sons (the eldest boy, John, was in Holland), three daughters and a twelve-year-old nephew Colin. His manservants were listed as a Mr Andrew Thomson who was overseeing the children and teaching them grammar, and two others, and he also employed four women servants.[11] Of the other law lords who were guests at the dinners, Hope of Rankeillor was invited four times, as was Swinton of Mersington (Alexander, brother of Patrick's close friend John, the Laird of Swinton). Falconer of Phesdo and Baird of Newbyth were sent invitations three times each, as was Dundas of Arniston.

The last of those named in the October 1659 Commission who was a dinner guest was William Enstruther of that Ilk, better known to us as Sir William Anstruther, who was a member of parliament for Fife and also a privy councillor. His wife was Lady Helen Hamilton, daughter of the 4th Earl of Haddington and sister of Lady Hopetoun; she obviously enjoyed going to roups, for we know that she was a successful bidder when the household plenishings of a Writer to the Signet, Andro Hog, were sold in October 1691.[12] It was a six-day affair and, judging by the range and the sequence of her successful bids, she probably went along on most of those days, accompanied by 'her lass' who was also a successful bidder for some items — 'ane copper tank at £1–6s, ane whyt iron filler at 4s, ane frame for smoothing irones at 5s, and ane stone chamber pott at 4s'. On the whole, Lady Anstruther herself bought rather more costly items, such as 'ane naprie preis' at £4–16s, her friend

Lady Arniston getting 'ane ffir presse' for £10–18s. Her most expensive lot, for which she paid £13–14s, was 'ane feather bed bolster and two cods with ane Lang-sadle [couch convertible into a bed]'; she also bought, for £12, 'ane fether bed bolster and two cods', and paid £7–7–6 for four pewter plates. Some of her purchases may have been for the use of the servants; for although, when the blankets were being auctioned, she paid £2–10s for one pair, she also bought 'four paire of course blankits at 36s pr paire'. And, like all roup addicts, she could not resist an obvious bargain, as when 'six old cusheones' went for only £1–16s.

One other law lord received as many as eight invitations to these dinners, and that was Campbell of Cessnock, but his was rather a special case. Although he had been persuaded, much against his will, to give up the post of Lord Justice Clerk in 1693, he was, as we have seen, the father of the heiress whom Patrick's son Alexander married in July 1697, so that an even closer bond than before was being forged between the two families at the time the dinners were taking place. There were two further points of past history linking Patrick with Cessnock. They had been fellow prisoners confined in the Bass in 1675; and they were both promoters of the Carolina scheme in 1682 (whereby some land in that province in North America was to have been acquired for settlement — the project having to be abandoned in the aftermath of the Rye House Plot). So on all counts it was natural that he should get more than the usual share of invitations. In 1696-8 much more topical than the defunct Carolina scheme was the Darien affair, and two of the people actively involved in this, who could bring the other dinner guests up-to-date as to what was happening, were invited to come along. Mr Francis Montgomerie, of Giffen in Ayrshire, whom Edinburgh Burgh Council had honoured by making him burgess and gild brother without payment in 1693 (he was made a Viscount in April 1700), was invited to four of the dinners.[13] Two invitations went to John Hamilton, 2nd Lord Belhaven who, in addition to his participation in the Darien scheme, was one of the farmers both of the poll tax and of the excise.

However pleasant it might be to have guests at these dinners who were personal friends, or who were not first and foremost politicians, the primary purpose of organising the events was to try and promote more political harmony, and to make the machinery of government work with the minimum of friction. From this point of view the most important group to have fully represented at as many of the dinners as possible was the members of the reconstructed administration of 1696. Patrick, as the new Lord Chancellor, was inviting his colleagues in the governing of Scotland to join him in a series of convivial occasions when past animosities (of which there were all too many) would, it was hoped, be forgotten. For it must be remembered that the new administration was made up of a varied assortment of people, some of whom actively disliked each other, or were strongly suspicious (often rightly) of each other's motives and intentions. To get them to pull together was a difficult, if not impossible, task, especially for someone lacking the political muscle of one of the powerful families of the land.

The particular member of the new administration whom Patrick was clearly determined to make the centrepiece of his special dinners was James Douglas, second Duke of Queensberry, who attended more of them than anyone else — as many as nineteen. He had succeeded to the title on the death of his father in 1695, and as the representative of an important magnate interest, King William's advisers went to great lengths to bring him into the government at this point, which involved persuading Melville to switch from his post as Privy Seal to another position. He had already played quite an important part in politics, and had been authorised in 1693 to sit and vote in parliament as Lord High Treasurer; earlier he had been branded by a supporter of the Stuarts as 'the first Scotsman that deserted over to the Prince of Orange, and from thence acquired the epithet (among honest men) of Proto-rebel . . .'[14] Except with those who hated the Douglas family, he was personally popular and regarded as a skilled diplomatist, and in making him a star turn at the dinners Patrick was anxious to make use of those qualities, and also to gain and retain his goodwill for the future.

George, Earl of Melville, who reluctantly gave up his privy seal post which he had held for five years, to enable Queensberry to be brought in, was now president of the council. He had known Patrick for a long time — they had been exiles together in Holland — and from his first appointment as secretary in 1689 had been much involved in government and administration. Patrick got on well with him, to judge by the tone of the large number of letters they wrote to each other. He was invited to eight of the dinners, though a few years later one unkind critic, whilst conceding that a steadiness of principle and a firm boldness for presbyterian government had enabled him to sustain the important positions he had held, also said, 'he hath neither learning, wit, nor common conversation'.[15]

The other member of that family in the 1696 administration was Alexander Melville, styled Lord Raith. He was the Earl's eldest son and had managed — or some would have said *mis*managed — the public revenue in his capacity as treasurer depute, a post he held from 1689 to 1698. He was invited to six of the dinners, and to one of them his Lady

(Barbara, daughter of Walter Dundas of that Ilk) was also asked to come, together with two of her nieces, neither of her own children having survived beyond infancy. That particular dinner (on Saturday 6 February 1697) was quite a family affair; Earl Melville was also invited, the only non-family guest being the ubiquitous Queensberry.

One of the features of the reconstruction of the administration in 1696 was the attempt to bring in several of the magnate interests, and as the Duke of Atholl had retired from public life, his son Lord John Murray was made joint secretary with Ogilvy. And a few months later, in order that he should also fulfil the duties of commissioner to the parliament, he had to be made an Earl, and chose as his title Tullibardine. Relations between him and Patrick seemed at first to be reasonable — he stayed at Polwarth House in May 1697 — but for some reason, although a key figure, he was invited to just two of the dinners. Macaulay's description of him as 'the falsest, the most fickle, the most pusillanimous of mankind' has, rather unfairly, stuck in the memories of most people.[16] Sir James Ogilvy, joint secretary with him, came to four of the dinners. A younger son of the Earl of Findlater, he carried little family weight but had taken a legal training and came to be regarded as a highly skilled administrator and manager. He represented the burgh of Cullen in parliament and had been an active member of the club, who signed the address (the significance of which has been explained in Chapter 8). He was later raised to the peerage as Viscount Seafield and took over from Patrick as Chancellor in 1702. A remark of his at the signing ceremony at the time of the Union in 1707 is widely remembered: 'now there's ane end of ane auld sang'.[17]

Sir James Stewart of Goodtrees had managed to hold on to his post as Lord Advocate in 1696. Riley sums him up in the comment 'nobody completely trusted him, and wisely'.[18] Rather surprisingly, Patrick seems to have remained on friendly terms with him — they had been exiles together in Holland — and he was invited to three of the dinners. Another untrustworthy character was Sir Patrick Home of Renton, the advocate, who was Solicitor General in the 1696 administration. He had been involved in a variety of dubious dealings, including the dispossession of his brother's relict. But he continued to be a protégé of Patrick's, often visiting Polwarth House, and he was invited to four of the special dinners. Adam Cockburn of Ormiston, the new Lord Justice Clerk, received six dinner invitations. His political career had followed a similar pattern to Patrick's, but without being firmly linked to any particular grouping (though he did sign the address).

Of the new treasury commissioners appointed in 1696, William

Johnston, first Marquess of Annandale, had changed sides more often than most of his contemporaries, and his political career, as well as his life, had for a time been put in jeopardy by his involvement in Montgomerie's plot in 1690 (though, like the ringleader, he had been a club member who signed the address). The plan, thought out by Sir James Montgomerie of Skelmorlie, had been to organise the restoration of James to the throne in return for very substantial rewards to the conspirators. Perhaps because he had talked himself out of so many tight corners Patrick clearly thought of him as an effective dinner guest, and he received eleven invitations. Another treasury commissioner invited almost as many times was Patrick's close friend Sir John Maxwell of Pollok, whose career we outlined in Chapter 4. But the most uncomfortable person to have as a treasury commissioner, or indeed as a colleague in any capacity, must have been Archibald Campbell, 1st Duke of Argyll, recently returned to the political scene, whose powerful family support William's advisers were particularly anxious to secure. He was no stranger to Patrick, who had known him in exile, and on more than one occasion Polwarth House was one of his staging points in his horseback journey to London. If in conversation his behaviour bore any resemblance to the contents of his letters, the eight dinners he attended would be lively affairs. One of the people he particularly disliked, Sir Thomas Livingstone, commander-in-chief of the forces in Scotland (made Viscount Teviot late in 1696), was asked to three dinners, but they were not ones at which Argyll was a fellow guest. A junior member of the 1696 administration, Mr Robert Pringle, who thanked Patrick for his help in obtaining the position of under-secretary, was abroad with the King during part of the time when the dinners were held, but did get the chance to attend one on 3 February 1698 when he was in Scotland. A more important person whose attendance on the King made it impossible for him to attend any dinners was Charles Douglas, second Earl of Selkirk (son of the late Duke of Hamilton) who had replaced Tarbat as lord clerk register in September 1696.

Apart from the primary purpose of trying to foster friendlier feelings towards each other amongst the members of the new administration, it is fair to assume from studying the names of the other politicians invited that another important aim was to try and ensure the continued support in parliament of people who had hitherto been on the same side as Patrick. Some of the guests we have already met came into this category, but we can now look at a few more and see (by knowing what happened afterwards) what success attended these endeavours. In one of the cases, success or failure cannot be measured. Sir Charles Halkett of Pitfirrane

(Fife), who was M.P. for Dunfermline, was invited to a dinner but died in 1697. The successes, from Patrick's point of view, were those who in the 1698 parliament showed themselves to be on the administration's side. One of these was Sir Archibald Murray of Blackbarony (Peebles) who had been at three of the dinners. Another, who had had nine invitations, had been a fellow member of the club and signed the address. He was James Douglas, Earl of Morton. Archibald Douglas, Earl of Forfar, attended five dinners and continued to support the administration, as did Robert Kerr, Earl of Lothian (Commissioner to the General Assembly in 1692), who received three invitations. John, Lord Carmichael, was at seven of the dinners. He had the unusual distinction of having once previously turned down the offer of being made Secretary, but he was prevailed on in 1698 to change his mind. George Mackenzie, Viscount of Tarbat (a Fellow of the Royal Society), had resigned as lord clerk register when the new administration was formed, but lent his support in the 1698 parliament; he was at three of the dinners.

These six cases where continued political support was forthcoming were matched by four other guests who later joined the opposition. Here, however, no amount of wining and dining could possibly have influenced the outcome. The key figure in the rather sorry story was William Hamilton of Whitelaw, an extremely able and ambitious lawyer, M.P. for the burgh of Queensferry, who had been made a member of the court of session in 1693. Up to the time of the dinners (to eight of which he was invited) he had always been closely associated politically with Patrick, culminating in the crucial help he gave in the parliamentary session of 1696 to enable the administration to get two years' cess for the army. As a reward for the key role he played in this, he was promised the position of president of the court of session, but the maneouvres of his enemies prevented the fulfilment of this promise, and from 1698 he became a leading member of the opposition. George Home, on 7 April 1698, claimed that 'his partiality and huffiness' had done him harm, 'at least they are made use of against him'.

Much to Patrick's disappointment, several more of his closest political allies went with Whitelaw. One of these was Thomas Burnet of Leys (Kincardine), at three dinners. Another to be invited the same number of times was Alexander Monro of Bearscrofts, an active club member who had signed the address. The third, invited to six dinners, was David, Lord Ruthven, who, with Forbes of Culloden, Patrick and one or two others, had been a member of the Melville clique, sometimes called the 'secret committee' which had virtually run the country for a time after 1690.

Patrick made great efforts to secure the goodwill of someone else who was becoming politically important, and invited the Duke of Hamilton's fourth son John to no fewer than eight dinners. He became Earl of Ruglen in April 1697, and thereafter became the only representative in parliament of this important magnate interest (Selkirk not being free to attend); it was a major blow when he joined the opposition in 1698. His appointment in 1696 as general of the mint and as a commissioner of the exchequer had been intended to make him feel part of the administration. The fifth and sixth of the Duke's sons, George who became Earl of Orkney and was a military man, and Lord Basil Hamilton who remained at home to look after the estates, were also each invited to a dinner, but it was John whose future backing for Patrick and the new administration would have been of real value.

Perhaps less important politically were John and Charles Hay. They were the sons of John Hay, first Marquess of Tweeddale, Patrick's predecessor as Lord Chancellor. The father died on 11 August 1697 but, before that happened, Patrick invited him and both his sons to the dinner held on 25 June 1696, John styled as Lord Yester and Charles as Master of Yester. John had already been invited on his own to two of the earlier dinners; he, incidentally, was a Fellow of the Royal Society. Then, on their father's death, they continued to receive invitations. John, now second Marquess of Tweeddale, attended one more dinner. Charles, now Lord Yester, also attended one more, but, most unusually in this series of dinners, his Lady was invited to accompany him. She was Susan, relict of the Earl of Dundonald, but she was also the third daughter of the Duke and Duchess of Hamilton, so the exception may have been made for this reason.

These special dinners were not the only ones that Patrick and Grisell organised. Margaret Warrender, in Appendix I of her book, prints 'The Countess of Marchmont's Bills of Fair while her husband the Lord Chancellor was Commissioner to the Parliament in 1698'.[19] The four dates are 23 July, and 26, 27 and 28 August 1698. Unfortunately no lists of those invited seem to have survived, and the weekly statements of what Patrick and Grisell spent on food in Edinburgh do not go beyond 1697. That they continued to hold formal dinner parties at the Abbey is clear from an entry in George Home's diary for 4 January 1699: 'I went to the Chancellours to have dined, but many being ther on invitation I came home to my Chamber'. But for the unfortunate fact that the pages of his diary cut out and destroyed are for the period 7 April 1696 to 19 September 1697, we would certainly have had his comments on the formal dinners he himself attended in May 1696. One of the 'Bills of Fair' is worth reproducing:

SUNDAY THE 28 DAY OF AUGUST 1698.

BILL FOR DINNER.

pottaig alla ryne.		rost mutton in blood.
gellie.		could bark powding.
Rost beefe.		a dish of tarts.
Lobesters.		gellie.
a pigeon paye.		Rost geese, 3.
portigall eges.		Ragow of Rabets, 3.
Rost hens, 6.		Ragow of Lamb.
pigeon compost, 8.	*To Relleve.*	grand sellet.
Rost mutton with Cuttllots.	wyld foull 8, & Chickns 6.	pottaige.
boyld powding.	Chickns 6, and pigeons 14.	olives of Mutton.
Rost Rabets, 7.		Rost Mutton with Couttllots.
scots collopes.		gellie.
Rost pigeons, 20.		Rost hens, 6.
gellie.		frydd skaite.
Rost kid.		chickn pay.
green sellet.		portigall eges.
a dish of tarts.		pottaige.

TO THE COMPTROLLER'S TABLE.

Rost Lamb.	Rost beefe.	Rost mutton.
	Pottaige.	
	Boyld mutton.	

Rost hens 5, *to Relleve.*

We are also told that on this occasion the wine for my Lord's table included 18 claret, 7 sherry, 2 gins, and 4 port, though the size of bottle is not specified.

Although these events had a serious political purpose, there was much more to being Chancellor than organising and participating in convivial dinner parties. So some account must now be given of what was happening in the political arena from the point at which we broke off in Chapter 8. When, against all the odds, Patrick was made Chancellor in May 1696, everyone, not least himself, knew exactly what was expected of him. First, to carry out faithfully the policies laid down by the King and his advisers, Portland and Carstares, neither going beyond his instructions nor failing to implement any of the crucial ones. Secondly, he was to keep what in today's jargon would be called a low profile, being particularly careful not to upset or annoy any powerful people or groups, either inside or outside the government. His own awareness of what he was required to do is clearly shown in the letters he wrote to Lord John Murray, to Sir James Ogilvy, to the Earl of Portland, William Carstares and the King himself (the last three all in Flanders at the time) immediately after taking over his new post. Almost every sentence of these letters makes this clear: 'I will set myself with all earnestness to endeavor the reconcilement of parties, and the removal of animosities, and the preventing of heats among those whom the King employs . . .'[20] He hopes before long they will 'have satisfying account of my deportment from honorable persons . . . for I am well resolved to commit as few errors as I can . . .'[21] His early efforts seem to have satisfied all concerned, for a few months later, writing from Whitehall on 19 December 1696, Lord John Murray (now the Earl of Tullibardine) pats him on the back: 'I have also acquainted his Majestie with your lordships zeale and diligence at this time and the unanimity and concurrence you have of the Duke of Queensberrie and others in the Councill . . . I am very glad you agree so very well with the Duke of Queensberrie and Argile; I wish it may continue . . .'[22] Congratulations were, indeed, in order. For although it helped to have good parliamentary working majorities among peers, barons and burgh representatives, and although the opposition made a rather poor showing, the skill of Patrick and the other managers, greatly helped by Hamilton of Whitelaw and others, had carried the day in the 1696 parliament. Patrick's reward for this, and for his past loyalty — he was made Earl of Marchmont on 23 April 1697 — was a necessary preliminary to his replacing the departed Tullibardine as commissioner for the next parliament in July 1698. But well before this last exciting opportunity came along, the cracks in the administration created in 1695-96 had become so wide that they could no longer be papered over.

The King himself had had ugly evidence of these cracks as early as April 1697. As Patrick learned by a letter from Whitehall on the 15th of that month (when he himself was probably too elated by his Earldom to be unduly worried by the news), Tullibardine had tried to persuade the King to rescind an appointment he had just made on Ogilvy's recommendation. The writer of the letter, the under-secretary Robert Pringle whom Patrick had recommended for his post, gives a graphic and secret account of what took place when the King called the two secretaries before him: 'At their first comming in he told them he was not willing to think of being anie more troubled with such differences . . . the King told them he would have no more of it . . . After they left the King, and had reasoned a little betwixt themselves before my Lord Selkirk, there was a seeming reconciliation made and they carry nou to on another as formerlie'.[23] How 'seeming' this and other reconciliations were was shown when, a year or so later, Tullibardine offered his resignation (which was, to his surprise, accepted) over the blocking of his proposed reward to Hamilton of Whitelaw, the post of president of the court of session, by Queensberry, who secured it instead for his candidate, Sir Hugh Dalrymple. Tullibardine, writing to Patrick just before resigning, blamed Carstares as well for what was happening: 'That a churchman should meddle with Court and State is intolerable . . . This honest man, Carstairs, pretends he goes about private business, and Secretary Ogilvy sayes the same, but I have grounds to know that he has other affairs to manage . . .'[24]

Patrick's position as commissioner for the 1698 parliament, and his job as chancellor, was made infinitely more difficult by Tullibardine now being in opposition and having been joined by Hamilton of Whitelaw. For the time being, Argyll decided to join forces with Queensberry, but such an alliance was bound to break down sooner or later, for the same underlying reason that had caused Tullibardine's resignation: the impossibility of satisfying the demands of the rival magnate interests. Patrick could hardly be blamed for not being able to reconcile the irreconcilable. And even had this been possible, his own power base was quite inadequate for any such venture.

With the opposition greatly strengthened in ability, if not numerically, by the presence of Tullibardine, Whitelaw and others, it might have been expected that Patrick's first (and, as it turned out, his last) parliamentary test as commissioner would be a gruelling one. However, despite famine-level harvests, and economic grievances with considerable potential as sticks with which to beat the administration, careful drafting of an address on the Africa Company (responsible for the Darien scheme) secured unanimous support, and the government emerged at the end of the session relatively unscathed. Carmichael was persuaded to accept the post of secretary and to act jointly with Ogilvy (now Seafield). But Queensberry was pursuing a remarkably successful policy of bypassing the secretaries, ignoring Patrick, and steadily extending his family's influence throughout the administration. And adverse developments in the Africa Company's affairs began to provide the opposition with just the issue they needed to make the government's position untenable.

The depressing story of the Darien disaster is too well known to need more than a brief reminder of the stages by which that position was reached. Right from its beginning, the Company of Scotland trading to Africa and the Indies had been political dynamite. Whether or not the dismissal from office of Tweeddale and Johnston was due to the part they were supposed to have played in the 1695 Act establishing the Company becoming law, there is no doubt that King William was against what he regarded as the far too sweeping powers conferred by the Act, and so were many protectionist interests in England, who thought the Navigation Act arrangements were bound to be gravely weakened thereby. And when the company's directors decided to found a Scottish colony in such a peculiarly inhospitable place as Darien, claimed by the Spanish, the scene was set for very large losses of capital on the part of the many subscribers, for loss of life, for the further poisoning of relations with England, for sparking off mob violence in Edinburgh on several occasions (the most alarming of which was in June 1700), and for acutely embarrassing everyone in Scottish politics except the opposition.* Patrick himself believed the whole scheme to be ill-conceived and virtually incapable of succeeding but, like everyone else, he was intensely worried as he saw his worst fears being realised. Writing to George Home (not the diarist, but Edinburgh's Lord Provost) from Polwarth House on 19 October 1699, he shows this, and seeks up-to-date information as to the company's response to what is happening: 'I cannot tell you how uneasie I have been by the news of our Colony tho I cannot hinder myselfe from hopeing that things are better than the common accounts give them out to be'.[25] The disastrous outcome of the Darien scheme was meat and drink to the opposition (though many of them suffered financially). For it not only provided a common cause to unite the otherwise disparate groups of which that opposition was composed, but the patriotic element involved made it extremely difficult for Patrick, and other members of the administration, openly to oppose any addresses and other proposals for a last-minute rescue or retrospectively helping the company, however impractical or extreme these might be. And it also gave the Hamiltons just the cause they needed to re-enter the political arena.

So in spite of a good harvest in 1699, following a succession of very poor ones in the years preceding, the administration found itself in grave difficulties, over Darien and for other reasons, in the last years of William's reign. The opposition demanded an Act stating the Africa

---

*Almost every prominent figure in Scottish politics had his windows broken or his house set alight at one time or another as a result of mob violence in Edinburgh. Patrick was one of the few who escaped such treatment, though George Home reported on 20 December 1699: 'there was a foolish paper put on the Crosse last night wherein was writt to this purpose "Murther Marchmont Murther Annandale &c Traitors to their Country K James is our righteous King"'.

Company's legal right to New Caledonia (the name given to the colony at Darien in the isthmus of Panama), but the administration's instructions from the King and his advisers did not permit them to agree to this. The first parliamentary session, in May 1700, was only survived with difficulty. A three-man delegation (Argyll, Seafield and Annandale) then went to London to report and to seek guidance, and Argyll and Seafield made great efforts on their return to Scotland to recruit support for the administration in the forthcoming parliament; but Queensberry, as before, seemed more interested in expanding his empire with the active (if sometimes secret) support of Carstares. The parliamentary session, 29 October 1700 to 1 February 1701, was by far the stormiest since Patrick had become Chancellor. To Robert Pringle the under-secretary on 19 November, he writes: 'We have hitherto had a contentious and hot session; I never saw the like'.[26] But worse was to come, and writing to him again on 9 January 1701, Patrick describes the latest sitting as 'the hottest, most contentious and disorderly that ever I saw; and I wish and hope never to see the like'.[27] He sums the whole session up in his next report to Pringle on 6 February 1701: 'but I must say, the King's servants did what they could; and I am sure, I have had a more difficult and burthensome post, than any who has been in my station in the last century, of which very many are sensible'.[28] Scotland was rapidly showing itself to be ungovernable under existing arrangements. Patrick himself, in an earlier letter to Pringle on 23 December 1699, said there was increasing support for the idea of a full union of Scotland with England; many were realising that in the long term this might be the only solution.[29] But things came to a head in the much shorter term, when Queensberry refused to countenance a plan which had the support of Argyll and Seafield as well as Patrick. This was to get Whitelaw into the administration (and secure the parliamentary votes of his henchmen), by arranging for him to have Selkirk's post of lord clerk register. And around the same time Queensberry succeeded in getting rid of Sir Patrick Home as solicitor general, and in having him replaced by one of his own nominees. Patrick was so infuriated that he wrote to the King on 19 April 1701 in unusually frank terms: '. . . your Majesty has been pleased to put off some, who have been in your service, particularly Sir Patrick Hume [Home], from being your solicitor, which I cannot easily believe, knowing him to be as able for that post as any who can be employed . . . Besides that, he has been useful to me in your Majesty's service, so as, I am sure, would please your Majesty, when I have an opportunity of telling particulars'.[30] Such an opportunity was not going to be provided if Queensberry had anything to do with it. The stage was set for the abjuration crisis of 1702, following King William's death in March.

For the first time since he had become Chancellor, Patrick's role in the 1702 parliament was decisive, but decisive in splitting the government, not in holding it together. King William having died, the opposition boycotted the meeting; those who remained were all government supporters. Queensberry, as Commissioner, decided to go ahead with the session despite the mass exodus of seventy-four members. His instructions made it possible for him, if he thought it desirable, to allow an Act imposing an abjuration of the pretender to the throne. He knew that to do so would bring into the open for all to see the fact that the government was split on this issue, as on many others. Patrick, on the other hand, wanted to press for such an Act, both because he believed in it, and in order that those who opposed it would have to stand up and be counted. Queensberry instructed him not to raise the issue, but he did. The expected split in the administration immediately showed itself, and the abjuration was passed, but by so few votes that the two incompatible groups of whom the government was now seen to be composed were also seen to be almost numerically equal. A crisis in which the Chancellor defied an instruction from the Commissioner, and publicly raised an issue calculated to wreck the government, was bound to lead to his no longer being kept in office. Immediately after the episode, parliament was adjourned on 30 June 1702, and was then dissolved on 8 August, Patrick being relieved of the Chancellorship a few months later.

From the vantage point of this crisis in 1702, we can look back to 1696 and ask ourselves how such a complete reversal could have come about. What had happened in those six years to cause Patrick (who had, entirely on his own initiative, made Queensberry the star turn of the special dinner parties he and Grisell organised in 1696-98, inviting him to no fewer than nineteen of them) to become Queensberry's arch-enemy in 1702? Part of the explanation lies in the ambivalence of Queensberry's beliefs and behaviour. The side that Patrick admired, and for which he was prepared gladly to follow him, was that of a key figure in the revolution, a fellow-exile who was completely committed to that cause, and whose personal credentials (unlike his father's) were unchallengeable. In the intervening six years, however, another side of Queensberry had become increasingly apparent and had, by 1702, made him seem no longer a revolution man, but a greedy self-seeker bent on advancing his relations and friends, totally without regard to their suitability or their beliefs. And it was not only Patrick who had decided enough was enough. Argyll, in alliance with Queensberry for much of the period, had certainly come to the same conclusion by September 1701, when he planned to detach Whitelaw and his followers from the opposition by securing for him Selkirk's post as lord clerk register, only to find that Queensberry was more interested in appointing one of his own nominees than in making parliamentary management easier.

But this was not all. For a very long time Patrick had been a prey to fears that those on whose advice the King relied might recommend his dismissal as Chancellor and replacement by someone else. To show how early in his Chancellorship these fears developed, it is revealing to look at some of his correspondence in December 1697, only some nineteen months after being given the post. This particular scare was started by a letter written to him by Tullibardine, dated Kensington, 16 December. Tullibardine talks of ill-disposed persons with access to the King and his advisers insinuating 'that there is no government in Scotland, which is the very words are saide, and that your Lordship has no authority, and that crimes are lett falle or but slightly noticed. I am informed within these two days that it is concerted that Earl Argile should be Chancellor. I challenged the Duke of Queensberry on itt to-day, but he sweares he knowes nothing of itt. The last continues to work by the back door, and I realy belive has been a black sight as we say, to Scotland, by mis-representing honest men, and other methods which I shall not now insist on . . . The King asked me yesterday if your Lordship was not grown old'.[31] This letter illustrates only too well the atmosphere of suspicion, double-dealing, betrayal and uncertainty in which Scotland's affairs were conducted. Exhortations for everyone in the administration to sink their differences and pull together were clearly useless in this sort of climate. Patrick wrote frantically to Ogilvy and Carstares, and although their replies were insistent that no such proposal was in the wind, no-one's reassurance could really be relied on.

Only about six months later we find George Home trying to alert his friend and protector the Chancellor to dangers of just the same kind. This time it is Tullibardine who is cast in the role of villain of the piece. He is credited (or debited) with having made a fool of Patrick and with having done everything in his power to get the Earl of Arran (James Douglas, afterwards fourth Duke of Hamilton) made Chancellor instead of him. The trouble all stemmed, in George's view, from Patrick's not having asked Carstares to dinner, or made sufficient fuss of him, when he was last in Scotland. Tullibardine had by the time of the diary entry of 11 July 1698 resigned, and 'now the Chancellour is like to have trouble enough to get things carried in parliament; Tullibardin is doing all he can to obstruct a cesse and break the army'. There is also ample evidence that Queensberry had been trying at intervals, in the four years preceding Patrick's ultimate dismissal as Chancellor in 1702, to replace him by one of his own nominees, of whom there were so many from his own family and friends always waiting in the wings for any available post that the actual name of the prospective Chancellor may well have changed from one month to the next. Patrick himself told Seafield in strict confidence on 19 December 1699 that both of their posts were threatened: 'Now, I must tell you, and take it from me to keep with yourself, I see evidently and by clear tokens, that both you and I need to stand back to back, if we will be upon our guard . . . for the Earl of Annandale and the Treasurer Depute are aiming with much earnestness to be upon our saddles'.[32]

Apart from his gradually increasing suspicion and dislike of Queensberry, and fears for his own position, Patrick certainly felt more and more isolated, with fewer and fewer friends around him as the months went by. This feeling of isolation really began when Tullibardine left the administration and Whitelaw's disappointment caused him to support the opposition in 1698. To understand how increasingly isolated Patrick must have felt, we have only to look at how many of those who had previously been his supporters and colleagues had, in 1698 or 1700, joined the opposition. Even a bare list of five of the 1698 defectors makes depressing reading — Sir Thomas Burnet of Leys, Ludovic Grant of Grant, Alexander Monro of Bearscrofts, James Pringle of Torwoodlee, and Sir John Lauder of Fountainhall. And when we add those who were either absent in 1698 or in only half-hearted support, but had by 1700 clearly moved to the other side, three of his closest associates — Duncan Forbes of Culloden, Sir John Home of Blackadder, and George Baillie of Jerviswood — are joined by at least two others, Sir Archibald Murray of Blackbarony and Robert Craig of Riccarton. For someone whose suitability for high office had always been in doubt because he had so few vote-carrying followers whose allegiance he could guarantee, the loss of even ten such sympathisers was nothing short of catastrophic. Viewed through the eyes of these ten, of course, it was not they who had defected but Patrick who, by clinging to office in an administration increasingly consisting of people whose loyalty to the revolution and to presbyterianism was highly suspect, had betrayed both his principles and his friends. When he at last saw the light and precipitated the abjuration crisis in 1702, an important lost sheep seemed to be returning to the fold with a vengeance.

Epilogue

Patrick's dismissal from his post as Lord Chancellor, though a bitter (if partly self-inflicted) blow, was not the end of his participation in the political and public life of Scotland. The blow was slightly softened by his being allowed to continue as Commissioner to the General Assembly of the Kirk. What happened there was that he had been given the responsibility by King William on 23 February 1702; but the King's death on 8 March was followed by Queen Anne immediately confirming both his appointment as Commissioner, and that the Assembly should carry on its deliberations as planned. The Assembly was an annual affair, and the Queen continued for another two years to nominate Patrick as her representative, but this came to an end after that, as George Home reports in one of his last diary entries, for 25 March 1705: 'The Commission for the Earl of Marchmont being Commissioner to the General Assembly was ready to be signed by the Queen, but the Duke of Argyll hindered it'. More importantly, he was still to have a significant part to play in helping to achieve an objective which had been dear to his heart for a long time: the complete union of Scotland and England. Though he never again held high office, these were certainly compensations. He was, after all, only sixty-one at the time of his dismissal as Chancellor, and although, when writing to the Earl of Leven (who had just been made commander-in-chief of the forces in Scotland) on behalf of his son on 28 January 1706, he says 'I am old, and off the stage of business; it is no matter for me', it is doubtful whether he meant it.[1] And he probably also had his tongue in his cheek when writing on 9 July 1709 to Robert Pringle: 'Some things which have happened of late relating to me, inclined me to think, that friends there began to look on me as a decayed man; and, I am sure, they can better judge of me, than I can do myself'.[2]

Locally as well as nationally, Patrick's life did not grind to a complete halt in 1702. He was still high sheriff of Berwickshire, as he had been ever since the revolution. He did not, however, remain entirely undisturbed in that position, for on 9 September 1710 we find him sending a letter of protest to the Queen: 'Now, being informed that your Majesty will be dealt with to give that office to the Earl of Home, who has as yet given no proof of his affection to your government, or done any service therein . . .'[3] The seventh Earl apparently felt that his claim was a hereditary one, but a few years later Patrick was restored to the office. And when the Earl of Home called a meeting of heritors at Duns in 1715, Patrick wrote to the sheriff clerk telling him to turn up at Duns on the day of the proposed meeting, and to invoke the law if his efforts peacefully to persuade people not to assemble there were unsuccessful.[4]

Another matter of great importance to Patrick locally is mentioned by George Home on 13 March 1704, when the diarist is trying to get hold of 'a copy of the Earl of Marchmont's signature of a new regality he has erected under the title of the Regality of Marchmont'. John Dickson (Patrick's factor) sent him a copy a week or so later. The gist of the matter was that on 31 January 1704 the baronies of Polwarth, Redbraes and Greenlaw were united and incorporated into 'ane haill and free lordship and regality of Marchmont . . . The town and burgh of Greenlaw [was] to be the principal head burgh of the said regality in all time coming'.[5] By doing this Patrick was, with royal permission, carving a little kingdom (as one writer described it) out of the realm. By such a grant the sovereign devolved all her royal rights upon the lord of regality, including the power of ordering capital punishment, and of dealing with virtually all crimes except treason. Indeed, these powers were so wide that the sheriff could be ordered to send back any culprit living in the regality to be tried and dealt with by the lord. Such powers might be useful to Patrick or his successors at some future time should the office of sheriff of Berwickshire (as was to happen for a while in 1710) fall into other hands. So what he persuaded the Queen or her advisers to grant him in March 1704 was no mere formality. Perhaps it was no accident that it was only a few weeks later that he changed the styling of Polwarth House to Redbraes Castle.

But although there were developments both in the national and in the local arena to take his mind off the major blow he had suffered in November 1702, there was also a succession of family matters, some a cause for rejoicing, others for grief. On the pleasurable side, a good deal of time was taken up, in the months following January 1703 when the decisions were first made, by the arrangements for two weddings, both of which took place in April — Jean's to Lord Torpichen, and Patrick's to Jean, the Earl of Home's daughter. And grandchildren from the marriages of his other children were now coming along, so that by 29 August 1711, when he wrote a letter full of family news to his relative Sir Gustavus Hume in Ireland, he was able to report that, although he had only two sons (Alexander and Andrew) and three daughters (Grisell, Julian and Jean), 'yet of those I have had many grand-children, in all, twenty-seven, whereof six have died and twenty-one I still enjoy . . .'[6]

Inevitably there were family occasions for grief as well. Saddest of these was the death of his wife Grisell, on 11 October 1703 of cancer of the breast, after a long illness. She died in Edinburgh, where she had been taken because of the better medical help to be had there. According to Lady Anne Purves she had said nothing about it, 'but Lord Marchmont found it out, and applied to the Physicians in Edinbro' who gave her Mercurial Vomits, which threw the Cancer through her Blood'.[7] Oddly enough, her funeral is the only one of which no account survives, for George Home's diary is missing at that point, and although there is an entry in her daughter's published accounts for 'the expence of my mothers funerals', it clearly relates to someone else, possibly her mother-in-law.[8] We know that both Patrick himself and his daughter Grisell were deeply affected by the loss. Patrick, writing to his relation the Duke of Devonshire on 12 December 1704, explains why he has not written for two years: 'Not that the honor and respect I have for you is lessened, but that the sad affliction which I have been under, by the death of my wife after long sickness, had so much disordered me, that I did not think of many things, which formerly I was in use to mind'.[9] Another great tragedy for Patrick was the death of his son Patrick Lord Polwarth on 25 November 1709 at Kelso, to which he had been persuaded to go, Lady Anne Purves had been told, because of 'the Smell of the New Lime' at Redbraes being bad for his consumption.[10]

Meanwhile, Patrick's own health had not improved, following back strain shortly after Grisell's death, which gave him intermittent trouble for a long time afterwards. George Home reported on 25 November 1703: 'I wrote to my Lord Polwart to know how my Lord his father was, he having strained his back some days ago with lifting a weight of 8 stone and ¼'. It seems the weight he lifted was a stone, for on 13 May 1704 we hear that 'Lord Marchmont looks well, but since his strain with lifting the stone he is not able to ride or go in a coach, and it has raised a rupture in him which he had been subject to a long time but by bandaging has kept within bounds. I remember when he was at Bordeaux he was talking of bandages, but he did not tell me his trouble'. This same problem must have been the reason for his consulting Dr Pitcairne some eight years later, as mentioned in Chapter 6.

We do not propose, however, to follow Patrick in his political activities after he lost the chancellorship in 1702, though in the end his virtually joining forces with the 'squadrone', and the support he was able to bring with him, was crucial in the final stages of securing the union of Scotland and England. Nor will we become involved in attempting to examine, still less to adjudicate upon, the distribution of the 'sweetener' of £20,000 of arrears provided by the English court in 1705-6 to secure the goodwill of those who had held office in Scottish administrations. Patrick's enemies claimed that his share was excessive, and constituted a bribe to betray his country, while Sir George Henry Rose flatly refutes such a charge in great detail and at considerable length in 1831.[11] Nor will we study the time, effort and money spent in extensive repairs and extensions to Polwarth House (styled Redbraes Castle after April 1704), almost up to the eve of work beginning on its mid-century replacement, Marchmont House. And it is not proposed to do any of these things because, for several reasons, the early 1700s form a sensible point at which to bring our story to a close. It is not only that two of the principal characters have gone — Grisell in 1703 and George Home the diarist in 1705 — it is also that with them, and by this stage in other cases too, the previously virtually unused *manuscript* sources, which have shed such a flood of light on what life was like in late seventeenth-century Scotland, have come to an end — the Compt Book, the Diary, the records of what was spent on food when living in Edinburgh, the lists of guests at the special dinners, the hearth and poll-tax rolls. To carry the story further would mean relying solely on *printed* sources, already so well utilised that they could yield little that is new. The excitement of being able to produce completely fresh evidence, and to put things in a contemporary diarist's words rather than one's own, would have gone out of the enterprise.

So it is time to draw the threads together and attempt some assessment of Grisell and of Patrick, a summing-up of George Home having already been given in the chapter devoted to him. As a mother, Grisell clearly gets full marks and she had, at least by today's standards, a particularly hard time of it — childbearing and -rearing for a very large slice of her adult life, and the trauma of taking most of the children with her to Holland. All the evidence points to her having been a very caring and thoughtful person, both in her dealings with her children and with others. Andrew did, it is true, half complain at one point to George Home that his mother was not as good to him as she was to his brothers and sisters. But when it came to the hard bargaining over the terms of his marriage contract with Douglas of Cavers's widow, it was his mother who persuaded his father to agree to contribute a much larger sum of money, thus saving the marriage at the outset. Reporting all this, the diarist quotes her as saying that if on occasion Andrew felt he had got less than he should have done, it was his own fault for not asking, as others always did. In such family misunderstandings as there were, it was usually mother, or failing her their eldest sister Grisell, whose help was sought by the children in persuading father to come round to their point of view, and their pleas seem usually to have succeeded.

That she was an unfailing help to her husband cannot be doubted. The Compt Book shows her looking after many things for him that went well beyond a housewife's normal duties. In his political dealings, we know that he relied on the reports she sent him when she was in London; and her help in organising the series of Edinburgh dinners, by which he set such store after becoming Chancellor and Commissioner to parliament, was clearly invaluable. To feminists she may seem too readily to have accepted a subsidiary role, in contrast to that played by her daughter Grisell Baillie in *her* marriage. One perhaps trivial matter illustrates this every year. When my Lord's birthday comes along on 13 January, his Lady sees to it that the occasion is suitably marked — the Compt Book explains that that is why more was spent on ale on that particular day. George Home records finding unusual visitors in 1698: 'this being his birthday the Earl of Home was ther and several others'. (They were always in Edinburgh in January.) Of his Lady's, we hear nothing at all; the event may not have passed completely unnoticed, but it certainly escapes mention in the sources available to us. This lack of information may be partly due to the male chauvinism that so constantly rears its head in George Home's diary — if Patrick hurts his toe, this is worthy of record, but Grisell has to be extremely ill before any notice is taken. Indeed, it is hardly too much to say that, for their situation to warrant inclusion in the diary, women have either to be dying or to have been 'brought to bed'; for in the latter case the outcome might, after all, be a son and perhaps an heir.

If, as families went, theirs was a relatively harmonious one, part of the credit must go to Patrick as well. Though he was a man of strong views on moral and other issues, he did not impose these beliefs on unwilling recipients. Only once were relations really strained, when Julian ran away and married someone who was, as she herself soon realised, quite unsuitable. And even here, as we have seen, reconciliation soon took place; and Julian ultimately made amends when, in her widowhood, she looked after her father in the last stage of his long life. And right up to his eighties, so often a time when people become more cantankerous or domineering than before, the picture we get of Patrick in his family setting is a highly favourable one. Lady Murray gives us this account of what happened when her mother Grisell Baillie visited Patrick in Berwick two or three years before he died, when many of her relatives had come to see her before she went to London: 'As mirth and good humour, and particularly dancing, had always been one characteristic of the family, when so many of us were met (being no fewer than fourteen of his children and grand-children) we had a dance. He was then very weak in his limbs, and could not walk down stairs, but desired to be carried down to the room where we were, to see us; which he did with great cheerfulness, saying that he could not dance with us, but could yet beat time with his foot, which he did, and bid us dance as long as we could, that it was the best medicine he knew, for at the same time that it gave exercise to the body it cleared the mind. At his usual time of going to bed, he was carried up stairs, and we ceased dancing, for fear of disturbing him; but he soon sent to bid us go on, for the noise and musick so far from disturbing that it would lull him to sleep. He had no notion of interrupting the innocent pleasures of others tho' his age hindered him to partake of it'.[12]

In public life also, his behaviour was normally comparatively free of many of the less attractive features characteristic of most of his political colleagues, particularly the abuse of power and patronage by securing posts for one's family and friends to the exclusion of all others. But there is one small if nevertheless disturbing case where Patrick's behaviour sank to the level so commonly found amongst his contemporaries. The story is told by Archibald Allan who in 1900 wrote the *History of Channelkirk*.[13] In 1697 a new minister had to be appointed by the local church, so the elders approached the presbytery asking that the man they had selected after hearing him preach, and who had been liked by the members, could be asked to preach again, and that the presbytery would then send a moderator to approve the appointment. As a heritor in the parish (he owned some of the lands of Headshaw), Patrick was entitled to have a say in the choice of minister. He apparently had a protégé of his own, and soon made it quite clear to the presbytery who was to be called to fill the vacancy. The presbytery were in a dilemma; on the one hand, the farmers and workpeople in the parish were in agreement with the choice offered to the presbytery by their elders, and on the other the eminent statesman, whom they were afraid of displeasing, was adamant that his choice was to be forced on the local people regardless of their wishes. In desperation the presbytery referred the matter to the synod as a superior court, and as nothing happened they also sought advice from the Commission of the General Assembly (a kind of ecclesiastical Court of Chancery). None of these events took place overnight. The acrimonious arguments dragged on for more than five years (June 1697-September 1702), with neither side willing to give way, and no counsel being offered by the church authorities. We know that as early as 10 November 1697 George Home, breaking his journey to Edinburgh at

Channelkirk, reported that he encountered Patrick: 'He had been long there and was at a meeting with the Heritors for choosing a minister. My Lady, My Lord Polwarth and Lady Jane and Mrs Betty were with him in the coach'. In the course of the long-drawn-out struggle that followed, the local people became disheartened and sickened by Patrick's dictatorial attitude in not allowing them the man of their choice. Moreover, Patrick did not leave it at that, and according to Archibald Allan, resorted to a variety of devious procedures in an effort to bring the local resident heritors to heel.

Eventually, in 1701 new elders were chosen and ordained, and by this time the local people had changed their minds about who might be called to fill the vacancy. The new elders approached the presbytery again with three new names, and after much procrastination a meeting was called in August 1701. Patrick was still determined to decide who was chosen. There were a number of heritors who were not resident in the parish, so they were drummed up when they were people on whom he could rely. On the appropriate day he chose not to attend the meeting himself, but saw to it that his son, Lord Polwarth, and a number of lairds who were also heritors, were there. The outcome was indecisive, as no unanimity was achieved. Later, in September of the same year, the presbytery called another meeting at which the moderators and the heritors (local and non-resident) attended; this time Patrick himself was there in person. He also had ceased to press for his original choice, and of the two men still in the running he decided to give the full weight of his support to Mr Henry Home, who was not the one favoured by the majority of the local people. The outcome of the meeting, after much acrimony, was that Home's name went forward; and a year later, in September 1702, in spite of protests by five out of the six elders, he was duly ordained. The fact that Patrick chose to make such an issue of the affair is disturbing. He was at considerable pains to get his own way regardless of the views of those who attended the church regularly, and who were left without a minister for more than five years.

It was rare, however, for Patrick to behave as badly as this. Macaulay's judgement of him is clearly grossly unfair: 'He was a man incapable alike of leading and of following, conceited, captious, and wrongheaded, an endless talker, a sluggard in action against the enemy, and active only against his own allies'.[14] On the contrary, he was certainly much more honest and straightforward than most of his contemporaries on the political scene. His speeches (and his letters) may have been rather long-winded, but his assessment of the situation faced by his country and what needed to be done about it was usually right, if not always popular.

Not much evidence, perhaps, of a sense of humour, but in his very last moments he demonstrated that he could crack a joke even under trying circumstances. Lady Murray tells us how Charles, Lord Binning (husband of Grisell Baillie's daughter Rachel), 'was sitting by his bedside before he expired, saw him smiling, and said, My Lord, what are you laughing at? He answered, I am diverted to think what a disappointment the worms will meet with, when they come to me expecting a good meal, and find nothing but bones'.[15]

He died of a fever at the age of 84 on 2 August 1724. As John Dickson's manuscript account book for 1724-28 provides detailed information on the cost of his funeral, totalling £263.3.4½ sterling (he gives all sums in sterling, this being the 1720s), we can end our story by saying something about the arrangements, as they throw a good deal of light on what was thought necessary to honour the departure of a Scottish Earl, even if his own and his family's elevation to that rank had only taken place a mere twenty-seven years earlier.[16] Thomas Balderstane, surgeon in Berwick, had attended him in his final illness, but could do little more than prescribe drugs to reduce his fever. For drugs for Patrick, attendance on him, and drugs for the women in the family, £39.1.5 was paid. The days following the death were inevitably very busy both at Redbraes and at Berwick (where Julian looked after the arrangements).

Contact was made at once with the Canongate Kirk in Edinburgh, with instructions about the funeral. The grave-maker was to clean and weed the burial place, and wrights and painters were to put in order the timber paling round the Earl's burial ground in the graveyard. At Redbraes Castle two 'quaires' of mourning paper, silk and thread 'to mend the pall velvet cloath', and quantities of nails 'for mending the hirse in case of need' had to be obtained. The hearse and horses were provided by Thomas Baillie, Coachmaster, at a cost of £7, with a further charge of 7s. for hats and black gloves for his men. Large amounts of black 'cloath' were bought at McKerstoun (Makerston), some to be hung at Redbraes, some to be attached to the mourning coach and some to be taken by carrier to Berwick to be hung in the dining-room there; he also took the 'Mort Cloath'. On 5 August a messenger was despatched to Haddington with 'ane letter to Provost McAla to make ready Supper to-morrow Night for 30 Gentlemen beside Servants'. From there the messenger was to proceed to Edinburgh to see that the Helmet, the Cornet (for which 'ane orrang Silk Tasel' was bought) and branches for the mortcloth were made ready. And also in Edinburgh, Roderick Chalmers, herald, was instructed to see to the painting of the Earl's

Escutcheons and Honours; he was paid £14.4.4 for his work. 'Cadees' were paid 5½d. for running errands. Mourning clothes for the family were bought at Greenlaw, Kelso, Berwick and Edinburgh; presumably one merchant would have been unable to supply such a large order quickly enough. The Redbraes servants were also fitted with mourning clothes, and some of the men with leather britches.

At Berwick, Alexander Dods 'joyner' supplied the 'Coffine' for £5.17.6. Julian was allowed £20 for mourning clothes on instructions by letter from her older sister Lady Baillie. She was also paid £10.15s. for 'Grave Cloathes, plumb cake etc.' (the latter presumably required when they all foregathered before setting out on the journey north). The party dined at Cockburnspath, the meal costing £18.2.10½; they then stayed overnight at Haddington as arranged with Provost McAla. Later he was paid £10 for 'ye Intertainment at his house', which seems to have been provision of beds, for the party of gentlemen had supper on 6 August, and breakfast next morning, provided by John Wilson, the vintner, whose bill came to £5.3.9. On 7 August the cortège set out on the last lap of its journey. As was customary, the poor were given alms at the staging points — Berwick, Cockburnspath, Haddington and Edinburgh — the sums varying from £1.1s. to 5s; a large amount, of course, had to be spent on drink money for workpeople, their servants, and for all the church attendants at Haddington and Edinburgh: bedals, bellmen, sextons, grave-makers etc.

At Edinburgh many other friends joined the sad group as they made their way to the Canongate churchyard, where Patrick was finally interred alongside Grisell in accordance with his wishes. After the burial, the mourners foregathered, and bills were paid to Esther Smith for 'ane Entertainment as per acct. £32.14.1½', and to Mr Stenton for 'wine to ye funerall £7.0.6'. The payment of half-a-crown to 'a poyet who had made an elegy on the Earl of Marchmont' may provide an appropriate ending to our rather longer elegy bidding farewell not just to Patrick, but to all of his family and the whole of their social network, on whose story we have tried to shed a flood of new light after a gap of some three centuries.

Suggestions for Further Reading

The references relating to each chapter should provide those who want to follow up any of the topics covered in this book with what they require. A few suggestions can, however, be made.

The general historical background is excellently sketched-in by Rosalind Mitchison, *Lordship to Patronage: Scotland 1603-1745* (London, 1983). On parliament, R. S. Rait, *The Parliaments of Scotland* (Glasgow, 1924), and Edith E. B. Thomson, *The Parliament of Scotland 1690-1702* (Oxford, 1929). The political complexities of the post-revolution period are particularly well explained in two books by P. W. J. Riley, *King William and the Scottish Politicians* (Edinburgh, 1979) and *The Union of England and Scotland* (Manchester, 1978). For economic history, S. G. E. Lythe and J. Butt, *An Economic History of Scotland 1100-1939* (Glasgow, 1978) and Bruce Lenman, *An Economic History of Modern Scotland 1660-1976* (London, 1977). The Scottish History Society's *Miscellany on Scottish Industrial History* (Edinburgh, 1978) will also be found useful. On social history, Robert Chambers, *Domestic Annals of Scotland* (2nd edition, 3 volumes, Edinburgh, 1861), Henry G. Graham, *The Social Life of Scotland in the 18th century* (London, 1901), I. F. Grant, *Everyday Life in Old Scotland, Part 2, 1603-1707* (London, 1932), Marion Lochhead, *The Scots Household in the 18th century* (Edinburgh, 1948), Marjorie Plant, *The Domestic Life of Scotland in the 18th century* (Edinburgh, 1952), and John Warrack, *Domestic Life in Scotland 1488-1688: a sketch of the development of furniture and household usage* (London, 1920). On clothes and costume, Marjorie Plant's article in volume 27 of the *Scottish Historical Review*, 'Clothes and the 18th century Scot', and Stuart Maxwell and Robin Hutchinson, *Scottish Costume 1550-1850* (Edinburgh, 1958). For medicine, John B. Comrie, *History of Scottish Medicine* (2nd edition, 2 volumes, London, 1932) and David Hamilton, *The Healers: a History of Medicine in Scotland* (Edinburgh, 1981). On the Scottish lyric, two books by Thomas Crawford, *Love, Labour and Liberty in the Scottish Lyric* (Edinburgh, 1976) and *Society and the Lyric: a study of the song culture of 18th century Scotland* (Edinburgh, 1979). On Scottish diaries, J. G. Fyfe, *Scottish Diaries and Memoirs 1550-1746* (Stirling, 1928) and Arthur Ponsonby, *Scottish and Irish Diaries, 16th-19th century* (London, 1927). On other specific topics, Stella Margetson, *Journey by Stages: some account of the people who travelled by stage coach and mail* (London, 1967), G. P. Insh, *The Company of Scotland trading to Africa and the Indies* (London, 1932), H. M. Hyde, *John Law: the history of an honest adventurer* (London, 1948), P. Hume Brown, ed., *Early travellers in Scotland* (Edinburgh, 1891) and the Scottish Record Society's *Painters in Scotland: a Biographical Dictionary* (Edinburgh, 1978). And, of

201

course, the subsequent fortunes of the Marchmonts can be traced in Margaret Warrender, *Marchmont and the Humes of Polwarth* (Edinburgh, 1894).

References

Chapter 1. Principal Sources

1. Manuscript. Grisell's Compt Book. Own collection.
2. Manuscript. Memorandum Book. Scottish Record Office GD158/957.
3. Baillie (*Lady* Grisell). The Household Book . . . 1692-1733. (Scottish History Society.) Edinburgh, 1911.
4. Manuscript. Dame Magdalen Nicolson's Account Book 1671-93. National Library of Scotland MS 2987.
5. Manuscript. George Home's Diary. Scottish Record Office GD 1/891/1-4.
6. Manuscript. George Home's Parchment Notebook 1681-84. Scottish Record Office GD 158/674.
7. Historical Manuscripts Commission. 1st Report on Marchmont MSS., p. 96. London, 1894.
8. Swinton (A. C.). The Swintons of that Ilk and their Cadets. Edinburgh, 1883.
9. Warrender (Margaret). Marchmont and the Humes of Polwarth, p. 165. Edinburgh, 1894.
10. Hume (*Sir* David), *Lord Crossrig*. Domestic Details. Edinburgh, 1843.
11. Manuscript. List of Dinner Guests 1696. Scottish Record Office GD 158/908.
Manuscript. List of Dinner Guests 1697-98. Scottish Record Office GD 158/910.
12. Edinburgh Burgh Records Extracts.
    1681-1689. Edinburgh, 1954.
    1689-1701. Edinburgh, 1962.
    1701-1718. Edinburgh, 1967.
13. Murray (*Lady* G.). Facts relating to my Mother's Life . . . 1749. In Rose (G.). *Observations on . . . C. J. Fox*. London, 1809.
14. Warrender. *Op. cit.*
15. *Ibid*. p. 147.
16. *Ibid*.

Chapter 2. Dark Days and Exile

1. Warrender (Margaret). Marchmont and the Humes of Polwarth, p. 22. Edinburgh, 1894.

2. *Ibid.* p. 29.

3. *Ibid.* p. 33.

4. *Ibid.* p. 41 and Hume (*Sir* David), *Lord Crossrig.* Domestic Details, p. 34. Edinburgh, 1843.

5. Gibson (Robert). An Old Berwickshire Town, pp. 116-119. Edinburgh, 1905.

6. Murray (*Lady* G.). Facts relating to my Mother's Life . . . 1749. In Rose (G.). *Observations on . . . C. J. Fox,* p. viii. London, 1809.

7. *Ibid.*

8. Warrender. *Op. cit.* pp. 142-143.

9. *Ibid.* p. 41.

Chapter 3. George Home the Diarist

1. Foulis (*Sir* John). Foulis of Ravelston's Account Book 1671-1707, p. 145. (Scottish History Society.) Edinburgh, 1894.

2. Manuscript. Accounts relating to George Home's brother. Scottish Record Office GD 158/673.

3. Manuscript. List of Hearths, Berwickshire 1690. Scottish Record Office E69/5/1.

4. Manuscript. List of Pollable Persons, 6 Berwickshire parishes 1695. Scottish Record Office GD 86/770A.

5. Manuscript. George Home's Parchment Notebook 1681-4. Scottish Record Office GD 158/674.

6. Foulis. *Op. cit.* pp. 247-249.

7. Scottish Record Office GD 158/674.

8. Wood (Marguerite). Edinburgh Poll Tax Returns for 1694. (Scottish Record Society.) Edinburgh, 1951.

9. Thanks are due to Dr Eric Mackerness of Sheffield University for tracking this down.

10. Scottish Record Office GD 158/674.

11. Manuscript. Letters from Marie Douglass and others to Sir Patrick Hume 1684-94. Scottish Record Office GD 158/1015.

Chapter 4. Close Friends of the Family

1. McCormick (J.), ed. State Papers and Letters addressed to William Carstares, p. 442. Edinburgh, 1774.

2. Hume (*Sir* David), *Lord Crossrig.* Domestic Details, p. 42. Edinburgh, 1843.

3. Cunningham (William) *of Craigends.* Diary and General Expenditure Book 1673-80, p. 115. (Scottish History Society.) Edinburgh, 1887.

4. Manuscript. List of Pollable Persons, 6 Berwickshire parishes 1695. Scottish Record Office GD 86/770A.

5. Hume. *Op. cit.*

6. *Ibid.* p. 17.

7. *Ibid.* p. 5.

8. *Ibid.* p. 18.

9. *Ibid.* p. 22.

10. *Ibid.* p. 25.

11. *Ibid.* pp. 63-64.

12. *Ibid.* p. 71.

13. Wood (Marguerite). Edinburgh Poll Tax Returns for 1694, p. 49. (Scottish Record Society.) Edinburgh, 1951.

14. Hume. *Op. cit.* p. 51.

15. *Ibid.* pp. xxiv-xxv.

16. *Ibid.* p. vi.

17. Foulis (*Sir* John). Foulis of Ravelston's Account Book 1671-1707, p. 226. (Scottish History Society.) Edinburgh, 1894.

18. A Description of Berwickshire or the Mers. In *Macfarlane's Geographical Collections*, III. (Scottish History Society.) Edinburgh, 1908.

19. Scottish Record Office GD 86/770A.

20. Manuscript. Letters from Marie Douglass and others to Sir Patrick Hume 1684-94. Scottish Record Office GD 158/1015.

21. Bannatyne Club. Letters . . . addressed to . . . Melville . . . 1689-91, pp. 76-77. Edinburgh, 1843.

22. Warrender (Margaret). Marchmont and the Humes of Polwarth, p. 159. Edinburgh, 1894.

23. Foulis. *Op. cit.* p. 164.

24. Manuscript. List of Hearths, Berwickshire 1690. Scottish Record Office E 69/5/1.

25. Manuscript. List of Pollable Persons, Hutton parish 1695. Scottish Record Office GD 158/679.

26. Warrender. *Op. cit.* p. 149.

27. Chambers (Robert). Domestic Annals of Scotland, 2nd ed., III, p. 183. Edinburgh, 1861.

28. Scottish Record Office GD 86/770A.

29. Swinton (A. C.). The Swintons of that Ilk and their Cadets, p. 84. Edinburgh, 1883.

30. Wood (J. P.). Cramond, p. 145. Edinburgh, 1794.

31. Scott-Moncrieff (R.). Household Plenishings . . . of Andro Hog . . . 1691. In *Proceedings of the Society of Antiquaries of Scotland*, 10 February 1919, p. 54.

32. Edinburgh Burgh Records Extracts 1689-1701, pp. 89-90. Edinburgh, 1962.

33. Kalmeter (Henry). Journal of . . . Travels in Scotland 1719-20. In

Campbell (R. H.), ed., *Scottish Industrial History: A Miscellany of Documents.* (Scottish History Society.) Edinburgh, 1978.

34. Foulis. *Op. cit.* p. 262.

35. Duff (H. R.), ed. Culloden Papers . . . 1625-1748, p. 275. London, 1815.

36. Chambers. *Op. cit.* p. 184.

37. Manuscript. Letter from Marchmont to Culloden. National Library of Scotland MS 2963.

38. Fraser (*Sir* William), ed. Memoirs of the Maxwells of Pollok, I, p. 81. Edinburgh, 1863.

39. *Ibid.*, II, p. 105.

Chapter 5. Children Growing Up

1. Historical Manuscripts Commission. 2nd Report on Marchmont MSS., p. 115. London, 1894.

2. *Ibid.*

3. Murray (*Lady* G.). Facts relating to my Mother's Life . . . 1749, p. x. In Rose (G.). *Observations on . . . C. J. Fox.* London, 1809.

4. Warrender (Margaret). Marchmont and the Humes of Polwarth, p. 168. Edinburgh, 1894.

5. Rose (*Sir* George Henry), ed. Marchmont Papers, III, p. 369. London, 1831.

6. Warrender. *Op. cit.* p. 62.

7. *Ibid.* p. 63.

8. Rose. *Op. cit.*, III, p. 368.

9. Warrender. *Op. cit.* p. 54.

10. Baillie (*Lady* Grisell). The Household Book . . . 1692-1733, p. x. (Scottish History Society.) Edinburgh, 1911.

11. Murray. *Op. cit.* p. xiii.

12. Wood (Marguerite). Edinburgh Poll Tax Returns for 1694. (Scottish Record Society.) Edinburgh, 1951.

13. Hay (Andrew) *of Craignethan.* Diary 1659-60, p. 185. (Scottish History Society.) Edinburgh, 1901.

14. Manuscript. List of Hearths, Berwickshire 1690. Scottish Record Office E 69/5/1.

15. Murray. *Op. cit.* p. x.

16. Warrender. *Op. cit.* pp. 187-189.

17. Murray. *Op. cit.* p. xii.

18. *Ibid.* p. xxiii.

19. *Ibid.* p. ix.

20. Warrender. *Op. cit.* p. 162.

21. *Ibid.* p. 163.

22. Historical Manuscripts Commission. *Op. cit.* pp. 127-128.

23. Warrender. *Op. cit.* p. 152.

24. *Ibid.*

25. *Ibid.* p. 160.

26. *Ibid.* p. 84.

27. *Ibid.* p. 166.

28. Marshall (Rosalind K.). The Days of Duchess Anne, p. 147. London, 1973.

Chapter 6. Lifestyle of the Merse Lairds

1. Manuscript. List of Pollable Persons, 6 Berwickshire parishes 1695. Scottish Record Office GD 86/770A.

Manuscript. List of Pollable Persons, Hutton parish 1695. Scottish Record Office GD 158/679.

2. Manuscript. List of Hearths, Berwickshire 1690. Scottish Record Office E 69/5/1.

Manuscript. List of Hearths, Roxburghshire 1690. Scottish Record Office E 69/21/1.

3. Foulis (*Sir* John). Foulis of Ravelston's Account Book 1671-1707, p. 152. (Scottish History Society.) Edinburgh, 1894.

4. Firth (C. H.), ed. Scotland and the Protectorate, p. 410. (Scottish History Society.) Edinburgh, 1899.

5. *Ibid.*

6. Foulis. *Op. cit.*

7. Baillie (*Lady* Grisell). The Household Book . . . 1692-1733, p. 11. (Scottish History Society.) Edinburgh, 1911.

8. Cunningham (William) *of Craigends*. Diary and General Expenditure Book 1673-80, p. 107. (Scottish History Society.) Edinburgh, 1887.

9. Edinburgh Burgh Records Extracts 1689-1701, p. 179. Edinburgh, 1962.

10. A Description of Berwickshire or the Mers. In *Macfarlane's Geographical Collections*, III, p. 184. (Scottish History Society.) Edinburgh, 1908.

11. Edinburgh Burgh Records Extracts 1689-1701, p. 280.

12. Stewart (*Lady* Marie), *Countess of Mar*. Compte Book 1638-42, p. 46. Edinburgh, 1846.

13. Jeffrey (Alexander). History and Antiquities of Roxburghshire and adjacent districts, III, p. 32. Edinburgh, 1859.

14. Chambers (Robert). Domestic Annals of Scotland, 2nd ed., III, p. 268. Edinburgh, 1861.

15. *Ibid.* p. 269.

16. Jeffrey. *Op. cit.*, III, p. 33.

17. Stevenson (Ronald). Harps of Their Own Sort. (National Library of Scotland.) Edinburgh, 1981.

18. Marshall (Rosalind K.). The Days of Duchess Anne, p. 73. London, 1973.

19. Stewart. *Op. cit.* p. 29.

20. *Ibid.* p. 53.

21. Sharp (James), *Lord Archbishop of St. Andrews.* Household Book 1663-66, p. 79. Forfar, 1929.

22. Spalding Club. The Book of the Thanes of Cawdor . . . 1236-1742, p. 362. Edinburgh, 1859.

23. Cunningham. *Op. cit.* p. 101.

24. Warrender (Margaret). Marchmont and the Humes of Polwarth, pp. 149-150. Edinburgh, 1894.

25. Manuscript. List of Hearths, Berwickshire 1690. Scottish Record Office E 69/5/1.

26. Chambers. *Op. cit.*, III, pp. 201-202.

27. Manuscript. List of Pollable Persons, 6 Berwickshire parishes 1695. Scottish Record Office GD 86/770A.

28. Malcolm (Charles A.), ed. Minutes of the Justices of the Peace for Lanarkshire 1707-1723, pp. 10-21. (Scottish History Society.) Edinburgh, 1931.

Firth (C. H.), ed. Scotland and the Protectorate, pp. 405-411. (Scottish History Society.) Edinburgh, 1899.

29. Baillie. *Op. cit.* p. 278.

30. *Ibid.* p. 280.

31. Plant (Marjorie). The Servant Problem in Eighteenth Century Scotland. In *Scottish Historical Review*, XXIX, 1950, p. 143.

32. Baillie. *Op. cit.* p. 173.

33. Foulis. *Op. cit.* pp. 315-317.

34. Brown (P. Hume), ed. Early Travellers in Scotland, pp. 230-290. Edinburgh, 1891.

35. *Ibid.* p. 231.

36. *Ibid.* p. 260.

37. *Ibid.* p. 275.

38. Allan (Rev. Archibald). History of Channelkirk, p. 197. Edinburgh, 1900.

39. Warrender. *Op. cit.* pp. 146-147.

40. Chambers. *Op. cit.*, III, p. 200.

41. Stewart. *Op. cit.* pp. 24-53.

42. Cunningham. *Op. cit.* pp. 30-116.

43. *Ibid.* p. 41.

44. Foulis. *Op. cit.* p. 160.

45. *Ibid.* p. 293.

46. Lauder (*Sir* John), *Lord Fountainhall.* Journals and Accounts 1665-1676, p. 267. (Scottish History Society.) Edinburgh, 1900.

47. Comrie (J. B.). History of Scottish Medicine, 2nd ed., I, pp. 272-277. London, 1932.

48. Johnston (W. T.). The Best of Our Owne: Letters of Archibald Pitcairne

1652-1713. Edinburgh, 1979.

49. Hamilton (David). The Healers: the History of Medicine in Scotland. Edinburgh, 1981.

50. Chambers. *Op. cit.*, III, p. 326.

51. Manuscript. Letters from Marie Douglass and others to Sir Patrick Hume 1684-94. Scottish Record Office GD 158/1015.

Chapter 7. How People and News Got Around

1. Fraser (*Sir* William), ed. Memoirs of the Maxwells of Pollok, I, pp. 78-79. Edinburgh, 1863.

2. Historical Manuscripts Commission. Report on Polwarth MSS., V, pp. 136-137. London, 1961.

3. Marshall (Rosalind K.). The Days of Duchess Anne, pp. 109-111. London, 1973.

4. Early issues of the *Edinburgh Gazette* and other Edinburgh Newspapers on File. National Library of Scotland RyIIa 20.

5. Baillie (*Lady* Grisell). The Household Book . . . 1692-1733, p. lxx. (Scottish History Society.) Edinburgh, 1911.

6. *Ibid.* p. lxix.

7. *Ibid.*

8. Sharp (James). *Archbishop of St. Andrews.* Household Book 1663-1666, p. 241. Forfar, 1929.

9. Baillie. *Op. cit.* p. 1.

10. Graham (Henry G.). The Social Life of Scotland in the Eighteenth Century, p. 43. London, 1901.

11. Allan (*Rev.* Archibald). History of Channelkirk, p. 476. Edinburgh, 1900.

12. Sharp. *Op. cit.* p. 25.

13. Edinburgh Burgh Records Extracts 1681-89, p. 187. Edinburgh, 1954.

14. Edinburgh Burgh Records Extracts 1701-18, pp. 79-80. Edinburgh, 1967.

15. *Ibid.* pp. 219-220.

16. Early issues . . . (as in note 4 above).

17. Hume (*Sir* David), *Lord Crossrig.* Domestic Details, p. 12. Edinburgh, 1843.

18. Early issues . . . (as in note 4 above).

19. Baillie. *Op. cit.* p. 29.

20. Chambers (Robert). Domestic Annals of Scotland, 2nd ed., III, p. 212. Edinburgh, 1861.

21. Manuscript. Letters from Marie Douglass and others to Sir Patrick Hume 1684-94. Scottish Record Office GD 158/1015.

22. Early issues . . . (as in note 4 above).

23. Edinburgh Burgh Records Extracts 1689-1701, p. 27. Edinburgh, 1962.

24. *Ibid*. pp. 31-32.

25. An elaborate cipher-key to the code used by William Carstares when writing to Patrick in 1697 is quoted in Historical Manuscripts Commission, 2nd Report on Marchmont MSS., p. 116. London, 1894.

26. Auckland (Bruce). Postal Markings of Scotland to 1808. Edinburgh, 1978.

27. Spalding Club. The Book of the Thanes of Cawdor . . . 1236-1742, pp. 382-384. Edinburgh, 1859.

Chapter 8. New Beginnings

1. Bannatyne Club. Letters . . . addressed to . . . Melville . . . 1689-91, pp. 95-100. Edinburgh, 1843.

2. Historical Manuscripts Commission. 2nd Report on Marchmont MSS., pp. 119-121. London, 1894.

3. *Ibid*. p. 109.

4. Riley (P. W. J.). King William and the Scottish Politicians, p. 57. Edinburgh, 1979.

5. Lauder (*Sir* John), *Lord Fountainhall*. Journals and Accounts 1665-1676, pp. 249-261. (Scottish History Society.) Edinburgh, 1900.

6. Graham (Henry G.). The Social Life of Scotland in the Eighteenth Century, p. 85. London, 1901.

7. Early Issues of *Edinburgh Gazette* and other Edinburgh Newspapers on File. National Library of Scotland Ry.IIa20.

8. Manuscript. Letters from Marie Douglass and others to Sir Patrick Hume 1684-94. Scottish Record Office GD 158/1015.

9. Bannatyne Club. *Op. cit.* p. 76.

10. Swinton (A. C.). The Swintons of that Ilk and their Cadets, p. 78. Edinburgh, 1883.

11. Warrender (Margaret). Marchmont and the Humes of Polwarth, p. 53. Edinburgh, 1894.

12. Historical Manuscripts Commission. *Op. cit.* p. 109.

13. *Ibid*. pp. 114-115.

14. Warrender. *Op. cit.* p. 53.

15. Manuscript. List of Pollable Persons, 6 Berwickshire parishes 1695. Scottish Record Office GD 86/770A.

16. Manuscript. List of Hearths, Berwickshire 1690. Scottish Record Office E 69/5/1.

17. Baillie (*Lady* Grisell). Household Book . . . 1692-1733, p. 71. (Scottish History Society.) Edinburgh, 1911.

Chapter 9. Housekeeping and the Compt Book

1. Manuscript. John Dickson's Account Book: Own collection.
2. Manuscript. Dame Magdalen Nicolson's Account Book 1671-93. National Library of Scotland MS 2987.
3. Fell (Sarah) *of Swarthmore Hall*. Household Account Book 1673-78. Cambridge, 1920.
4. Stewart (*Lady* Marie), *Countess of Mar*. Compte Book 1638-42. Edinburgh, 1846.
5. Scott-Moncrieff (R.). Household Plenishings . . . of Andro Hog . . . 1691. *Proceedings of the Society of Antiquaries of Scotland*, 10 February 1919, p. 60.
6. *Ibid.* p. 59.
7. Manuscript. List of Pollable Persons, 6 Berwickshire parishes 1695. Scottish Record Office GD 86/770A.
8. Baillie (*Lady* Grisell). The Household Book . . . 1692-1733, p. 165. (Scottish History Society.) Edinburgh, 1911.
9. Fairley (John A.). Lauriston Castle: the Estate and its owners, p. 139. Edinburgh, 1925.
10. Wood (Marguerite). Edinburgh Poll Tax Returns for 1694. (Scottish Record Society.) Edinburgh, 1951.
11. Manuscript. List of Pollable Persons, 6 Berwickshire parishes 1695. Scottish Record Office GD 86/770A.
12. Manuscript. John Dickson's Account Book: Own collection.
13. Manuscript. List of Hearths, Berwickshire 1690. Scottish Record Office E 69/5/1.
14. Manuscript. List of Pollable Persons, 6 Berwickshire parishes 1695. Scottish Record Office GD 86/770A.
15. Firth (C. H.), ed. Scotland and the Protectorate, p. 406. (Scottish History Society.) Edinburgh, 1899.
16. Manuscript. List of Pollable Persons, 6 Berwickshire parishes 1695. Scottish Record Office GD 86/770A.
17. Malcolm (Charles A.), ed. Minutes of the Justices of the Peace for Lanarkshire 1707-1723, pp. 16-21. (Scottish History Society.) Edinburgh, 1931.
18. Manuscript. List of Pollable Persons, 6 Berwickshire parishes 1695. Scottish Record Office GD 86/770A.
19. *Ibid.*
20. Manuscript. Dame Magdalen Nicolson (as in note 2).
21. *Ibid.*
22. Baillie. *Op. cit.*
23. Lauder (*Sir* John), *Lord Fountainhall*. Journal and Accounts 1665-1676. (Scottish History Society.) Edinburgh, 1900.
    Foulis (*Sir* John). Foulis of Ravelston's Account Book 1671-1707. (Scottish History Society.) Edinburgh, 1894.

Cunningham (William) *of Craigends*. Diary and General Expenditure Book 1673-80. (Scottish History Society.) Edinburgh, 1887.

24. Edinburgh Burgh Records Extracts 1689-1701, p. 223. Edinburgh, 1962.

25. Foulis. *Op. cit.* p. 249.

26. Manuscript. Dame Magdalen Nicolson (as in note 2).

27. *Ibid.*

28. Rankin (Eric). Cockburnspath. Edinburgh, 1981.

29. Baillie. *Op. cit.* pp. 71-79.

30. Manuscript. Dame Magdalen Nicolson (as in note 2).

31. Baillie. *Op. cit.* p. 72.

32. Manuscript. Dame Magdalen Nicolson (as in note 2).

33. Malcolm. *Op. cit.* pp. 16-20.

Firth. *Op. cit.* pp. 405-411.

34. Baillie. *Op. cit.*

35. Foulis. *Op. cit.*

36. Baillie. *Op. cit.* p. 256.

37. Foulis. *Op. cit.* p. 312.

38. *Ibid.* p. 323.

39. Spalding Club. A Genealogical Deduction of the Family of Rose of Kilravock, p. 390. Edinburgh, 1848.

40. Baird (J. G. A.). Papers of an Old Scots Family. In *Blackwood's Magazine*, July 1907, p. 68.

41. Baillie. *Op. cit.* pp. 204-205.

42. Foulis *Op. cit.* p. 395.

43. *Ibid.* p. 340.

44. *Ibid.* p. 331.

45. Baillie. *Op. cit.* p. 191.

46. Spalding Club. The Book of the Thanes of Cawdor . . . 1236-1742, p. 325. Edinburgh, 1859.

47. Baird. *Op. cit.* p. 68.

48. Montgomerie (A.). An East Lothian Executor's Accounts 1645-1650. In *Scottish Historical Review*, XXX, 1951, pp. 150-152.

Chapter 10. Crest of the Wave

1. Edinburgh Burgh Records Extracts 1689-1701, pp. 196-197. Edinburgh, 1962.

2. Edinburgh Burgh Records Extracts 1701-1718, p. 58. Edinburgh, 1967.

3. Manuscript. Account Book of Household Expenses in Edinburgh 1696-99. Scottish Record Office GD 158/967.

4. *Ibid.*

5. Foulis (*Sir* John). Foulis of Ravelston's Account Book 1671-1707, p. 399. (Scottish History Society.) Edinburgh, 1894.

6. Edinburgh Burgh Records Extracts 1689-1701, p. 295. Edinburgh, 1962.

7. *Ibid.* p. 194.

8. *Ibid.* p. 162.

9. *Ibid.* p. 295.

10. Manuscript. List of dinner guests 1696. Scottish Record Office GD 158/908.

Manuscript. List of dinner guests 1697-98. Scottish Record Office GD 158/910.

11. Wood (Marguerite). Edinburgh Poll Tax Returns for 1694. (Scottish Record Society.) Edinburgh, 1951.

12. Scott-Moncrieff (R.). Household Plenishings . . . of Andro Hog . . . 1691. In *Proceedings of the Society of Antiquaries of Scotland*, 10 February 1919, pp. 52-63.

13. Edinburgh Burgh Records Extracts, 1689-1701, p. 115. Edinburgh, 1962.

14. Dictionary of National Biography, XV, p. 324. London, 1888.

15. Cokayne (G. E.), ed. The Complete Peerage, VIII, p. 651. London, 1932.

16. *Ibid.*, I, p. 317.

17. Dictionary of National Biography, XLII, p. 30. London, 1888.

18. Riley (P. W. J.). King William and the Scottish Politicians, p. 122. Edinburgh, 1979.

19. Warrender (Margaret). Marchmont and the Humes of Polwarth, pp. 183-186. Edinburgh, 1894.

20. Rose (*Sir* George Henry), ed. Marchmont Papers, III, p. 103. London, 1831.

21. *Ibid.* p. 106.

22. Historical Manuscripts Commission. 2nd Report on Marchmont MSS., p. 129. London, 1894.

23. *Ibid.* pp. 133-134.

24. *Ibid.* p. 146.

25. Edinburgh Burgh Records Extracts 1689-1701, p. 310. Edinburgh, 1962.

26. Rose. *Op. cit.*, III, p. 213.

27. *Ibid.* p. 217.

28. *Ibid.* p. 218.

29. *Ibid.* pp. 197-198.

30. *Ibid.* pp. 220-221.

31. Historical Manuscripts Commission. *Op. cit.* p. 139.

32. Rose. *Op. cit.*, III, p. 195.

Epilogue

1. Rose (*Sir* George Henry), ed. Marchmont Papers, III, p. 301. London, 1831.

2. *Ibid.*, III, p. 352.

3. *Ibid.*, III, p. 373.

4. *Ibid.*, III, p. 385.

5. Gibson (Robert). An Old Berwickshire Town, p. 137. Edinburgh, 1905.

6. Rose. *Op. cit.*, III, p. 379.

7. Warrender (Margaret). Marchmont and the Humes of Polwarth, p. 173. Edinburgh, 1894.

8. Baillie (*Lady* Grisell). The Household Book . . . 1692-1733, p. 267. (Scottish History Society.) Edinburgh, 1911.

9. Rose. *Op. cit.*, III, pp. 273-274.

10. Warrender. *Op. cit.* p. 173.

11. Rose. *Op. cit.*, I, pp. cix-cxxiii.

12. Murray (*Lady* G.). Facts relating to my Mother's Life . . . 1749. In Rose (G.), *Observations on . . . C. J. Fox*, p. xvii. London, 1809.

13. Allan (*Rev.* Archibald). History of Channelkirk, pp. 192-207. Edinburgh, 1900.

14. Macaulay (*Lord*). History of England, I, p. 540. London, 1881.

15. Murray. *Op. cit.* p. xviii.

16. Manuscript. John Dickson's Account Book. Own collection.

Index

Items appearing in the chapter references have not been included in this index, nor are the acknowledgements and further reading covered.

Abercorn, 81, 96

Aberdeen, 124

Abernethy, Dr, 25, 37, 65, 165

abjuration crisis of 1702, 189-191

Agutter, Ralph, musical instrument maker, 119

Aikman, William, portrait painter, Plate 8

Allan, Rev. Archibald, 113-114, 197-198

Allan, Bessie, chambermaid in Polwarth House, 154

Allanbank, 81, 96

Allen, John, workman, 153

Allen, Patrick, servant in Polwarth House, 155

Allen, William, younger, servant in Polwarth House, 155

almsgiving, 35, 100-101, 200

architecture, 34, 55, 132, 176

Angiers (sic), 40

Angus, Thomas, weaver, 146

Annandale, William Johnston, fourth earl and first marquess of, 180-181, 187, 188, 191

Anne, queen of England and Scotland, 55, 62, 192, 193

Anstruther, Sir William, younger, of that Ilk, 177

Argyll, Archibald Campbell, ninth earl of, 22, 64

Argyll, Archibald Campbell, tenth earl and first duke of, 40, 130, 181, 185, 186, 188, 189-190, 192

Argyll, John Campbell, eleventh earl and second duke of, 113

Argyll, family interest of, 129, 181

Argyll's expedition, 22, 64

Arniston, 41, 42, 177, 178

Arran, James Douglas, earl of, see Hamilton, fourth duke of

Atholl, John Murray, first marquess of, 129

Atholl, family interest of, 129

Auchinleck, Mr, 36, 37, 48

autobiography, 10-11, 41-47

Ayton, 85, 95, 134

Baillie, George, of Jerviswood and Mellerstain, 14, 20, 22-23, 27, 66, 67, 68, 86, 87, 88, 112, 115, 128, 132, 191

Baillie, Lady Grisell, daughter of Patrick and Grisell: married to George Baillie, 2, 4, 5, 6, 13, 14, 17, 18-19, 20-22, 28, 55, 64, 65, 66, 67-70, 71, 74-76, 84, 97, 98, 112-113, 115, 128, 130, 132-133, 136, 138, 139, 140, 145, 155, 157, 160, 161, 164, 165, 166-167, 168, 169, 170, 193, 194, 195-197, 200

Baillie, Captain James, 175

Baillie, Rachel, daughter of George and Grisell Baillie: married to Charles, lord Binning, 70

Baillie, Robert, of Jerviswood, 17, 19, 22, 68

Baillie, Thomas, coachmaster, 199

Baird, Dame Margaret, wife of Sir Patrick Home of Renton, 95

Baird, Sir William, of Newbyth, 177

Balderstane, Thomas, 199

Bank of Scotland, 53

baptisms, 41, 61

Belhaven, John Hamilton, second lord, 178

Bellingham, Charles, married to Patrick and Grisell's daughter Julian, 71-72, 77

Berwick, 27, 44, 45, 72, 74, 98, 105, 108, 110, 121, 196, 199-200

Berwickshire, 11, 17, 24, 37, 40, 42, 44, 45, 47, 48, 52, 53, 54, 66, 67, 73, 81, 88, 107, 112, 113, 127, 133, 134, 161, 192, 193

Binning, Charles Hamilton, styled lord Binning, married to Rachel, daughter of George and Grisell Baillie, 70, 199
Binns, 105
Bishop, Henry, 124
Blackadder, 3, 24, 25, 26, 40, 41, 42, 44, 45, 52, 81, 82, 83, 90, 91, 96, 108, 111, 112, 175, 191
Blair, John, Edinburgh apothecary and postmaster, 120, 122
Boldry, Rebecca, cook in Polwarth House, 155
books, 31-32, 103
Bordeaux, 22
Borthwick, 42, 46
Brack, Thomas, tenant, 149
Brierson, Patrick, weaver, 153
Broomfield, Robert, miller, 19-20
Broun, Sir George, of Colstoun, 168, 170
Brounfield, Robert, alehouse keeper, 136
Brown, Peter, gardener, 151
Bruce, Sir William, architect, 55, 176
Brysson, Elizabeth, servant in Polwarth House, 155
Buccleuch, Duchess of, 131
Burnet, Sir Thomas, of Leys, 182, 191

Calder, 92, 124, 170
Callender, earl of, 17
Cambray, 73
Campbell, Colin, of Arbruchell, styled lord Arbruchell, 177
Campbell, Sir George, of Cessnock, father of Margaret Campbell who married Patrick and Grisell's son Alexander, 73, 178
Campbell, Sir Hugh, of Calder, 92, 124, 170
Campbell, Margaret, married to Alexander, son of Patrick and Grisell, 72-74, 178
candles, 160
Cardross, Henry Erskine, third baron, 129
Carmichael, John, second baron, cr. earl of Hyndford 1701, 182, 186
Carolina scheme 17-18, 178
Carre, John, of Cavers and West Nisbet, 14, 27, 34, 39, 48-49, 51, 81, 90, 96, 120
Carstares, William, 38, 40, 62, 128, 184-185, 186, 188, 190

Cavers, 14, 39, 48, 49, 51, 52, 75, 76, 81, 90, 96, 120
Cavers Carre, 15, 48
Cawdor, 92, 124, 170
Chalmers, Roderick, herald, 199-200
Chambers, Robert, 116
Channelkirk, 71, 99, 107, 108, 113, 173, 197-198
Charles II, king of England and Scotland, 18, 55, 61
Chato, Thomas, soap maker, 161
cheese, 6, 146, 159
Cheislie, Sir Robert, lord provost of Edinburgh, 176
chimney sweeping, 171-172
Christy, Nany, Lady Grisell Baillie's cook, 133
churchgoing, 30, 39, 72, 94, 197-198
clothes, 25-26, 28, 35, 39, 51, 66, 71, 77-78, 83, 97, 105, 166-170, 199-200
'club', the, 126, 129, 181
coal, 29, 86, 142
Cockburn, Adam, of Ormiston, 180
Cockburn, Sir Archibald, of Langtoune, 81
Cockburn, Sir James, of Duns Castle, 81, 88-89, 108, 165
Cockburnspath, 107, 108, 123, 160, 200
Cockran, John, gardener, 172-173
coin, shortage of, 165-166
Company of Scotland trading to Africa and the Indies, 53, 118, 129, 186-188
cost-of-living, *see* value of money
Coventry, John, 119
Craig, Robert, of Riccarton, 191
Craigends, 40, 81, 86, 93, 96, 100, 157
Cramond, 55, 83
Craw, Robert, Patrick's baillie, 142
Crawford, John (convicted of stealing), 89
crowned orange, 23, 127
Culloden, 57, 58, 127, 129, 175, 182, 191
Cunningham, William, of Craigends, 40-41, 81, 86, 93, 96, 100-101, 157
Currie, James, workman, 153

Dalmeny, Archibald Primrose, viscount, 34
Dalrymple, Sir Hugh, 186
Dalrymple, Sir James, of Stair, *see* Stair, first viscount

Dalrymple, Sir John, master of Stair, *see* Stair, first earl of
Dalrymples, the, 126, 129
Dalyell, Sir Thomas, of Binns, 105
Dalzell, Sir Thomas, of Abercorn, 81, 96
dancing, 66, 73, 78, 92, 96, 196-197
Darien expedition, 26, 30, 118, 178, 186-188
Davidson, John, hind, 151
Davidson, Sir John, of Thirlstoune, 81
Day, Barbara, my lady's gentlewoman and housekeeper, Polwarth House, 154
Defoe, Daniel, 117
Dempster, John, of Pitliver, 127
Denmark, 73
Devonshire, William Cavendish, fourth earl and first duke of, 194
diaries, 2, 6-10, 24-39, 49, 51-52, 65, 70-72, 74-76, 82-83, 107-109, 111-113, 123-124, 171
Dickson, Isobell, tenant, 150
Dickson, John, of Anton's Hill, factor to the earls of Marchmont, 25, 34, 35, 89, 120, 138, 142, 148, 199-200
dinner parties, 11, 53, 173-184
doctors, 10, 27, 36-38, 102-105, 141, 164-165
Dods, Alexander, Berwick joiner, 200
Dods, Will, hind, 151
domestic staff, 27-29, 41, 46, 52, 69, 96-97, 154-156
Donaldson, James, 116-117, 118
dotterels, 90
Douglas, Sir William, of Cavers (his relict, Lady Douglas, married Andrew, Patrick and Grisell's son, in 1700), 75-76, 195
Douglass, Marie, Lady Hilton, 27, 29, 35, 49-52, 75, 94, 131-132, 175
Douglass, Sophia, Lady Kettleston, 50-51, 52
Dover, 115
drink, 52-53, 58-59, 104, 146, 157-158, 172-173
drink money, 24, 156
Drumlanrig, James Douglas, earl of, *see* Queensberry, second duke of
Drummond, Thomas, of Riccarton, 127
Dublin, 89
Dumbarton, 72
Dunbar, 51, 98, 110
Dundas, Dr, 165

Dundas, Barbara, married to Lord Raith, 179-180
Dundas, Sir James, of Arniston, 41, 42, 44
Dundas, Sir Robert, of Arniston, 177
Dunglass, 65, 71, 86, 108
Dunglass, lord, son of Charles, earl of Home, 112
Duns, 26, 27, 29, 37, 81, 83, 88, 89, 93, 107, 108, 120, 142, 160, 193

Edinburgh, 2, 3, 6, 7, 8, 9, 12, 13, 17, 19, 22, 24, 25, 26, 27, 28, 29, 30, 31, 32, 34, 35, 37, 38, 39, 40, 41, 43, 44, 45, 46, 47, 49, 51, 52, 53, 54, 55, 56, 60, 61, 64, 65, 67, 68, 69, 70, 72, 73, 74, 77, 78, 82, 84, 85, 88, 89, 90, 91, 96, 101, 102, 103, 104, 105, 107, 108, 109, 110, 111, 112, 113, 114, 115, 116, 117, 118, 119, 120, 121, 122, 123, 124, 125, 126, 127, 128, 130, 131, 132, 134, 144, 145, 146, 147, 148, 150, 151, 152, 158, 159, 160, 162, 164, 165, 166, 167, 168, 171, 172, 173, 174, 187, 194, 195, 196, 197, 199-200
Edinburgh Courant, 115, 117
Edinburgh Flying Post, 117, 131
Edinburgh Gazette, 12, 112, 115-121, 130
education, 21, 25, 41, 42-44, 47, 49, 51, 60, 62-63, 68, 72, 103
Elliot, Sir Gilbert, of Stobs, married to Dame Magdalen Nicolson, 156
Elliot, William, Dame Magdalen Nicolson's stepson, 162
episcopalians, 16, 103, 129
exile, 20-22, 67, 70, 77, 125, 179
expenses claims, 87-88
Eyemouth, 108, 134

Fairbairn, Robert, tenant, 135, 149
Falconer, Sir James, of Phesdo, 177
famine conditions, 99-100
Fell, Sarah, 139, 140
Ferintosh, 57, 58
Fife, 103, 119, 177
fire hazard, 8, 46, 101
fish, 39, 49, 98, 159-160, 173
Flatman, Thomas, poet, 32
flax, 6, 97, 145-146
fleas, 39

food, 97-98, 100, 103, 146, 158-160, 172-173, 183-184, 200
Foord, Margaret, chambermaid in Polwarth House, 154
Forbes, Duncan, of Culloden, father of John and Duncan, 46, 57-60, 127, 129, 175, 182, 191
Forfar, Archibald Douglas, earl of, 182
Forrest, George, of Haddington, 170
Foulis, Sir John, of Ravelston, 24, 30, 47, 52, 56, 83, 84, 98, 101, 157, 164-165, 169, 170, 174
Fountain, Edward, dancing master, 78
Fox, George, founder of the Quaker movement, 139
fox-hunting, 49, 51, 90, 103
France, 22, 24, 40, 41, 43, 44, 45, 115, 148, 170
Friends, Society of 139
funerals, 24, 30, 41, 52, 58-59, 70, 83, 94-95, 106, 194, 199-200
furniture, 6, 27-28, 98, 144, 171, 177-178

Gainsborough, Thomas, portrait painter, 70
Galashiels, 15, 77
games, 25, 42, 89-92
gardens, 34-35
'George', 2, 3, 7-10, 12, 24-39, 44, 45, 48, 49, 51, 52, 65, 66, 69, 70, 71-72, 74-76, 77, 78, 80-83, 85, 86, 87-89, 90-91, 93, 94-96, 98, 105, 106, 107, 117, 120-124, 130, 131, 133, 136-137, 165, 171, 175, 182, 183, 187, 190, 192, 193, 194, 195, 196, 198
Gibson, Robert, 20, 134
Gifford Hall, 107, 108, 109
Glasgow, 62-3, 102, 173
Gordoune, George, Edinburgh wig-maker, 169
Graham, H. G., 130, 131
Graham, John, 122
Grant, Ludovic, of Grant, 191
Greenlaw, 6, 19, 43, 111, 133, 134, 135, 136, 137, 143, 145, 146, 147, 148, 149, 150, 155, 157, 160, 193, 200
Grieve, Margaret, tenant, 149
'Grisell', 1, 2, 3, 4, 5, 6, 9, 10, 11, 12, 14, 15, 16-23, 34, 40, 41, 50-51, 52, 56, 64-79, 83, 92, 100, 112, 113, 116, 118, 126, 127-128, 131-133, 136-137, 138-170, 171-184, 194, 195-196, 198, 200

Haddington, 107, 108, 109, 123, 160, 170, 199-200
Haddington, Thomas Hamilton, sixth earl of, 17, 175
Hague, The, 16, 117
Haliday, Robert, Fogo carrier, 121
Halkett, Sir Charles, of Pitfirrane, 181
Halkett, Grisell (Grisell's mother), 15
Hall, Sir James, of Dunglass, 66, 71, 77
Hamilton, Anne, duchess of, 183
Hamilton, lord Basil, 183
Hamilton, Christian, Patrick's mother, 15-16
Hamilton, family interest of, 129, 183, 187
Hamilton, David, carrying of lime, 142
Hamilton, Lady Helen, wife of Sir William Anstruther, sister of Lady Hopetoun, 177-178
Hamilton, James Douglas, fourth duke of, formerly earl of Arran, 190
Hamilton, Sir John, of Halcraig, styled lord Halcraig, 177
Hamilton, Lady Susan, daughter of the duke and duchess of Hamilton; married first to the earl of Dundonald and then to Charles, lord Yester, 183
Hamilton, Sir William, of Whitelaw, 182, 185, 186, 188, 190, 191
Hamilton, William, third duke of, 125, 126, 129, 183
hearth tax, 12-13, 27, 41, 45, 48, 52, 69, 81, 132, 134, 149-150
Henderson, Alexander, tenant, 150
Hepburn, Mr, of Humbie, 71, 77
Heude, Nicholas, portrait painter, 34, 41
highwaymen, 109-110
Hilton, 49, 51, 52, 85, 94, 95, 175
Hirsel, the, 37, 40, 66, 81, 82, 94, 175, 176
Hog, Andro, 56, 144, 177
Holiwell, George, minister, 135, 149
Holland, 17, 20, 21, 22, 40, 53, 56, 64, 65, 69, 70, 72, 74, 77, 103, 127, 131, 167, 173, 177, 179, 180, 185
Holyrood, 11, 55, 73, 89, 171-172, 173, 174-184
Home, Sir Alexander, of Renton, 94-95
Home, Alexander, seventh earl of, 192-193
Home, Alexander (Commissary Home), 7-8, 10, 47-48, 65, 82, 85, 175
Home, Charles, sixth earl of, 8, 30, 37,

46, 66, 81, 82, 93, 112, 175-176, 196

Home, David, George Home's brother, 26, 108

Home, Sir David, of Crossrig, styled lord Crossrig, 2, 3, 10-11, 12, 19, 40, 41-47, 88, 90, 115, 176-177

Home, Baillie George, lord provost of Edinburgh, 176, 187

Home, George, of Kimmerghame, the diarist, *see* 'George'

Home, Helen, chambermaid in Polwarth House, 154

Home, Henry, minister, 198

Home, Isobel, George Home's sister, 25-27, 32, 109

Home, Lady Jean ('bonnie Jean o' the Hirsel'), 66, 176, 193

Home, John, son of Sir Patrick Home of Renton, 123-124

Home, Sir John, of Blackadder, 24, 26, 27, 34, 35, 38, 40-41, 42-43, 44, 45, 81, 82, 83, 91, 95, 96, 108, 111, 112, 175, 191

Home, Julian, George Home's sister: married to Dr Trotter, 26, 27, 29, 37

Home, Sir Patrick, of Lumsden and then of Renton, advocate, 10, 65, 94-95, 123-124, 180, 188

Home, Robert, minister, 133

Home, Robie, son of George Home the diarist, 24-26, 27, 31, 35, 36, 37, 38, 49, 66, 76, 82, 90, 106, 109

Home, William, sixth earl's brother, 94

Hope, Sir Archibald, of Rankeillor, styled lord Rankeillor, 112, 177

Hope, Charles, of Hopetoun, later the first earl of Hopetoun, 55, 56, 175

Hope, Helen, daughter of Lady Hopetoun, married Thomas, sixth earl of Haddington in 1696, 175

Hope, Lady Margaret, of Hopetoun, 54-56, 175

Hopetoun, 54, 55, 56, 175, 176

household account books, housekeeping, 1-2, 5-6, 68, 74, 77, 92, 138-170

Humbie, 71, 77

Hume, Alexander, son of Patrick and Grisell: second earl of Marchmont, 1724, 17, 68, 72-74, 77, 135, 138, 140, 155, 178, 193

Hume, Andrew, son of Patrick and Grisell, 13, 17, 39, 51-52, 73, 74-76, 87, 90, 135, 140, 172, 193, 195

Hume, Anne, Patrick's sister, married to Commissary Home, 15, 47-48

Hume, Anne, daughter of Patrick and Grisell, 17, 71, 72, 75, 76-77, 116, 140

Hume, Christian, daughter of Patrick and Grisell, 17, 21, 69, 70

Hume, Elizabeth, married to Patrick's son Lord Polwarth, 65

Hume, Sir Gustavus, of Castle Hume, Ireland, 65, 193

Hume, Jean, daughter of Patrick and Grisell, 17, 20, 76, 77-79, 116, 140, 193

Hume, Julian, daughter of Patrick and Grisell: married to Charles Bellingham, 17, 20, 71-72, 76, 77, 113, 116, 140, 193, 196, 199, 200

Hume, Patrick, son of Patrick and Grisell: later became lord Polwarth, 17, 20, 21, 32, 34, 64-67, 72, 73, 77, 83, 120, 123-124, 128, 140, 175, 193, 194, 198

Hume, Sir Patrick, of Polwarth, eighth baron, later Lord Polwarth and earl of Marchmont: *see* 'Patrick'

Hume, Sir Patrick, of Polwarth, seventh baron, Patrick's father, 15-16, 127, 133

Hume, Sir Patrick, of Polwarth, sixth baron, Patrick's grandfather, 15

Hume, Robert, son of Patrick and Grisell, 17, 70-71

Hutton Hall, 49, 52, 75, 95

illness, 25-26, 35-37, 40, 48, 51-52, 65, 70, 77, 101-102, 194

imprisonment, 17, 19, 38, 51, 60-61, 64, 85, 118, 122, 178

Inverness, 57, 59

Ireland, 65, 100, 122, 159, 193

Irons, John, soldier, 119

jacobites, 57, 99

Jaffrey, James, workman, 153

James II and VII, king of England and Scotland, 61, 181, 187

Jedburgh, 96, 158

Jedburgh, Robert, third baron, Patrick's stepfather, 16, 49

Jerviswood, 14, 17, 22, 27, 67, 86, 87, 88, 128, 132, 191

Johnston, James, 'Secretary', secretary of state, 129, 187
Johnston, John, workman, 153
Johnston, Joseph, son of Marie Douglass, Lady Hilton, 51, 95-96, 175
Johnston, Joseph, of Hilton, husband of Marie Douglass, 49-50, 94, 175
Johnston, Katie, widow of laird of Manderston, 51-52, 75, 76
Johnston, Robert, son of Marie Douglass, Lady Hilton, 51, 175
journeys by coach, 41, 53, 83, 107-109, 111-115, 171
journeys by sea, 20, 21, 22, 26, 30, 31, 40, 43, 53, 55, 56, 64, 115, 119
journeys on horseback, 24-26, 40-41, 52, 107-111, 173
justices of the peace, 84, 97, 150-152, 162-164

Kalmeter, Henry (Dutchman, an industrial spy), 56
Kar, Agnes, daughter of Sir Andrew Kar, married to John Carre of Cavers and West Nisbet, 48-49, 106
Kar, Sir Andrew, Grisell's half-brother, 15, 48
Kar, Dame Grisell, married to 'Patrick': *see* 'Grisell'
Kar, Sir Thomas, of Cavers Carre, Grisell's father, 15, 48
Keir, Adam, Edinburgh baker, 148
Kelso, 26, 37, 67, 90, 91, 92, 107, 160, 161, 200
Kendall, Mrs, Edinburgh tavern keeper, 53
Kettleston, 50, 51
Kilravock, 168
Kimmerghame, 2, 7, 24, 25, 26, 27, 28, 29, 30, 42, 43, 45, 49, 74, 76, 81, 82, 85, 86, 93, 96, 98, 106, 107, 108, 110, 116, 175
Kirke, Thomas, English traveller in Scotland, 98-99
Kneller, Sir Godfrey, portrait painter, 70, Plates 6 and 7
Knox, Robert, miller, 147, 149

Lamb, John, master household, Polwarth House, 154
Lanarkshire, 55, 67, 100, 151, 152, 163

Lapearle, Mestr., Edinburgh tailor, 167
Lauder, 47, 48, 81, 134
Lauder, Sir John, of Fountainhall, 102, 130, 157, 177, 191
Lauderdale, John Maitland, first duke of, 17, 53
Law, John, financier, 148
Law, Lady (Jean Campbell, mother of John Law), 147-148
law lords, 177
Leadhills, 55
lead mines, 55-56
Leitch, Archibald, 120
Leith, 55, 56, 74, 90, 91, 114, 115, 159
Leslie, John Leslie, styled lord, *see* Rothes
letters, 11-12, 50-51, 57, 80, 106, 121-124, 126
Leven, David Leslie, fifth earl of, 192
Leyden, 103
Lidgate, John, George Home's servant, 86, 121
lime, 141-142, 194
Lindsay, James, 118
Linlithgowshire, 55, 81, 96, 176
litigation, 8, 46, 88, 95
Livingston, Sir Thomas, C-in-C Scotland, *see* Teviot
Lockie, David, of Lumsdean, 81
lodgings, 27, 45-46, 66, 68-69, 82, 130-131
London, 7, 31, 35, 41, 51, 53, 58, 59, 61, 62, 64, 71, 74, 87, 99, 104, 110, 111, 112, 115, 117, 119, 124, 125, 126, 127, 128, 132, 147, 181, 185, 190, 196
Longformacus, 54, 81
Lothian, 142
Lothian, Robert Kerr, fourth earl and first marquess of, 182
lotteries, 89
Lunham, Robert, candlemaker, 140, 148, 160
Lyon, Henry, cook in Polwarth House, 154

McAla, provost of Haddington, 199, 200
Macaulay, lord, 180, 198
McCracket, Finlay, gardener, 151
McMurray, Anne, Lady Campbell of Cessnock, 72-73
magnates, Scottish, 125, 129, 179, 180, 183

Maitland, Sir John, of Ravelrig, styled lord Ravelrig; after 1695 earl of Lauderdale, 177

Manderson, George, tenant, 149

Manderston, James, workman, 153

Manderston, Robert, butler in Polwarth House, 154, 155, 173

manners, 105-106

Marchmont, Alexander Hume, second earl of, *see* Alexander Hume

Marchmont, Patrick Hume, first earl of, *see* 'Patrick'

marriages, 15, 24, 27, 38, 40-44, 47-48, 51-52, 54, 65-66, 68, 70-79, 84-85, 101, 128

Marshall, Adam, coachman at Polwarth House, 155

Marshall, Dr Rosalind K., 112

Maxwell, Sir John, of Pollok, 60-63, 110, 181

meal, 6, 147-148

Medina, Sir John, portrait painter, 70, Plates 9 and 14

Medina, John, the younger, Plates 5 and 13

Mein, John, 116

Mein, Robert, 116, 122

Mein, William, son of Robert, 120, 122

Meldrum, George, minister, 39, 65

Mellerstain, 13, 27, 34, 67, 69, 70, 76, 86, 90, 97, 98, 145, 164

Melville, family of, 129

Melville, George Melville, fourth baron and first earl of, 46, 51, 80, 125-126, 127, 128, 129, 132, 179, 182

Mercurius Caledonius, 116

mill stones, 141

Miller, James, Edinburgh coppersmith, 118

Mississippi scheme, 148

Monorgun, George, 100, 139

Monro, Sir Alexander, of Bearscrofts, 59-60, 127, 182, 191

Montgomerie, Sir James, of Skelmorlie, 181

Montgomerie's plot, 181

Montgomery, Francis, of Giffen, 130, 178

Monthly Register, 121

Morer, Thomas, English traveller in Scotland, 98-99

Morton, James Douglas, eleventh earl of, 182

Mosman, George, Edinburgh bookseller, 31

Murdo, John, George Home's servant: porter in Polwarth House, 24, 108, 154

Mure, Sir Archibald, lord provost of Edinburgh, 176

Murray, Sir Archibald, of Blackbarony, 182, 191

Murray, Lady Grisell (Grisell Baillie's daughter), 13, 64, 67, 69, 70, 168, 196-197, 199

Murray, Sir James, of Philiphaugh, 177

Murray, lord John, *see* Tullibardine

music, 32-33, 69-70, 92-93, 100, 119, 174

Newcastle, 37, 108, 110, 115

newsletters, newspapers, 12, 115-121, 131

Nicholson, Sir James, of Cockburnspath, 160

Nicolson, Dame Magdalen, 2, 6, 138-139, 140, 156, 157, 158-159, 160, 161, 162, 167

Ninewells, 42, 85, 94, 130

Norham, 29

Northumberland, 29

Ogilvy, Sir James, *see* Seafield

Old, Robert, tenant, 135, 149

Orange, Jammy, George Home's servant, 28-29, 52

Orkney, George Hamilton, first earl of, 183

Ovens, John, miller, 136

Paris, 31, 103, 105, 117, 147

parliament, Scottish, 7, 10, 40, 52, 54-55, 57, 60-62, 78, 88, 125-130, 184-191

'Patrick', 1, 2, 3, 5, 6, 9, 10, 11, 12, 13, 14, 15, 16-23, 26, 27, 34, 36, 40, 41, 50-51, 52, 55, 56, 57, 59-60, 62, 64-79, 80, 81, 82, 83, 85, 87, 96, 100, 103-104, 111, 112, 115, 116, 118, 121, 122, 123, 125-136, 138, 140, 167, 171-192, 192-200

Pearson, William, dyer, 146

'penny weddings', 83-84

pets, 39, 40, 91, 94

pewter, 6, 27, 143-144

Pitcairne, Sir Archibald, physician, 10, 103-104, 165, 194

poems, 32, 66, 103, 200
poll tax, 12-13, 27, 45-46, 48, 52, 54, 69, 81, 96, 133-137, 149-152, 155-156
Pollok, 60, 61, 110, 181
Polwarth, 1, 6, 15, 18, 108, 133, 134, 135, 136, 137, 141, 142, 145, 147, 148, 149, 151, 152, 153, 160, 193
Polwarth House, previously Redbraes, later Redbraes Castle, 7, 15, 18, 19, 21, 23, 24, 27, 34, 36, 47, 48, 49, 52, 65, 66, 67, 68, 69, 72, 77, 79, 81, 82, 88, 96, 111, 113, 116, 120, 123, 128, 131, 132-133, 135, 138, 141-149, 153, 154-155, 156, 160, 165, 172, 173, 181, 187, 193, 199
Polwarth, Patrick Hume, first lord: later first earl of Marchmont, *see* 'Patrick'
Polwarth, William, tenant, 150
Portland, William Bentinck, first earl of, 128, 184-185
portraits, 33-34, 41, 47, 49, 51, 67, 70
pregnancies, Grisell's, 16-17
presbyterians, 16, 57, 61, 127, 129
Preston, Berwickshire, 107, 108, 109
Prestonpans, 36
Primrose, Archibald, of Dalmeny, *see* Dalmeny, viscount
Primrose, Margaret, George Home's second wife, mother of Robie, 24
Pringle, Frank, 34
Pringle, James, of Torwoodlee, 191
Pringle, Robert, undersecretary, 181, 185, 188, 192
privy council, Scottish, 10, 17, 85
public positions, 87-88
Purves, Lady Anne, 13-14, 22, 51, 65, 75, 100, 194

Quaker movement, 139
quarrels, 50, 79, 93-95, 114
Queensberry, family interest of, 129, 179, 188, 189-190, 191
Queensberry, James Douglas, second duke of, 179, 180, 185, 186, 188-190, 191
Queensberry, William Douglas, first duke of, 129, 179

race meetings, 89-90
Raith, Alexander Melville, styled lord, 62, 179-180

Ravelston, 24, 30, 47, 52, 56, 83, 84, 98, 101, 157, 164, 165, 169, 170
Ray, John, English traveller in Scotland, 98-99
Redbraes, *see* Polwarth House
Redbraes Castle, *see* Polwarth House
Redpath, Alexander, nerd, 151
Redpath, Christopher, workman, 153
Reidpath, James, tenant, 150
Renfrewshire, 62, 86
Renton, 94, 95, 108, 124, 180
Riley, P. W. J., 129, 180
Robison, John, carrying of lime, 142
Robisone, David, George Home's servant, 25, 27, 86
Rose, Sir George Henry, 195
Rose, Margaret, daughter of the laird of Kilravock, 168
Rothes, John Leslie, styled lord Leslie and then ninth earl of, 175
Rothes, Margaret, countess of, widow of Charles Hamilton, fifth earl of Haddington, 175
roups, 177-178
Row, Colonel Archibald, 26, 119
Roxburghshire, 1-2, 6, 134, 138, 157, 162, 176
Ruglen, John Hamilton, first earl of, 182-183
Ruthven, David Ruthven, second baron, 129, 182
Rye house plot, 18, 178

St Andrews, 47, 92, 113, 114, 159
St Clair, Dr, in Edinburgh, 165
salt, 70, 98, 103
Sanderson, Thomas, hind, 151
Scarborough, 37, 62, 105
Scot, Jammy, George Home's servant, 28
Scot, Magdalen, 162
Scott, Anne, daughter of Grisell's sister Isobel and Hugh Scott of Gala, 77-79
Scott, Isobel, of Gala, Grisell's sister, 15, 132
Scott, Dame Margaret, widow of Sir Alexander Home of Renton, 94-95
Scott, Sir Walter, the novelist, 54
Scott, Walter, of Raeburn, married to Anne Scott, Grisell's niece, 79
Scougall, John, portrait painter, 34, 49, 50, 67, 70, 165, Plates 4, 12, 15 and 16
Seafield, Sir James Ogilvy, first viscount

and first earl of, 130, 180, 185, 186, 188, 190, 191

Selkirk, Charles Douglas, second earl of, son of the duke of Hamilton, 181, 185, 188, 190

Seton, Sir Walter, 83

Seton, Sir William, of Kylesmuir, 122

Sharp, James, lord Archbishop of St Andrews, 92, 113, 114

Sheill, David, workman, 153

silver, 6, 21, 143

Sinclair, Sir John, of Longformacus, 81

Sinclair, Sir Robert, of Longformacus, 54

Smith, David, tenant, 135, 149

snuff, 158

soap, 160-161

songs, 33, 69

spelling, 2-3, 48, 139-140

Sprenel, John, wine merchant, 146

Stair, Sir James Dalrymple, first viscount of, 126

Stair, Sir John Dalrymple, master of Stair, second viscount and first earl of, 125, 126, 128, 129

Stenson, Thomas, half hind, 151

Stevenson, Dr, in Edinburgh, 26, 37, 65, 103, 164-165

Stevenson, Sir Archibald, Pitcairne's father-in-law, 104

Stewart, Sir James, of Goodtrees, lord advocate, 54, 84-85, 100, 129, 180

Stewart, Lady Marie, countess of Mar, 90, 92, 100, 139

Stewart, Sir Robert, of Allanbank, 81, 96

Stewart, Sir Thomas, of Coltness, 100

Stichell, 41, 66

Stirling, 17, 29

sudden death (including murder, suicide and execution), 17, 22, 47-48, 49-50, 51, 55, 78, 79, 89, 93, 94, 96, 118, 147, 187

superstition, 95-96

Swinton, 53, 54, 81, 83, 96, 112, 113, 132, 134

Swinton, A. C., 9-10

Swinton, Alexander, of Mersington, brother of Sir John Swinton of that Ilk, 177

Swinton, Sir John of that Ilk, 53-54, 81, 96, 105-106, 112, 113, 132, 177

Symenton, William, cook at Polwarth House, 143

Tarbat, George Mackenzie, first viscount of, 182

Taylor, John, workman, 153

Taylor, John, footman in Polwarth House, 155

teinding, 86

tenants' obligations, 29, 80, 86, 150

Teviot, Sir Thomas Livingston, first viscount of, C-in-C Scotland, 181

thieving, 88-89, 97, 118

Thirlstoune, 81

Thomson, Andrew, teacher of Lauder of Fountainhall's children, 177

Thomson, George, undermiller, 149

Thomson, James, miller, 136, 147

Thomson, Samuel, miller, 141

tobacco, 158

Torphichen, James Sandilands, seventh lord Torphichen, 78-79, 193

toys, 25

Trotter, Dr, 25, 27, 29, 36, 37

Trotter, Alexander, of Charter Hall, 81, 90

Trotter, Patrick, son-in-law of Robert Lunham the candlemaker, 148

Tullibardine, John Murray, earl of, 129-130, 180, 185, 186, 190, 191

Turnbull, John, workman, 153

Tweeddale, John Hay, second earl and first marquess of, formerly lord Yester, 17, 129, 130, 183, 187

Tweeddale, John Hay, third earl and second marquess of, formerly lord Yester, 183

Tynninghame, 56, 170

union of Scotland and England, ·62, 78-79, 180, 188, 194

Utrecht, 19, 20, 68, 69, 70, 72, 74

Valentine, John, 119

value of money, 156-165

Varelst, Maria, portrait painter, 70

Victoria, queen of Great Britain, 156

wage assessments, 84, 97, 150-156, 162-164

wages and working conditions, 97, 150-156, 162-164

Warrender, Margaret, 10, 14, 67, 69, 132, 133, 134, 183

water, 101-102, 172
Watherset, Andrew, 109
Watson, James, Edinburgh printer, 117
Watt, James, servant in Polwarth House, 155
weather, 35-36, 99, 111
Wedderburn, 41
West Nisbet, 14, 27, 48, 49, 81, 90
Whilas, Thomas, wright, 149
White, James (from Preston, acting as guide), 109
Whitehead, George, half hind, 151
Whitehead, Patrick, workman, 153
wigs, 36, 38, 93, 109, 169
William III and II, king of England and Scotland, 20, 22, 23, 58, 62, 64, 99, 125, 126, 127-129, 179, 181, 184-185, 187, 188, 189, 190, 192

Williamson, Robert, half hind, 151
Wilson, George, miller, 136
Wilson, George, tailor, 35, 93
Wilson, John, vintner in Haddington, 200
Winter, Jamie, carpenter, 18-19
Wood, Marguerite, 134
Wood, William, miller, 136

Yester, Charles Hay, styled master of, and then lord, 183
Yester, John Hay, styled lord, *see* Tweeddale, second marquess of
Young, Jean, miller, 147
Young, William, half hind, 151

Zeeland, 55